CW00767491

Jan Wacław Machajski

Jan Wacław Machajski

*A Radical Critic
of the Russian Intelligentsia
and Socialism*

MARSHALL S. SHATZ

University of Pittsburgh Press

Series in Russian and East European Studies No. 11
Published by the University of Pittsburgh Press, Pittsburgh, Pa., 15260
Copyright © 1989, University of Pittsburgh Press
All rights reserved
Feffer and Simons, Inc., London
Manufactured in the United States of America

The portrait of Machajski as a young man appeared in Zygmunt Zaremba, *Słowo o Wacławie Machajskim* (Paris: Księgarnia Polska w Paryżu, 1967).

Library of Congress Cataloging-in-Publication Data

Shatz, Marshall.
    Jan Wacław Machajski : a radical critic of the Russian intelligentsia and socialism / Marshall S. Shatz.
        p.   cm. — (Russian and East European studies)
    Bibliography: p.
    Includes index.
    ISBN 0-8229-3602-X
    1. Vol'skiĭ, A., 1866–1926.   2. Revolutionists—Soviet Union— Biography.   3. Communism and intellectuals—Soviet Union.   I. Title. II. Series: Russian and East European studies (Pittsburgh, Pa.)
HX313.8.V65S5   1989
306'.345'0924—dc19
[B]   88-19811
                                                                CIP

To Edith and Irvin
good friends

It took Mama and Galya two weeks to walk to Kiev [in 1919].
They deliberately dressed to look like beggars; in actual fact,
this is what they were. Galya went without glasses, and walked
holding on to Mama's shoulder, like a blind woman. No one
would have believed them to be poor if Galya had worn her
glasses. Everyone treated people in glasses suspiciously in those
violent times. They thought them cunning enemies, and hated
them bitterly. It is amazing that this distrust of people wearing
glasses has persisted up to the present time.

—Konstantin Paustovsky, *The Story of a Life*

Contents

Preface

Jan Wacław Machajski (1866–1926) is an exceedingly difficult figure to classify, in intellectual as well as political terms. Born a Pole, he repudiated the cause of Polish political independence early in his career in favor of proletarian internationalism. University educated, he made his mark on Russian history as a bitter critic of the intelligentsia and its role in Russian political life. Although he drew upon a number of the revolutionary currents that swirled through the Russian Empire in the early years of the twentieth century, he belonged to none of them and criticized all of them. One of the pillars of his social and political theory was Marxism, but he came to regard the Marxist movement as one of the greatest threats to the future well-being of the working class. The other pillar of his thought was anarchism, particularly its Bakuninist variant—so much so, in fact, that his doctrines have generally been treated as part of the history of anarchism. Yet he never acknowledged any influence of Michael Bakunin and denounced the anarchists just as roundly as he denounced the Marxists. He did not join any party but attempted instead, with little success, to create his own revolutionary movement called the Workers' Conspiracy.

This uncompromising sense of independence helps to account for his obscurity. Although his views on the intelligentsia were widely known, at least in general terms, little in the way of serious discussion of them took place during his lifetime; he had few adherents but many indignant critics. Even the term by which his doctrines were known contributed to the obscurity. Almost universally, they were referred to as *makhaevshchina*, formed from "Makhaev," a Russian corruption or misunderstanding of his name, coupled with the disparaging ending -shchina. It might be translated as "the notorious doctrines of Makhaev." Throughout this study I have chosen to use the term Makhaevism. It is essentially the name by which contemporaries knew this current of thought, but in a neutral form and without the negative associations of the Russian word; although it retains the corruption of its founder's name, it may prove less taxing for the English reader than the more accurate Machajskiism. In Russian, the disparaging label which its critics pasted on it doubtless helped to discourage serious analysis of just what it signified. It became simply a byword for hostility to the intelligentsia, and Machajski was relegated largely to the footnotes of Russian revolutionary history, usually in highly tendentious terms.

Why, then, should we be mindful of him? What is the justification for a detailed examination of his thought and his political activity? In part, it is the sheer originality of Makhaevism. Machajski adopted and adapted various elements of anarchism, Marxism, and syndicalism, but he put them together in a novel synthesis, with the intelligentsia as its centerpiece. Makhaevism was not simply a variation of some other doctrine but a unique creation. In turn-of-the-century Russia, where political life often seemed little more than a recapitulation of every idea and movement Western Europe had ever devised, this was an impressive intellectual achievement, and, as such, deserving of interest in and of itself.

The richness of this original doctrine in implications and suggestiveness makes it possible to treat it from a variety of perspectives. Paul Avrich, for example, has written on Machajski and his ideas in the context of the Russian anarchist movement.[1] While he did not consider himself an anarchist, Machajski did share many salient points with the anarchists; in other respects, he emphasized and developed elements of anarchist belief which were latent in anarchism or remained unexamined by the anarchists themselves. A second, closely related aspect of Makhaevism is its contribution to the anarchist dialogue with Marxism, and it is from this point of view that Anthony D'Agostino has approached the subject.[2] At least since Bakunin, anarchism had engaged in a prolonged critique of Marxian socialism — indeed, to some degree it fashioned its own identity in terms of its divergences from Marxism. Machajski both drew upon that anarchist view of the Marxists and made his own distinctive contribution to it. Yet a third possible approach to Machajski is in terms of the relevance of his ideas to the "sociology of intellectuals," the social, economic, and political role of intellectuals in the world today and their relationship to other classes. This was a concern of the late Alvin Gouldner, for example, who was familiar with Machajski's basic views.[3] It is a subject that includes the concept of the "new class" as applied to the Communist rulers of Eastern Europe, but its broader implications transcend the historical or geographical boundaries of Eastern Europe, and some of its early roots go back to Makhaevism.

Thus Machajski and his doctrines have something of significance to say about anarchism, socialism, the "new class," the role of intellectuals in the modern world. All of these themes will be dealt with to some degree in what follows. What interests me most, however, in the history of Makhaevism, is what primarily interested Machajski: the Russian intelligentsia and its historical role in Russian life. For all the ideological and sociological suggestiveness of Makhaevism, Machajski himself was primarily a revolutionary (or a would-be revolutionary), and the focus of his attention was the intelligentsia's domination (or, again, would-be domination) of the socialist and labor movements in Russia. Therefore, whatever else it may have been, Makhaevism was above all a mordant critique of the Russian intelligentsia. Just as Marxism sought to lay bare the class nature and ideology of the bourgeoisie, Machajski set out to unmask the identity, class character, and ultimate aspirations of the intelligentsia, not only in Russia, but in Russia especially. This is the issue that gives Makhaevism its larger historical significance and elevates it above the status of a minor intellectual current or revolutionary sect; and this, I believe, is what constitutes the principal justification for a book-length study of the subject. That is not to say that Machajski's critique of the intelligentsia was correct — though often penetrating, it was in many respects far off the mark. Machajski is one of those historical figures who are more important for the questions they raise than for the answers they give. Machajski posed the issue of the Russian intelligentsia in bolder and more novel terms than any of his contemporaries. A critical examination and

xiii

testing of his views against the historical reality of the intelligentsia is the central focus of this study, and it is hoped that the results will tell us as much about the intelligentsia as they do about Makhaevism itself.

The purposes of this book are threefold. The first is to provide a comprehensive biography of Machajski and history of Makhaevism; no full-length study of the subject currently exists in any language. This includes an account of Machajski's life, to the extent that it can be reconstructed from the extremely sketchy and fragmentary historical record; a detailed exposition and critical analysis of the doctrines of Makhaevism; and the history of the various Makhaevist organizations and the role they played in the Russian revolutionary movement. Though but a small part of the political history of the Russian Empire in its last decades and the Soviet Union in its first decades, Makhaevism and its creator made a distinctive contribution to it, and their story deserves, finally, to be told.

The second purpose is to examine the identity and the historical significance of the Russian intelligentsia in the light of Machajski's views. By no means did Machajski invent anti-intelligentsia sentiment; instead, to a large degree he articulated and systematized a variety of critical or hostile currents which preceded or paralleled his own. The Russian intelligentsia was under attack from many quarters throughout its existence, and Makhaevism helps to illuminate the sources of these attacks and the forms they took. It is for this reason that I have carried the story of Makhaevism past Machajski's own death in 1926 and into the 1930s, for Stalin's Great Purge, with the massive toll it took on the old intelligentsia, marks the real terminal point of this theme. To deal with such a vast and amorphous subject as the history of anti-intelligentsia sentiment in Russia — which amounts, one might say, to an anti-history of the intelligentsia — I have had to rely largely on familiar, or at least previously used, sources, as well as the works of other scholars. While little of this information is actually new, it has generally been presented in another context: labor history, Social-Democratic or Communist party history, and so forth. When pieced together to serve as the immediate background of Makhaevism, however, it comes to be seen in a new and revealing perspective.

The third and final purpose is to identify Machajski's contribution to the history of the concept of the "new class." This is the term that began to be applied to the new Soviet ruling elite under Stalin in the 1930s, and in the 1950s was widely popularized in Milovan Djilas's famous book. It has a long ideological and political pedigree. Originating in the anarchist critique of Marxism, it was first articulated by Michael Bakunin. It was Machajski, however, who gave it a systematic formulation, elements of which can be found in subsequent versions of it whose authors were quite unaware of Machajski. Without attempting an exhaustive review of the voluminous literature on this subject, I shall try to excavate the original foundations of the idea of the "new class" and Machajski's contribution to its development. It is a minor but oddly satisfying irony of history that despite the almost total obscurity that ultimately enveloped him, his spirit continues to be invoked, albeit unwittingly, whenever this now commonplace term is uttered.

The analysis of Machajski's views which forms the core of this book originated as a doctoral dissertation at Columbia University under the supervision of Marc Raeff. It is my great pleasure to thank Professor Raeff for his unfailing courtesy, attentiveness, and critical insight, qualities which have made him justly renowned among those privileged to have been his graduate students. Professor Norman Naimark of Boston University kindly read parts of the manuscript and gave me the benefit of his considerable knowledge of Polish affairs. I owe a particularly great debt to Professor Paul Avrich of Queens College of the City University of New York, who has read this work in several different versions and has contributed numerous suggestions for improving it. The support he has given this project over the years has been unstinting, and it is deeply appreciated.

I wish to offer a word of posthumous thanks to Max Nomad, who, already well into his eighties when I was working on my dissertation, generously supplied me with material from his archive as well as pieces of his still sharp mind. While not always agreeing with what I had to say, he gave a young American graduate student an invaluable glimpse into the mentality and temperament of the Eastern European revolutionaries of the early twentieth century, with whom virtually all living links have now been severed.

Finally, I would like to express my gratitude to the staff of the International Institute of Social History (Internationaal Instituut voor Sociale Geschiedenis) in Amsterdam for the kind assistance I have been given on my several visits there; and to Gabriel Grasberg and the reference staff of the Healey Library of the University of Massachusetts at Boston for the friendly and efficient service they have provided.

Dates of events within the Russian Empire and Soviet Union have been given according to the calendar in use there at the time: until early 1918 according to the Old Style or Julian calendar, which was twelve days behind the Western calendar in the nineteenth century and thirteen days behind in the twentieth; and thereafter according to the New Style or Gregorian calendar. Russian names and words have been transliterated into English in accordance with the Library of Congress system, slightly simplified. Exceptions have been made for a few figures well known to English readers by a conventional version of their names, such as Leon Trotsky and Maxim Gorky. Russian orthography has been modernized throughout the work. For Polish names, I have endeavored to retain the Polish spelling for those individuals primarily active in Poland itself, while using a transliterated Russian version for those principally engaged in Russian movements or essentially Russified. In doubtful cases, I have tended to use the Russian form, since this work is focused primarily on Russian history.

Jan Wacław Machajski

Chapter 1

Poland and Siberia

J AN WACŁAW MACHAJSKI was born poor, Polish, and a subject of the Russian tsar, a set of circumstances not sufficient to make him a revolutionary but certainly conducive to such a result. The place of his birth, on December 15 (December 27, N.S.), 1866, was the small town of Busko, in Kielce gubernia, twenty-eight miles south of the city of Kielce.[1] Kielce gubernia was part of the Congress Kingdom of Poland, established in 1815 by the Congress of Vienna and attached to the Russian Empire. Machajski's father, Konstanty, was a minor official and a former mayor of the town.[2] He died when Machajski was still a child, leaving his large family in considerable financial difficulty.[3] The family must have had aspirations, however, if not means, for Machajski received a good education. He prepared for admission to a gymnasium, the educational route to university training, first attending a progymnasium in the town of Pińchów, where his family may have resettled. To supplement the family's income he tutored fellow students whom his mother boarded in the family apartment. He then attended the gymnasium in Kielce, from which he graduated with a gold medal. In 1886 he entered Warsaw University, spending four years in the Natural Sciences Faculty and then transferring to the Medical Faculty, which he never completed.[4]

Machajski first became acquainted with socialist ideas in his student days. It will be useful, therefore, to identify some of the distinctive features of Polish socialism as Machajski encountered it in the 1880s, in order to assess the contribution it may have made to the formation of his later views.

Machajski came of age in a period of abrupt and far-reaching change in Russian Poland, change both socioeconomic and intellectual.[5] The traditional gentry domination of the Kingdom of Poland had been shattered by the events of 1863 and 1864. The defeat of the 1863 insurrection against Russian rule discredited, at least for some time to come, the romantic vision of a national uprising to restore the independence of Poland and physically decimated the gentry class (the *szlachta*) which had cultivated that vision and led the insurrection. A further blow came in 1864, when the Russian government emancipated the Polish peasants on terms considerably more favorable than those the Russian peasants had been granted in their emancipation, thereby successfully destroying the economic position of much of the middle and small-holding gentry which had been the bulwark of Polish nationalism.

One major effect of the peasant emancipation was to open the way to industrialization by creating an urban labor force. In fact, industrial development proceeded even more rapidly in Russian Poland than in post-emancipation Russia itself, and the Kingdom of Poland quickly became one of the leading industrial areas of the Russian Empire, particularly in mining and metalworking and in textile manufacturing. In response to this economic growth, as well as to the failure of the insurrection, Polish thought turned away from romantic nationalism and dreams of political independence and came to be dominated by the program of "organic work." As articulated especially by the so-called Warsaw Positivists, "organic work" promoted the virtues of peaceful social, economic, and cultural development through education and productive industrial and commercial activity, accepting Russian political domination and taking advantage of Poland's access to the large Russian market. It was this "bourgeois" program, and its materialistic and individualistic approach to things, that Polish socialism arose to challenge in the 1870s.[6]

A peculiar disparity had arisen by the seventies between development in Russia and in Poland. For the moment, at least, industrial growth was greater and an impoverished urban working class more in evidence in Poland than in Russia, where industrialization would achieve its most rapid development only in the late eighties and the nineties. Thanks to the severe political and cultural repression which the Russian authorities exercised, however, socialism was slower to develop in Poland; here, the political quietism of Warsaw Positivism prevailed even as the populist movement was reaching the peak of its activity in Russia. As a result of this disparity, when socialism did come to Poland, it came largely from Russia. This was due in part to admiration for the populists, particularly the Narodnaia Volia (People's Will party), whose determination in hunting down and ultimately assassinating Alexander II made a strong impression on many Poles. It was also a result of the influence of Polish students from the borderlands of European Russia, sizable numbers of whom chose to study at Russian universities rather than in the Congress Kingdom. There they were introduced to radical Russian authors such as Chernyshevskii, Dobroliubov, and Pisarev, then Lavrov and Bakunin, and to Lassalle, Marx, and other Western writers. They also came in direct contact with the Russian revolutionaries, and a number of them became active participants in the Russian revolutionary movement. Others, however, made their way to Warsaw, clustering particularly around Warsaw University, to proselytize their new ideas — including the use of terrorism as an instrument of political and social action which they accepted from Russian populism.

With its militancy and acute sensitivity to social injustice, the socialism of these radicalized students fell on fertile soil: increasing impatience with the prosaic materialism of "organic work," and increasing revulsion at the deprivations endured by the industrial workers. By 1876 and 1877, various socialist groups and study circles had arisen in Warsaw, not only in the student and intellectual milieu of the university but among some elements of the working class as well. (Like St. Petersburg, Warsaw was not only a cultural and administrative center but also a major industrial center, particularly of the metallurgical industry.) Despite a wave of arrests in 1878–1879, the ideas of socialism continued to make headway both at home and in the emigration, and in 1882 the first Polish socialist party was formed. It called itself the Social-Revolutionary "Proletariat" party, more familiarly known simply as the Proletariat party, or sometimes as Wielki (Great)

5

Proletariat to distinguish it from later parties of the same name. Its leadership consisted largely of former students at Russian universities, including the party's prime mover, Ludwik Waryński. The party's ideology was strongly Marxist-inspired, emphasizing class division and class conflict rather than social or national solidarity, and, most significant in the Polish context, staunchly rejecting patriotism and the struggle for Polish independence in favor of international class struggle. (Just as Plekhanov and the early Russian Marxists had to ignore Marx's kind words about the Russian peasant commune, these Polish Marxists found themselves more "orthodox" than Marx and Engels themselves, who consistently supported the cause of Polish independence as a way of striking a blow at the bastion of European reaction, tsarist Russia.) In a manifestation of the party's internationalism, the Proletariat cooperated closely with the remnants of the Narodnaia Volia in Russia.

Such a rejection of the national issue, however, could hardly have universal appeal in a country which was ruled by foreign conquerors and whose very cultural identity was under attack.[7] This is the issue that runs like a great fissure through the Polish socialist movement from its very beginnings: whether, and how, to combine national and social objectives, and which should take precedence over the other. Even before the founding of the Proletariat, Polish socialists had begun to divide over the subject of the national struggle. In 1881 a group led by Bolesław Limanowski had formed the Lud Polski (Polish People), rejecting Waryński's rigid class outlook and combining both socialist and patriotic principles. The Proletariat itself proved short-lived: the original leadership, including Waryński, was arrested in police operations of 1883 and 1884. The party managed to keep going until 1886, but even before its final destruction the influence of Polish nationalism had begun to reassert itself over some of the party's adherents. It would remain the fundamental issue that Proletariat's remnants and successors had to face, as well as the issue that confronted Machajski as he attained political awareness.

It is not surprising that at first he was drawn to the patriotic viewpoint. As a Polish gymnasium and university student, Machajski could hardly avoid direct and forceful experience of what Russian rule over the Poles meant. After the insurrection of 1863,

6

the tsarist government embarked on a ruthless policy of Russification, introducing a series of measures designed to obliterate Polish national identity. The Kingdom of Poland was integrated into the administrative structure of the empire, losing not only its autonomy but even its name: it was now officially referred to as Privislanskii Krai, the Vistula Territory. Russian was made the language of the courts and administrative institutions, and, increasingly, of the educational system as well. In 1867 Polish educational affairs were placed under the control of a newly created Warsaw Educational District, headed by an appointed curator directly subordinate to the Ministry of Education in St. Petersburg. In 1869 the Warsaw Central School, which had been established just seven years earlier as the first comprehensive institution of higher education in Russian Poland since the insurrection of 1831, was transformed into the Russian-language Warsaw University. By 1885 the entire Polish school system had become Russified: Russian was made the language of instruction in all Polish schools for all subjects, with the exception of religion and the Polish language. Machajski therefore was educated in a system where even Polish history and literature were taught to Polish students in Russian! In the spring of 1883, the so-called Apukhtin affair occurred. When Aleksandr Apukhtin, the particularly repressive curator of schools for the Warsaw Educational District, attempted to implement new and harsher regulations in institutions of higher education, he provoked a wave of student protests and street demonstrations. Numerous students were suspended or arrested, and one student (who was in fact Russian) became a national hero when he managed to slap Apukhtin's face.[8] With the school system a focal point of the tsarist government's Russification policy, the students inevitably became a focal point of resistance to that policy.

Fortunately for the historian, one of Machajski's closest friends both at the Kielce gymnasium and at Warsaw University was the future novelist Stefan Żeromski. Thanks to this famous literary figure, whose friendship with Machajski continued long after their school days, some details of Machajski's early life, and of his intellectual and political development, have been preserved which would otherwise be unobtainable. In Kielce, Machajski lived in a private home where he received room and board in return for tutoring the two boys in the family.[9] As in Russia, students even at the secondary-school level in Poland developed a kind of unofficial curriculum parallel to the official one, immersing themselves in disapproved and even contraband readings and doctrines. According to Żeromski, at the gymnasium in Kielce one of the students' favorite extracurricular activities was to gather for nocturnal readings of whatever literature they could lay their hands on. "We read whatever came to hand, in any bookcase: Victor Hugo and Karol Libelt, Słowacki and Turgenev, Henry Thomas Buckle and Brandes, Mickiewicz and Draper, Quinet and Sienkiewicz."[10] Machajski loved to declaim heroic speeches from romantic plays and for a time even aspired to go on the stage.[11] Many years later, Żeromski penned this vivid and affectionate portrait of Machajski as a schoolboy:

Jan Wacław, always the best pupil and candidate for the gold medal, imagined at that time that he was the most accomplished actor on the face of the earth, a great tragedian and fiery artist. He wore his hair long, so impermissibly and culpably long that he suffered more than a few persecutions at the hands of the director of the gymnasium. . . . But none of [the latter's] punishments, threats and blustering, foot-stamping, or peremptory focussing of his spectacles on the long-haired culprit could induce Jan Wacław to cut his Absalom-like locks.[12]

From exalted literature, students often went on to radical political and social ideas, to which all the efforts of the tsarist censorship were unable to bar their access. Machajski received at least some exposure at the gymnasium to both the socialist and nationalist currents of thought in circulation at this time. At one point in his diary for 1885, Żeromski recorded that he and Machajski and another friend had stayed up until 3:00 A.M. arguing about "socialism and patriotism," with Żeromski defending "patriotism and republicanism against communism and cosmopolitanism."[13]

By the time Machajski reached the university, Proletariat had been crushed and the revival of patriotism had begun to generate new currents of thought and new organizations. In contrast to the gentry democracy of the past, the goal of Polish political independence now appeared in combination with various radical ideas, both populist and socialist.[14] Within this framework Machajski, as seen through Żeromski's eyes, seems to have spent his first year or two in Warsaw experimenting with different ideological positions — trying on a variety of ideological roles, as it were. In his diaries for 1886 and 1887, Żeromski rebukes his friend on a number of occasions for betraying his ideals by adopting cosmopolitanism, materialism, and even a Bazarov-like nihilism. In May 1887, for example, he recorded a quarrel with Machajski over the latter's "cosmopolitan principles, his disrespect for Mickiewicz, and his materialism."[15]

In November 1886, however, Machajski told Żeromski that he accepted "the program of Zagłoba."[16] "Zagłoba" was the pseudonym of a student named Leon Wasilkowski, who was associated with the periodical *Głos (The Voice)*.[17] Begun in 1886, *Głos* was one of the first significant expressions of the new patriotism, espousing a nationalist position with a strongly populist tinge and emphasizing the interests of the Polish peasantry. In 1887, this current gave rise to an organization in Switzerland called the Liga Polska (Polish League, reorganized in 1893 as the Liga Narodowa, or National League, and, under the leadership of Roman Dmowski, increasingly right-wing in orientation). The Liga Polska combined the goal of political independence with socialist ideas and accepted the use of antigovernment terror. Shortly thereafter, the student youth of Warsaw organized a parallel group called the Związek Młodzieży Polskiej (Union of Polish Youth), known as Zet, which soon affiliated itself with the Liga Polska.[18] Wasilkowski was one of the leaders of Zet, and both Machajski and Żeromski were drawn into its activities.[19]

Zet, like the Liga Polska, was predominantly patriotic in orientation but with a socialist tinge, anticipating a democratic Poland based on the working classes and especially the peasantry. Its socialism was closer to English Fabianism than to revolutionary internationalism, and it recognized the necessity of education and a considerable period of preparatory work. Zet was organized along Masonic lines in a three-tiered conspiratorial structure, and its combination of socialism and nationalism proved highly appealing to Polish students. It established branches throughout the Polish territories and the Russian Empire, as well as in European cities where Polish students were concentrated. The Warsaw section soon had at least several dozen members.

They devoted themselves largely to educational activity among the artisans and workers of the capital. (Zet branches in the countryside conducted similar activity among the peasants.) Establishing secret libraries and reading rooms, lecturing and teaching literacy in small study-circles, they introduced the workers to the history and literature of Poland, arousing their patriotic moral fervor and attempting to win their support for Poland's independence.[20] This was Machajski's first venture into conspiratorial activity,[21] and he threw himself into it wholeheartedly, staying up nights to prepare maps, charts, and other materials for his geography and history lessons to the workers.[22] He proved an able and effective teacher — and at the same time his activity among the workers may have had a role in turning him away from idealization of the peasants and toward a greater awareness of the proletariat.

He was slow to take this step, however, even though he had the opportunity to familiarize himself with the program of proletarian socialism. Żeromski recorded that toward the end of 1888 a representative of the Proletariat turned up at a meeting of Machajski's worker circle and expounded the party's socialist program.[23] The reference presumably is to the short-lived Second Proletariat party, which, revived in 1888, upheld the commitment of its predecessor and namesake to class struggle and social revolution, and its opposition to nationalism, as well as placing a particular emphasis on terror in its tactical thinking.[24] According to at least one source, however, when a schism developed in 1889 within the Kielce student group in Warsaw, Machajski was considered the leader of the "socialist-nationalists" rather than the "international socialists."[25]

Hence, he was drawn to the views of the Paris-based Gmina Narodowa-Socjalistyczna (National-Socialist Commune). Founded in 1888, the Gmina had the active participation of Bolesław Limanowski, among others, and it was to some degree the successor to his Lud Polski; in 1889 it became a unit of the Polish League. As its name suggests, it was dedicated, at least in theory, to combining patriotism with socialism, regarding a revolution in Poland as the road both to national independence and a socialist order.[26] In 1890, Machajski had an opportunity to make contact with the Paris émigrés: when the remains of Adam Mickie-

Jan Wacław Machajski

wicz were exhumed in June of that year for reburial in Cracow's Wawel Castle, Machajski and Żeromski traveled to Paris to attend the ceremony as representatives of the youth of Warsaw.[27] In the following year he journeyed to Cracow and in April was arrested by the Austrian authorities in Galicia while attempting to smuggle illegal literature across the border into Russian Poland. After four months in a Cracow prison he was expelled from Austrian Poland, and since the Russian police were now aware of his activities and he could not return to Warsaw, he emigrated to Switzerland and settled in Zurich.[28]

Here he became acquainted with the Polish émigré circles located in Switzerland and the Polish student groups at the University of Zurich. It was at this point that he finally began to turn away from the nationalist sentiments which he had previously held. In January 1892 he published a report on the work of the "national socialists" in the Congress Kingdom. Entitled "Underground Life in the Congress Kingdom," it appeared in *Pobudka (Reveille)*, the Paris journal of the Gmina Narodowa-Socjalistyczna. As far as is known, this was Machajski's first publication, and it marked a crucial step in his ideological evolution. Some of the sentiments expressed in this article, as well as the periodical in which it appeared, indicate that he had not yet broken completely with the socialist-patriot position. Clearly, however, he had begun to feel an acute contradiction between the socialist and nationalist components of that position and was moving toward a repudiation of the latter and a firm commitment to proletarian socialism.

The article was highly critical of the patriotic student circles among which he had lately worked in Warsaw. By contrast with the energetic activities of the "social democrats," or internationalists, he found the national socialists lethargic, lacking a clear political profile, and, worst of all, narrowly concentrating on intellectuals and students while refusing to participate in May Day demonstrations and remaining aloof from the rising labor movement.

We agitate among the intellectual proletariat, or rather among the youth. Although this is very receptive material for any revolutionary activity (and therefore for socialist propaganda), as the basis for a party it is very elastic, irresolute, and highly susceptible to the blandishments of those parties which have nothing in common with socialism. In particular, the symptom is distinctly appearing among us whereby all strata of the people are in some measure in opposition to the partitional regime and to the gullible may be viewed as revolutionaries.[29]

The main hindrance to the efforts of the national socialists was their insistence on making common cause with democratic elements who held them back from any effective revolutionary activity.

We have apparently gone blind and do not see that those who seem to us sincere friends are our most dangerous enemies in the field of socialist propaganda, that we are doing nothing at all through them, that they hold us back from any bold step, and therefore above all from sincere participation in the socialist movement; we do not perceive that each one of those people is a skilled "secret Jesuit" who, representing himself to us as a socialist, at the same time behind our backs paralyzes the growth of socialism more effectively than the government and the bourgeoisie.[30]

He concluded with the hope that this blindness would clear and that instead of joining forces with other "revolutionary" Polish parties "we will come to understand that the labor question is not a question of a single class . . . but a question of millions, a question of whole societies." Then, "by the solemn celebration of the workers' holy day, our youth will show the world that it understands the pulse of the people's life, that it itself lives and that Poland lives!"[31]

Now Machajski began to draw a firm line of demarcation between patriotism and revolutionary socialism. According to his wife, Vera, he later recalled his thinking in this period in the following terms: "The patriots were becoming socialists. And I felt that they were becoming socialists only in order to draw the masses of the people into the struggle for the 'fatherland,' that these aristocrats were thinking not at all about the liberation of the masses but about an independent Polish state." Henceforth, his wife's account adds, he would reject "any sort of 'national-liberation' movement, any struggle for the fatherland."[32]

He now joined a student organization of the Second Proletariat party in Zurich.[33] In May 1892 the workers of Lodz, the major textile center of Russian Poland, organized a general strike which turned into a virtual uprising. Lasting eight days, the strike involved over twenty thousand workers, there were street battles with the authorities, and more than two hundred people were killed or wounded and hundreds more arrested.[34] In June, Machajski set out for Poland bearing copies of an appeal to the Polish workers; although the appeal urged no immediate action, it sought to draw lessons from the events in Lodz and define the course that the workers' movement should take in the future. The appeal was printed by the Proletariat group and was signed "The Polish Social-Revolutionary Party," but its author was in fact Machajski himself.[35] The keynote of the appeal was militant internationalism. It urged the workers not to rest content with local strikes, but to organize a nationwide general strike — a tactic that would later reappear as a feature of Makhaevism. "In the future, we will organize a strike not in one city but in the entire country; we will carry our workers' banner to the farthest corners, we will call all the working people to battle. And then our strike and our struggle will last not eight days but as long as it takes to obtain our demands."[36] Cooperation with the Russian revolutionary movement had been one of the central tenets of the original Proletariat party, and Machajski echoed this principle in assuring the Polish workers that bold action on their part would arouse the Russian workers to a joint assault on the tsarist regime: "Then our brothers, the Russian workers, seeing how weak the tsar is in the face of the people's might, will awaken from their age-old bondage; they will call their own rich men to account, and together with the Polish working people they will crush the tsar, the greatest tyrant on earth."[37] In contrast to the principles he would adopt later, he still considered the autocracy the workers' main enemy and the overthrow of tsarism the immediate objective of the workers' movement; ultimately, he would reject political goals entirely and urge the workers to confine their strike activity to strictly economic demands. The militancy of this appeal, however, including the acceptance of violence, would remain a permanent part of his outlook.

In taking up the struggle with the factory owners, we are at the same time calling tsardom itself to battle. To the fusillades of the troops the workers of Lodz replied with rocks, and were therefore obliged to retreat. In the future, we will reply to bullets with bullets and bombs, and we will blockade the streets against cavalry attacks. And we will bear in mind that in the struggle with a regime like the tsar's, any means of battle that the mind and hand of man can devise is noble.[38]

Neither Machajski nor his proclamation reached Poland. On June 17 he was arrested on the Prussian border by the tsarist police, and his participation in the Polish socialist movement came to an end. Shortly thereafter the national issue, which had preoccupied Polish socialism for so long, finally produced an irrevocable split in the ranks of the Polish socialists. In 1892–1893 the Polska Partia Socjalistyczna (Polish Socialist party, or PPS) was organized and came under the leadership of Józef Piłsudski. The PPS squarely adopted a national approach to socialism, with the struggle against tsarism for the resurrection of Polish independence taking precedence over social revolution. It was, in effect, the ideological culmination of Lud Polski, Zet, Liga Polska, and other manifestations of the patriotic current which had been gathering strength within the Polish socialist movement in the course of the 1880s, and even drew in some remnants of the old Proletariat party. The minority who rejected the nationalist position and adhered to the Marxist orthodoxy of internationalism, viewing themselves as the ideological heirs of the Great Proletariat party, formed the Socjaldemokracja Królestwo Polskiego (the Social Democracy of the Kingdom of Poland, SDKP; with the adhesion of the Lithuanian Social Democrats in 1899, it became the Social Democracy of the Kingdom of Poland and Lithuania, or SDKPiL). Rosa Luxemburg was its leading light.[39] Machajski could only follow these events from a distance, if at all. He was imprisoned in the Warsaw Citadel for a year and a half, and then for another year and a half in the "Kresty" prison of St. Petersburg. He was finally exiled for five years to Viliuisk, in the Iakutsk region of Siberia.[40]

In what ways, and to what degree, did Machajski's early political experience in Poland influence the development of his later critique of the intelligentsia? Some of the seeds of Makhaevism may well have been planted in this period. The element of revolutionary militancy, for example, a salient feature of Makhaevism, emerges clearly toward the end of this period, especially in the 1892 manifesto. Doubtless, it was the product of a personality already inclined in this direction interacting with a political culture favorable to its development. The biographical information available on Machajski is too thin to support any but the most general kind of psychological profile. At the very least, however, it can be said that Machajski was a highly intense, strong-willed individual who made commitments passionately and whole-heartedly. "Even in his childhood and youth," Żeromski wrote of him, "an unbridled fanaticism characterized him. Initially it was adoration of the poetry of Słowacki, of the theater, then it was materialist, patriotic, social fanaticism."[41] Żeromski also attributed to him an "inflexible character and iron will."[42] At the same time, bitterness was easily bred in the Polish situation, where political repressiveness and social injustice were exacerbated by national oppression. The fact that the Polish socialist movement developed in close ideological and organizational interaction with the Russian Narodnaia Volia further encouraged in its adherents a tendency to regard terror as an acceptable weapon of struggle. There was no lack of heroic martyrs to serve as examples for the young Machajski: at the beginning of 1886, in fact, just a few months before he entered the university, the Warsaw Citadel had been the scene of the execution of four leaders of the Proletariat party.

A more specific element of the Polish scene may also have made a lasting impact on Machajski. After the insurrection of 1863, there was a noticeable tendency in Russian Poland for impoverished members of the *szlachta* to enter the ranks of the intelligentsia. Considerable numbers of them went into the professions or assumed managerial positions in the new industries.[43] The Proletariat party's newspaper, *Proletariat*, even classified the "bourgeois-gentry intelligentsia" among the reactionary and exploiting classes, with only a tiny segment (including, presumably, the Proletariat's own leaders, many of whom, such as Ludwik Waryński, were drawn from this group) capable of becoming allies of the proletariat.[44] This phenomenon could, perhaps, have established the first link in Machajski's mind between the intelligentsia and the privileged classes, his unshakable image of the intelligentsia as the servant of the bourgeoisie. Although it may have been more pronounced in Russian Poland, however, this social development

16

was not unique to it and could be observed in Russia itself. There, state service provided an alternative for members of the gentry leaving the land (while in Russian Poland state service was largely barred to non-Russians), but they were also moving into the professional intelligentsia.

Finally, and most important, it was Machajski's Polish experience that first opened his eyes to the possibility that forces within the socialist movement itself were holding back the kind of all-out class struggle to which he had become committed. As he picked his way through the various Polish political groups and currents of the 1880s, he became increasingly critical of what came to be known as the "socialist-patriots." Most of all, he rejected their view of the nation as an organic whole with certain common interests that transcended class conflicts—a reprise of the notion of social solidarity which the early Polish socialists had criticized so vehemently in the proponents of "organic work." Machajski's growing militancy impelled him to repudiate such an outlook because it seemed to pose the threat of reformism and the restraint of working-class radicalism; this, too, would reappear as a fundamental component of Makhaevism.[45]

Given the position he had reached by 1892, it is easy to see why the PPS would have had little appeal for him. The question arises, however, as to why he did not ultimately throw in his lot with the SDKPiL. With its Marxist internationalism and unremitting antipatriotism, it would seem to have been the natural political destination toward which he was headed at the time of his arrest. Yet he eventually rejected it, along with all other forms of socialism, no less firmly than he rejected the PPS. Quite possibly he would have joined the SDKPiL had he remained in Polish politics. Fate—in the person of the Russian authorities— intervened, however, and he emerged from his prolonged imprisonment and exile with a different, and much broader, perspective than he had had previously. This new perspective was based not merely on a reexamination of Polish socialism, but even more on an analysis of developments within the German Social-Democratic party, which he was able to follow in Siberia. As the largest and apparently most successful of Marxist parties, German Social Democracy had exemplary significance for many other socialists, especially in Eastern Europe, who minutely examined its evolution and heatedly debated its doctrines and practices. It was his investigation of German Social Democracy that formed the main subject of Machajski's first essays, and by the time these began to appear at the end of the 1890s he was moving well to the left of Marxism itself.

The relationship between Machajski's Polish experience and his later views, therefore, was complex and somewhat indirect. Certainly it would be a mistake to regard Machajski's critique of the intelligentsia and socialism merely as a kind of projection of his earlier reaction against Polish nationalism. This is the implication of Vera Machajska's statement that Machajski's rejection of the socialist-patriots was his "first lesson in how the intelligentsia was using socialism in its own interests."[46] Although revolutionaries in the Russian Empire did tend to mature early, it should be kept in mind that Machajski was not quite twenty when he entered Warsaw University, and only twenty-five when he was arrested. Makhaevism was the product of an older man who had gone through the fire of prison and exile, and not just the continuation of an earlier path. Furthermore, it is worth noting that except for a brief period after the 1905 revolution Machajski never again directly involved himself in Polish affairs, in itself a reflection of the shift in his interests and preoccupations. Most significantly, however, it is a considerable leap from rejection of Polish patriots to rejection of the intelligentsia. After all, the Polish situation, where the national issue was of paramount importance, was hardly typical of socialist movements in general, and Machajski could not have been unaware of this. It was only when he was forcibly removed from the Polish context that he reached the conclusion that the threat of socialist reformism came not just from some misguided or self-interested Polish nationalists but from a much more widespread and significant social force, and, indeed, from the theory and practice of Marxism itself. His early years in Poland may have first raised in his mind the question of the "corruption" of socialism, but the answer he arrived at, and began to voice in his initial essays, was largely the product of his years in exile.

The Siberian exile to which Machajski was subjected was neither a desired nor a desirable experience, but it had little in common with the Gulag of Stalin's time. For the most part, the tsarist government was interested in isolating from the Empire's population centers those whom it considered to be political subversives, not in brutalizing them or in exploiting their labor. Isolation was certainly accomplished: the Iakutsk region, or Iakutiia, comprising most of eastern Siberia, was an area about two-thirds the size of European Russia and very sparsely settled. Political exiles were dispersed in small groups, or "colonies," across this immense and nearly empty space. For some, that was punishment enough; loneliness and inactivity drove a number of exiles to madness or suicide.[47]

For those able to withstand the isolation, the living conditions, the boredom, and, in the northernmost settlements, the winterlong Arctic darkness, exile was, at worst, tolerable, and, at best, provided a kind of graduate course in political science. In the prisons and convoys en route to their places of exile, the "politicals" were separated from the common criminals and were generally treated more carefully and more respectfully by their keepers. Although the exiles were subject to police surveillance, climate and lack of transportation made escape from the more remote settlements unlikely (though not impossible), and there the exiles were left pretty much to their own devices. There was no shortage of books, even on sensitive subjects, and there was plenty of time for political debate, which could be carried on with a greater degree of freedom and openness than at home. Especially if an exile received financial help and reading matter from family and friends, Siberia could prove a refreshing and educational respite from the anxieties of underground life. Those who resumed their political activity when their term of exile was over were no less determined to overthrow the tsarist government, but, thanks to their reading and their discussions with other exiles, they were often much better informed as to how to go about doing it. Lenin provides the most famous example: during his term of exile his relatives kept him well supplied with books and journals, and in between salubrious outdoor activities he was able to compose a series of Marxist treatises and articles for publication in St. Petersburg.[48] Even for Machajski, in a much more remote and uncomfortable location than Lenin, Siberian exile had positive benefits. It gave him the leisure (albeit enforced) to work out his new ideas, and it gave him the opportunity to disseminate them to a receptive audience of fellow exiles. Far from hindering him, the conditions of Siberian exile played a decisive role in enabling him to develop Makhaevism and to introduce it into the Russian revolutionary movement.

Viliuisk itself was hardly a spot that any revolutionary would have chosen as a place of residence. Though not as far north as some of the exile communities (it was at least below the Arctic Circle), it was one of the more remote locations to which political exiles were sent, situated several hundred miles northwest of the town of Iakutsk. It had a total of fifty buildings and contained, according to the 1897 census, all of 609 inhabitants. Even the prerevolutionary Russian encyclopedia which soberly reported these statistics could not refrain from characterizing Viliuisk as a "sorry settlement."[49] Its chief claim to fame in radical circles was that Chernyshevskii had endured eleven years of exile there. When Machajski arrived, however, he was greeted by a small but lively and harmonious community of exiles. According to Mikhail Romas', who was living there when Machajski reached the settlement in the winter of 1895, there were some two dozen exiles in and around Viliuisk, including several whose wives had accompanied them.[50] If the political exiles in Iakutiia as a whole formed a broad cross-section of the revolutionary movement in the Russian Empire, the Viliuisk colony reflected that movement in microcosm: there were Poles and populists, and Social Democrats of various stripes. Henryk Dulęba, for example, had been a member of the old Proletariat party, while Romas' himself was a *narodovolets*. A bit later came the Social-Democratic "economists": Liubov' Aizenshtadt, who, according to Vera Machajska, became one of Machajski's adherents, was of this persuasion.[51]

Most of the exiles managed to find some work, such as giving lessons, or kept themselves busy in other ways, and were on friendly terms. "Only Machajski, a man of great intellect and crystal-clear soul, immediately upon his arrival pounced upon the books and refused any work or assistance; he was in very great material need. Quite often, especially in the winter, we gathered in one apartment or another, and arguments and endless discussions would begin. Iudelevskii [a populist exile] and Machajski, who were studying Marx, often did not see eye-to-eye on the interpretation of one or another of his positions."[52]

Machajski had no lack of books to pounce upon, now that his years of imprisonment had come to an end. "As far as books were concerned," his wife wrote, "conditions in Viliuisk were exceptionally favorable," with the exiles in possession of "not only the basic works of Marx, Engels, and Kautsky, not only Russian journals, but whole runs of *Neue Zeit* for several years."[53] New books arrived as well, including Eduard Bernstein's works of Social-Democratic revisionism, which played a crucial role in the formation of Machajski's ideas. Bernstein's *Voraussetzungen des Sozialismus* was circulating in Iakutiia in 1899, the year of its publication, and copies of it quickly made their way to Viliuisk.[54]

Between 1898 and 1900, Machajski composed the first two of the essays that were to form his major work, *The Intellectual Worker (Umstvennyi rabochii)*. His fellow exiles in Viliuisk helped him to duplicate them on a hectograph and send copies to other exile colonies.[55] The exiles seem to have had a remarkably effective distribution network for what would today be termed *samizdat* literature, for Machajski's work quickly made its way across the vast spaces of Siberia. The effect of these hectographed pamphlets was electrifying, and for months they dominated the exiles' discussions. To some degree, Makhaevism aroused interest simply as an intellectual novelty, bringing a breath of fresh air into the stale ideological debates of the exiles. In some cases, however, its criticism of the intelligentsia caught the conscience of individuals who, of course, were themselves *intelligenty*. "On many people it made an enormous impression. Not a few exiles became 'Makhaevists' under its influence."[56]

There is ample evidence of the widespread circulation of Machajski's essays in the Siberian exile community. To the northeast, in the Verkhoiansk colony, "the question of the intelligentsia" became an acute issue, thanks to Machajski.[57] By the end of 1899 a copy of the first part of *The Intellectual Worker* had reached the Polish socialist Jan Strożecki in the settlement of Sredne-Kolymsk, in the far northeastern corner of Iakutiia. Strożecki, a schoolmate of Machajski's in Kielce and Warsaw, had been associated with the Second Proletariat party and subsequently with the PPS; he referred to Machajski's essay in a letter dated December 16, 1899 (N.S.).[58] South of Viliuisk, in Olekminsk, the pamphlets came into the hands of B. I. Gorev, a Social Democrat who would later write on the history of anarchism — and at one point Gorev helped to bury them in the ground in anticipation of a police search.[59] Far to the southwest, the pamphlets reached Leon Trotsky, then in exile in Ust'-Kut, in Irkutsk gubernia.

Down from Viliuisk, Machajski's lithographed booklets were delivered to us. The first booklet, in which he subjected the opportunism of Social Democracy to criticism, made a great impression on everyone with its array of facts and quotations. The second booklet, as far as I remember, was in the same mode, but weaker. The third one, however, in which the author spelled out his positive program, slipping in part into revolutionary syndicalism and in part into trade-unionism, seemed to me, as it did to the majority of the Social-Democratic exiles, extremely weak. Machajski had a few followers, primarily from the Viliuisk colony. The old populists seized upon his criticism as a weapon against Social Democracy in general, without worrying unduly about his conclusions.[60]

This was not the last of Trotsky's encounters with Makhaevism. In fact, he later had the opportunity to become personally acquainted with its creator. On a visit to Irkutsk in the summer of 1902, he was present at an evening-long argument between Machajski and K. K. Bauer, an adherent of the Legal Marxist and liberal Peter Struve. When Trotsky tried to intervene in the debate, both of its participants turned on him, and, in what was certainly a rare act of forbearance on Trotsky's part, he deemed it best to keep his silence.[61]

From Siberia, the exiles subsequently carried word of Machajski's views to their revolutionary comrades in Russia and Europe. Trotsky provides a noteworthy example. When he turned up on Lenin's doorstep in London late in 1902, the two strolled around the city while Trotsky filled Lenin in on the news from Siberia, telling him, among other things, "about the three essays by Machajski."[62]

Shortly after composing these essays, Machajski himself was able to begin disseminating them to a somewhat broader audience, and to begin creating an organization based on them. He was released from exile in 1900, but in the course of his journey westward he was accidentally arrested, having been mistaken for the future Bolshevik (and biographer of Michael Bakunin) Iurii Steklov, who had escaped from Iakutsk exile in November 1899.[63] When the police found a number of copies of *The Intellectual Worker* in his possession, they put him in jail. A group of exiles in the city of Irkutsk put up 5,000 rubles in bail for him, which facilitated his release from prison but prevented him from fleeing the city. He remained in Irkutsk under police surveillance.[64]

In Irkutsk, Machajski formed the first group of "Makhaevists" and began to make contact with the railroad workers, bakers, and typesetters of the city.[65] *The Intellectual Worker* was reproduced on a mimeograph, a small printing press was established, and in April 1902 the group printed a May Day appeal to the workers. This manifesto embodied the basic Makhaevist position that the workers must struggle solely for their own economic demands and not for political goals, which would benefit only "educated society." It berated the Social Democrats for politicizing the workers' movement, and it called for mass economic strikes and demonstrations.[66]

At the beginning of 1903, the Makhaevist group was broken up by arrests—although, as the Social Democrats were to discover, it left lasting traces on the labor movement of Irkutsk. According to one source, the immediate cause of the arrest of Machajski and his adherents was their organization of a bakers' strike and their publication of leaflets calling for an "insurrection of the hungry."[67] Machajski and three of his associates were sentenced to six years of exile each in the forbidding settlement of Sredne-Kolymsk.[68] First, however, they were taken to Aleksandrovskii Tsentral, a transit prison located a few miles outside Irkutsk—where the warden was instructed to keep them under the strictest surveillance as "especially dangerous persons."[69]

The *starosta*, or elected spokesman, of the political prisoners at the time of Machajski's arrival at Aleksandrovskii Tsentral was the Social Democrat Petr Garvi, whose memoirs provide a detailed account of Machajski's stay there. Machajski's ideas had by now created such a sensation throughout Siberia that Garvi himself had heard about him while en route to the prison; when Machajski was brought there he was received by the other politicals almost as a celebrity. A hectographed copy of his *Intellectual Worker* circulated among them and was read "to shreds," provoking, as usual, heated debates, and overshadowing even the old arguments between the Marxists and the populists.[70]

Machajski himself made a vivid, and for the most part favorable, impression on his fellow prisoners. When he arrived, an agreement was in effect between the prison administration and the political prisoners which gave the latter certain liberties in return for their promise not to attempt escape. Machajski, though he expressed disapproval of such arrangements in principle and was in fact hoping to make an escape, agreed to abide by the arrangement — and Garvi adds that he soon came to realize that Machajski was a man who would not go back on his word. As Garvi describes him, Machajski had considerable personal charm. "Of medium height, well built, with the eyes of a Polish revolutionary fanatic set in an energetic face framed by a thin beard, he had a striking vitality." Though unyielding when it came to defending his views, he was extremely cheerful, delighting in gymnastic tricks, chess, and dancing. He also turned out to be an excellent cook and considerably upgraded the prisoners' cuisine — which was perhaps just as well for his own health, for Garvi also noted in him a weakness for alcohol.[71]

During the few months that Machajski spent at Aleksandrovskii Tsentral, a dramatic confrontation took place between the political prisoners and the prison administration. Following a precedent set by the previous year's batch of exiles, the prisoners bound for the various colonies in Iakutiia demanded to be told their precise destination before their departure instead of en route, in order to notify relatives and maintain uninterrupted mail deliveries. When the authorities in Irkutsk refused their request, the prisoners barricaded themselves in their barracks — and then faced the question of what to do next. Garvi depicts Machajski as a firebrand in this episode, and not just figuratively speaking. If Garvi is to be believed, Machajski first argued that the prisoners should offer armed resistance to any attempt to storm the barracks, even though they had only a few revolvers and knives amongst them. Then he proposed that the prisoners threaten to burn down the barracks, with themselves inside, rather like the Old Believers of yore, if their demands were not met. He must have had considerable powers of persuasion, because a majority of the prisoners adopted his proposal, over Garvi's strenuous objection, and an ultimatum was issued to the authorities. It worked, in a manner of speaking: after two weeks, the prisoners were finally informed of their specific destinations — but in many cases discovered that those destinations were now more remote than their original sentences warranted.[72]

With this episode, the gentlemen's agreement between the prisoners and the warden broke down, and Machajski was now morally free to make an escape attempt. He was assisted by one of his adherents, A. Shetlikh, who had met him in prison in St. Petersburg and been exiled with him to Viliuisk. Shetlikh, having been released from exile, now came to the area and helped to organize Machajski's escape.[73] At the end of May or beginning of June, on the very day the prisoners were to set off from the transit prison under armed guard (thus making flight virtually impossible), Garvi persuaded the too-trusting warden to allow him to go into the free settlement to buy provisions for the journey, accompanied by Machajski and his comrade Mitkevich. They talked their guard into allowing them to pay a last visit to a "sick" friend who lived in the village, and while Garvi sipped coffee with the guard in the next room, first Machajski and then Mitkevich climbed out the invalid's bedroom window and down a ladder. Even at such a delicate moment, Machajski had sufficient aplomb to wave good-bye to Garvi, behind the guard's back, as he climbed over the windowsill. Garvi learned later that after wandering about in the taiga for some time, the two made their way back to Irkutsk, where they found refuge with friends and completed their escape. Machajski returned to European Russia and from there went abroad, finally settling in Geneva. "In 1904," Garvi concludes his narrative, "I met him — very warmly — in Paris."[74]

During the next two or three years Machajski published most of his major writings, developing the theoretical foundations of Makhaevism that he had first laid out in his Siberian essays. It is clear, however, that even before he left Siberia, Makhaevism was already very well known. The hectographed and mimeographed copies of his writings continued to circulate. Familiarity with Makhaevism had begun to seep into the various branches of the revolutionary movement and, thanks to the Makhaevists' efforts in Irkutsk, into the labor movement as well.[75] Whatever the degree of obscurity that may have enveloped Machajski subsequently, in the early years of the twentieth century his criticism of the intelligentsia as a "new class" of exploiters, and of socialism as its class ideology, were the subject of widespread interest, discussion, and debate.

Chapter 2

The "New Class"

FROM 1903 TO 1906, when the revolution in Russia permitted him to live briefly in St. Petersburg, Machajski remained in Switzerland. Now married to a Russian woman who went by the name of Vera and had been a fellow exile in Siberia,[1] Machajski devoted himself mainly to elaborating the theoretical foundations of Makhaevism. At the beginning of 1904, he turned for financial assistance to his old friend Stefan Żeromski, who had now achieved fame as a novelist. They had not been in contact for thirteen years. In a letter of February 24, written from Geneva, Machajski described himself as destitute. Not surprisingly, his views on the intelligentsia had alienated all political groups both in Russia and in Poland: "Here in emigration I have not counted, nor can I count, on any cooperation at all from the Polish and Russian intelligentsia."[2] He had found some occasional work as a translator from German into Russian and as a typesetter at one of the Russian presses, but now even these odd jobs were no longer available to him. He seemed less concerned with subsistence, however, than with the publication of his writings, including one which he described as "a comparison of my own views with the latest currents."[3] Among other money-making projects which he had in mind, he asked whether Żeromski might commission him to translate one of his works into Russian, providing an advance large enough to enable him to survive and to print a book some two hundred pages in length.[4] In subsequent letters he told Żeromski that he had worked as a house-painter and again as a typesetter. He also tried giving lectures in Geneva and Bern, and, through Russian émigré circles, in Berlin as well, but few paid to come and hear him.[5]

Although the translation project did not come to pass, Żeromski on more than one occasion did supply financial assistance.[6] Another source, however, casts some doubt on the degree of deprivation Machajski was suffering. Max Nomad met Machajski in Geneva in 1905 and for several years was an adherent of his views and an activist in Makhaevist groups. As Nomad describes him, Machajski had a compelling physical presence: "He was thirty-eight at that time, but looked at least fifty. His ascetic face reminded me of the pictures of John the Baptist."[7] According to Nomad, however, while Machajski and his wife were in Geneva their living expenses and the printing of Machajski's writings were financed by "a rich convert." This was a young woman named Janina Berson, the daughter of a Petersburg banker. Having been won over to Machajski's views by Vera Machajska, Berson contributed a large part of her allowance to the Makhaevist cause.[8] Like the Bolsheviks and other Russian revolutionaries, Machajski was able to find at least one wealthy "angel" willing to back the destruction of her own class.

By one means or another, Machajski succeeded in getting his writings into print. The work in progress that he mentioned to Żeromski was probably part 3 of *The Intellectual Worker*, comprising two sections entitled "Socialism and the Labor Movement" and "Socialist Science As a New Religion." They joined the two Siberian essays, "The Evolution of Social Democracy" and "Scientific Socialism," which, respectively, formed parts 1 and 2. All three parts of *The Intellectual Worker*, the major theoretical exposition of Makhaevism, appeared in Geneva in 1904–1905.[9] Also in Geneva in 1905, Machajski published two shorter works: *The Bourgeois Revolution and the Workers' Cause (Burzhuaznaia revoliutsiia i rabochee delo)*, which was reprinted in St. Petersburg in the following year, and *The Bankruptcy of Nineteenth-Century Socialism (Bankrotstvo sotsializma XIX stoletiia).*[10] Two other works round out his theoretical writings. In 1906, he published in St. Petersburg a translation of excerpts from Marx's *The Holy Family*, with extensive notes by the translator.[11] Finally, there is an unpublished manuscript, written in Polish in 1910–1911 and subsequently translated into Russian by Vera Machajska.[12] Two journals, each of which appeared in only a single issue, complete the corpus of Machajski's writings: *Rabochii zagovor (The Workers' Conspiracy)* of 1908, devoted mainly to revolutionary tactics, and *Rabochaia revoliutsiia (The Workers' Revolution)*, Machajski's response to the Bolshevik seizure of power, dating from 1918.[13]

Thus, around the time of the 1905 revolution, Machajski's writings began to circulate in print, both within Russia and in emigration. For the most part, however, all of his subsequent writings amounted to restatements and minor amplifications of the basic positions he had worked out in Siberia. For an analysis of the theoretical bases of Makhaevism, therefore, his body of writings is best taken as different expressions of the same fundamental set of ideas rather than as a chronological progression.

His views did undergo one major shift, however, as he was writing his very first essay, "The Evolution of Social Democracy." The question that preoccupied him in Siberia was why Marxism, particularly in Germany, seemed to have lost its revolutionary impetus. The essay was devoted to this subject, beginning with a lengthy analysis of the German party and then proceeding to consideration of the PPS, the Bund (the General Jewish Workers' Union in Russia and Poland), and the Russian Social-Democratic party. All these parties, according to Machajski, had succumbed to the fatal preoccupation with winning political freedom that Marx himself had introduced into the movement. In the *Communist Manifesto*, Marx had urged the communists to "labor everywhere for the union and agreement of the democratic parties of all countries," and, as the first step of the proletarian revolution, "to raise the proletariat to the position of ruling class, to win the battle of democracy."[14] Machajski maintained that only a revolutionary, economic struggle could further the workers' cause, not a democratic, political one. It was utopian to believe that the proletariat could utilize legal institutions, howsoever democratic, to attack the property structure of capitalist society. "The economic foundations of the bourgeoisie's exploitation and domination can be *destroyed* only by the *domination* of the proletariat, only by its 'despotic attack on the right of property,'" as he felt the *Communist Manifesto* had much more accurately phrased it in another passage.[15]

Machajski claimed that Marx had formulated just such a policy in his militant *Address of the Central Committee to the Communist League* of 1850. That statement had urged the German communists to break with the democratic parties rather than to make common cause with them, and it contained the famous reference to "permanent" revolution. Here, Machajski declared, the communists had no thought of trying to use the legal rights and institutions of the class state to express the will of the proletariat. But the tactics outlined in the *Manifesto* rather than the positions taken in the *Address* had determined the future policy of Social Democracy. That policy was expressed in the formula: "the proletariat can fight for its emancipation only by using the political rights of the democratic state."[16] Its adoption by the First International had been the source of the Bakuninist opposition to Marx. The workers who supported that opposition were not protesting against the centralization that Marx had imposed on the International, as Bakunin and his anarchist followers claimed, but against the fact that this centralization lacked revolutionary content. It arose not because the General Council, the leadership of the International which Marx controlled, consisted of "Jacobins" who were plotting their own dictatorship on the morrow of the revolution, but because it did not consist of revolutionaries.[17]

The emphasis on politics had led the International to concentrate on separate national revolutions. The *Communist Manifesto* made the first step in the workers' revolution nationalist in form: the proletariat of each country must contend with its own bourgeoisie. The International had continued this policy of encouraging the proletariat to participate in the political life of individual countries. But the seizure of power by the proletariat must be an international act; it could result only in reformism if confined within national limits.[18] Whether the objective was a parliamentary majority, as in the case of German Social Democracy, a constitutional replacement for autocracy in the case of Russian Social Democracy, political independence for Poland or equal rights for the Jews, such a pursuit inevitably led to a compromise between the cause of the proletariat and the cause of the liberal and radical bourgeoisie. The results of such political compromises were necessarily fatal for social revolution. Only the Polish Proletariat party — to which Machajski himself, of course, had belonged —

won his praise as a "party of revolutionary Marxism," for it had devoted itself not to gaining the independence of Poland but to immediate economic revolution. (He also had a good word to say for Rosa Luxemburg as a critic of opportunism within the German Social-Democratic party.) The workers themselves would respond eagerly if Social Democracy changed its ways and pursued truly revolutionary objectives, Machajski argued, as the Lodz May Day strike of 1892 had clearly demonstrated.[19]

Machajski began this first essay as a Marxist revolutionary, an impatient but loyal critic of Social Democracy. His critique reflected the experiences and preoccupations of his Polish period: his rejection of the increasingly nationalist orientation of the Polish socialist movement, the impression made on him by the 1892 Lodz strike. It was not a particularly unusual or original critique. The *Address of the Central Committee to the Communist League*, which Marx composed at a moment when his expectations of revolution were at a high point, was a favorite text for Marxist militants opposed to the political pragmatism of other Marxists.[20] Machajski's essay assumed that the "opportunism" of the Marxist parties in Germany and the Russian Empire was merely an ideological or tactical error which could be corrected; his purpose was to persuade them to renounce their absorption in legal tactics and political goals and return to their true Marxist labor of overthrowing the economic and social system of capitalism. It was an objective many of Machajski's Social-Democratic readers in Siberia, such as Trotsky, shared, and they could welcome his essay as a useful salvo in the battle against Revisionism. There was little in it that was distinctively "Makhaevist."

By the time he reached the conclusion of his essay, however, Machajski had become convinced that persuasion was useless, for Social Democracy's turn to "opportunism" stemmed from a more fundamental source of corruption than mere tactical errors or loss of nerve. In a newly written preface to the Geneva edition of this essay, he warned his readers that he had worked out his point of view only in the course of writing the work and had expressed it clearly only in the conclusion. The earlier parts of the essay, he conceded, displayed a serious defect: "the author kept trying to find a way to turn Marxism away from its errors and onto the true revolutionary path, an effort which later investigation showed

31

was completely utopian."[21] Only in the conclusion had he realized that the evolution of Social Democracy revealed the presence within the movement of "forces which, by their very nature, cannot wish the abolition of the capitalist contradiction." The doctrines of Marxism permitted the "continual penetration of non-proletarian elements into the revolutionary army of the proletariat, elements which hinder its development and its definitive attack on the bourgeois order."[22]

In the course of the essay Machajski had made some passing references to these elements but had not singled them out for special attention. He had referred to "the ruling bourgeois classes" as comprising "not only the owners of industrial and commercial capital, but also the privileged employees of the capitalist state: politicians, journalists, scholars, and all the 'noble' professions."[23] In regard to the June Days of Paris in 1848, he argued that the suppression of the workers by the newly established republic "showed the proletariat that its enemy was not just the owners of capital . . . but the whole mass of *privileged employees* of the capitalist state: lawyers, journalists, scholars."[24] Finally, however, he realized that he had made a fundamental discovery: socialism, and particularly Marxism, represented the class interests not of the workers but of a rising new class—the intelligentsia, or, as he termed them, the "intellectual workers," who sought a profitable accommodation for themselves with the capitalist order rather than its definitive overthrow.[25] This now became the core idea of Makhaevism, the doctrine which gave it its unique character and distinguished it from other revolutionary currents in the Russian Empire.

The key that unlocked the true nature of Social Democracy for Machajski was a series of articles which Karl Kautsky had published in *Die Neue Zeit* in 1894–1895. Under the conditions of capitalist production, the German Social-Democratic theorist wrote, "intellectual work becomes the special function of a particular class, which as a rule does not directly—nor, by its nature, necessarily—have an interest in capitalist exploitation: the so-called intelligentsia [*Intelligenz*], which makes its living from the sale of its special knowledge and talents."[26] To some extent, the intelligentsia provided a refuge for ruined small property-owners: "A new, very numerous, and continually growing middle class is formed in this way," masking to some degree "the decline of the middle class as a whole."[27] The end result was a significant new socioeconomic formation: "in the intelligentsia a new middle class is arising, growing in part because of the requirements of the capitalist process of production, in part through the decline of small business, a middle class whose size and significance in relation to the petty bourgeoisie is steadily increasing, but which is also more and more depressed by the mounting oversupply of labor and thereby is permanently discontented."[28] Both the power of the intelligentsia and the power of its discontent merited the attention of Social Democracy.

Having identified this "new middle class" and its growing numbers, Kautsky proceeded to deny it any independent significance. The intelligentsia was a very heterogeneous group, composed of many different strata; it had no specific class interest of its own, only professional interests within a particular specialty. An actor and a clergyman, a doctor and an attorney, a chemist and an editorial writer could have neither intellectual nor economic interests in common.[29] What distinguished the intelligentsia from the proletariat was a kind of caste or guild mentality, a sense of the intelligentsia's privileged position as the "aristocracy of the spirit," and a desire to maintain that exclusiveness by limiting entry into the intelligentsia.[30] A good part of the intelligentsia, Kautsky felt, could be won over to the side of the proletariat. Excepted were those groups whose work required them to justify the bourgeoisie and share its sentiments: certain kinds of teachers and journalists, legal and administrative officials, direct participants in the extraction of surplus labor from the workers (Kautsky seems to have had managers in mind here). By and large, however, the intelligentsia was a potential ally of the proletariat by virtue of its role as a bystander in the process of capitalist exploitation, its lack of a homogeneous class interest, and its broader intellectual horizon, which gave it a greater capacity than any other part of the population for rising above its own interests and looking at the needs of society as a whole.[31]

Machajski viewed the position of the intelligentsia in an entirely different light. He maintained that Kautsky had revealed the existence of a new class of exploiters but had refused to draw the appropriate conclusions. The doctrines of Social Democracy denied the possibility of the growth of the middle classes and insisted that the fruits of capitalism were being usurped only by a small number of capitalists and large landowners.

Meanwhile, the evolution of capitalism displays the indisputable growth of bourgeois society. Even if small enterprises inevitably perish, the middle classes of bourgeois society, in the form of the continually growing number of privileged employees of capital, increase all the same, and so "all the advantages of the gigantic growth of productive forces are monopolized" *not by a "handful" of plutocrats alone, but by the continually growing bourgeois society.*[32]

Here was the real enemy of the proletariat: "the privileged employees of the capitalist order, . . . the 'intelligentsia,' the army of intellectual workers,"[33] no less interested than the capitalists themselves in the continued exploitation of the manual workers.

In Marxism, the crucial factor determining class relationships is ownership of the means of production. Machajski, however, denied the central importance of property ownership. The intelligentsia owned neither factories nor land, and yet, he observed, it bore the same relationship to the workers as the property owners did.

In every country, in every state, there exists a huge class of people who have neither industrial nor commercial capital, yet live like real masters.

They own neither land nor factories nor workshops, but they enjoy a robber's income no smaller than that of the middling and large capitalists. They do not have their own enterprises, but they are "white-hands" just like the capitalists. They too spend their whole lives free from manual labor, and if they do participate in production, then it is only as managers, directors, engineers. That is, in relation to the workers, to the slaves of manual labor, they are commanders and masters just as much as the capitalist proprietors.[34]

Although the intelligentsia did not own the means of production, it did possess and exploit a special form of "property," namely, education.

A larger and larger part of bourgeois society receives the funds for its parasitical existence as an intelligentsia, an army of intellectual workers which does not personally possess the means of production but continually increases and multiplies its income, which it obtains as the hereditary owner of all knowledge, culture, and civilization.[35]

Hence the fundamental class conflict in contemporary capitalist society was not the antagonism between the owners and nonowners of the means of production: it was the larger conflict between those who did manual labor and those who did not, between the uneducated and the educated. As Machajski summarized his position several years later, the intelligentsia consisted of all those who had any sort of higher education, in short, of everyone with a diploma. Each year the secondary and higher educational institutions of every country turned out tens of thousands of people who would occupy a privileged position in society, free from the yoke of manual labor. Only a small minority were capitalists; the vast majority, the "professional intelligentsia," received not a return on their own capital but a comfortable income in the form of a "salary" or "fee." "Some of the more able or more cunning of those equipped with diplomas, in state administration or industry, in public or literary careers, attain such high posts that they live in no less luxury and wealth than any big capitalist."[36] Throughout the world, "knowledge, just as much as land or capital, furnishes the means for the parasitic lordly existence of the present-day robbers."[37]

Kautsky was wrong, Machajski declared, in claiming that the various components of the intelligentsia did not share a common class interest. The class interest of the intelligentsia was the preservation of its hereditary monopoly on education, the source of which was the economic exploitation of the proletariat. Marxism regarded the higher income of nonmanual workers as a just reward for their "skilled labor power." Machajski maintained a much stricter interpretation of the labor theory of value and refused to admit that nonmanual workers could create value. Such workers lived on "net national profit," the total national sum of the proletariat's surplus labor. This fund constituted the hereditary property of bourgeois families and enabled successive generations of *intelligenty* to educate themselves. Then, in the form of payment for their skilled labor, they too acquired the right to appropriate the unpaid labor of the proletariat. "Bourgeois society passes on to its offspring surplus value appropriated under the guise of a

35

reward for labor 'of a higher quality,' and the greatest riches of mankind — knowledge, science — become the hereditary monopoly of a privileged minority."[38]

The position of the European proletariat as a whole had not significantly altered in the half-century of Social Democracy's existence, according to Machajski; the contradictions of capitalism were no weaker than before. The evolution of Social Democracy, therefore, must reflect something else: the changing composition of "bourgeois society" itself, namely, the rise of the "intellectual workers" and their growing stake in the capitalist order. The task of a truly revolutionary socialism was not to deny the rise of this new class but to declare it "the new enemy of the proletariat."[39]

• In developing his theory that the intelligentsia was a rising new class of "intellectual workers" using socialism to pursue its own interests at the expense of the workers, Machajski utilized basic Marxist principles of social analysis. He adhered to Marx's economic materialism and class theory, broadening and adapting them somewhat and turning them against the Marxists themselves. Nor did he have to go outside the Marxist movement itself to find inspiration for his initial criticism of Social-Democratic policies. He could draw, for example, on the revolt of the so-called *Jungen* (the Young Ones), or Independents, within the German Social-Democratic party in the early 1890s.[40] The *Jungen* were young intellectuals of a radical bent whose criticism of the party leadership broke into the open with the party's decision in 1890 to reject a general walkout of the German workers on May 1 and to limit observance to after-work meetings and peaceful festivities. This alone would have been enough to attract Machajski's attention. The celebration of May Day played a particularly important role in early Polish socialism,[41] and Machajski himself placed great emphasis on May Day strikes and demonstrations as a way of mobilizing the working class. The controversy regarding May Day brought to the surface deeper frustrations over the German party's seeming loss of revolutionary spirit, and the *Jungen* erupted with accusations that the socialist movement and its leadership had been corrupted by the preoccupation with parliamentary practices. The *Jungen* voiced their criticism at the Halle Party Congress of 1890 and the Erfurt Congress of 1891, where they were read out of the party. Machajski had become familiar with their views while living in Zurich before his arrest and sympathized with their position. He referred approvingly to them in the early pages of his first essay.[42]

His ultimate rejection of Marxism itself, however, raises the complex issue of just how much Makhaevism owed to anarchism. Machajski's unyielding opposition to political activity strongly echoed the central tenet of anarchism, while his emphasis on the general strike as an instrument of working-class action was closely reminiscent of anarchosyndicalism. His preoccupation with the intelligentsia, however, was not present in the same form, or to the same degree, in anarchism, and this was enough to give Makhaevism a distinctive profile. For his part, Machajski never considered himself an anarchist, and he denounced anarchism in much the same terms that he applied to Marxism. Nevertheless, not only was there a considerable degree of doctrinal similarity, but when Makhaevism as an organized movement got under way there was a good deal of exchange of personnel between Makhaevist groups and anarchist groups. Of particular interest is the question of Machajski's familiarity with the writings of Michael Bakunin. Though Marxism formed the starting point of Makhaevism, its general tone and a number of its specific features seem to have been inspired by, if not directly borrowed from, Bakunin. Machajski admitted no indebtedness to Bakunin and rarely mentions him at all in his writings (though even when he wrote his first essay he displayed some familiarity with Bakunin's criticism of Marx in the First International[43]). Nevertheless, Bakunin appears to have been the main intellectual precursor of Makhaevism. Most notably, it was Bakunin who first raised the issue of a connection between the personal interests of the intellectuals and the ultimate objectives of Marxism. In a number of scattered but trenchant passages in his writings, he adumbrated much of what Machajski was later to develop.

One significant theme that was to figure prominently in Makhaevism appeared in a series of articles that Bakunin wrote on the subject of education for the Swiss socialist newspaper *L'Égalité* in 1869. Here he argued that educational inequality contributed to the exploitation of the workers, and that unequal knowledge could of itself generate class inequality.

One who knows more will naturally dominate one who knows less; and should there exist at first between two classes only this one difference of instruction and education, this difference in a little while would produce all the rest. The human world would find itself back where it is now, i.e., it would be divided anew into a mass of slaves and a small number of rulers, the former working as they do now for the latter.[44]

Instead of just *more* education for the workers, Bakunin demanded complete equality of educational opportunity, "integral and complete education" for the proletariat, so that "there may no longer exist above it, to protect it and direct it, that is to say, to exploit it, any class superior by virtue of its knowledge, any aristocracy of intelligence."[45]

The present domination of the bourgeoisie, according to Bakunin, was in large part a result of its educational superiority. All the inventions of science, and all their applications to social life, had profited only the privileged classes and increased the power of the state apparatus through which they ruled.

By what force do the privileged classes maintain themselves today . . . against the legitimate indignation of the masses? Is it by an inherent force? No, it is solely by the force of the state, in which, moreover, their children occupy today, as they always have, all the ruling posts and even all the middle and lower posts, minus those of worker and soldier. And what is it that today chiefly constitutes the power of states? It is science.[46]

Since the existing social structure enabled only the bourgeoisie to receive an education, it alone was able to participate in the march of civilization; the proletariat was condemned to ignorance, just as the progress of industry and commerce condemned it to poverty. Intellectual progress and material progress contributed equally to the workers' enslavement. Therefore, Bakunin concluded, the destruction of the existing social order was necessary in order to make both cultural and material wealth the patrimony of all men.[47]

When Bakunin spoke of "knowledge" and "education" he usually had in mind not technical or professional expertise but an abstract, theoretical comprehension of social and political principles. He defined "the man who knows more" as the man "whose

spirit [has been] enlarged by science, and who, having better understood the associations of natural and social facts, or what are
called the laws of nature and society," can more easily understand
the character of his environment.[48] For all his respect for such
knowledge, a recurrent theme in his writings toward the end of
his life was a rejection of all claims to power based on scientific
understanding. On this count he vigorously criticized the followers of Auguste Comte, rejecting the elitist pretensions of "savants"
who claimed superior sociological insight. As his struggle with
Marx in the International intensified, he began to criticize the
"scientific socialists" in the same terms. "The government of
science," he wrote in an essay that was to achieve wide circulation, "and of men of science, whether they call themselves positivists, disciples of Auguste Comte, or even disciples of the doctrinaire School of German Communism, can only be impotent,
ridiculous, inhuman, cruel, oppressive, exploitative, and mali-
cious."[49] Although he valued the liberating effect on the individual
of knowing "the laws of nature and of society," he held that any
attempt to force a society to conform to such laws would result
in the sacrifice of the individual to bloodless abstractions. The
liberty of man consisted in obeying natural and social laws because he recognized their legitimate authority, and not because
they were forced on him by another's will.[50] "Monopolists of
science" formed a distinct caste, he declared, and they were interested not in individuals, not in "Peter or James," but in abstractions; they regarded living individuals merely as the flesh of intellectual and social development. True to form as the arch-rebel
of his age, Bakunin preached *the revolt of life against science,
or, rather, against the government of science.*"[51]

   As he continued his attack on the Marxists, he began to use
the term "new class" in regard to them, warning that those who
claimed to possess "scientific socialism" might use this claim to
assert political power. Bakunin may well have been the first to
apply the phrase "new class" in this now familiar fashion. In an
unpublished fragment of the work just cited, he wrote: "The partisans of the communist state, as their name alone indicates, are
partisans of collective, communal property, administered and exploited by the state for the benefit of all the workers." The result,
even if based on universal suffrage, would necessarily be a new

form of tutelage, "the creation of a new political class, the representative of the domination of the state."[52] In another such fragment, written in 1872 but published only decades later, Bakunin was even more explicit.

In the popular state of Mr. Marx, we are told, there will be no privileged class. Everyone will be equal, not only from the legal and political but also the economic point of view. At least, that is what they promise, though I doubt very much that their promise can ever be kept, given the path they wish to follow. There will be no classes, but a government, and, mind you, an extremely complex one, which will not content itself with governing and administering the masses politically, as all governments do today, but will also administer them economically, concentrating in its hands the production and the *just* distribution of wealth, the cultivation of the earth, the establishment and development of factories, the organization and direction of commerce, and, finally, the application of capital to production by the sole banker, the state. All this will require immense knowledge. . . . There will be a new class, a new hierarchy of real and fictitious savants, and the world will be divided into a minority ruling in the name of science and an immense ignorant majority.[53]

Bakunin gathered together his charges against the Marxists in somewhat more systematic fashion in an important work entitled *Statism and Anarchy (Gosudarstvennost' i anarkhiia)*, which he published in 1873 in the aftermath of his defeat by Marx in the International. In the disorderly but sometimes strikingly penetrating manner characteristic of his writings, he made the bold prophecy that the triumph of Marxism would produce a "scientific" and technological elite to rule over the workers.

Because they believed that thought precedes life and that sociology must therefore be the starting point of all social reform, idealists, metaphysicians, positivists, and "doctrinaire revolutionaries" — Bakunin's term for the Marxists — considered the state a necessity. The small minority possessing scientific theory must direct the reconstruction of society after the revolution, representing their dictatorial regime as the will of the people.

Now it is clear why the *doctrinaire revolutionaries*, who have as their objective the overthrow of the existing governments and regimes in order to found their own dictatorship on the ruins, have never been and will never be enemies of the state. . . . They are enemies only of the existing authorities, because they want to take their place, enemies of the existing political institutions because these preclude the possibility of their own dictatorship. But at the same time they are the warmest friends of state power, for if it were not retained the revolution, once it had truly liberated the masses, would deprive this pseudo-revolutionary minority of all hope of putting them in a new harness and conferring on them the benefits of its own governmental decrees.[54]

Adding a reference in the next paragraph to "the doctrinaire revolutionaries under the leadership of Mr. Marx," Bakunin left no doubt as to the specific target of these accusations.

Some pages later, Bakunin raised the question of the real meaning of Marx's concept of the "dictatorship of the proletariat." Marx had spoken of raising the proletariat "to the level of a ruling class." But retention of the state — instead of its immediate abolition, as Bakunin advocated — would necessarily mean government of the people by a new elite, even if that elite consisted of workers.

Yes, of *former* workers, perhaps, who as soon as they become rulers or representatives of the people will cease to be workers and will start viewing the laborer's world from the heights of the state; they will no longer represent the people, only themselves and their pretensions to rule the people. Anyone who doubts this is just not familiar with the nature of man.[55]

Nor would the commitment of these new rulers to socialism have any significance. Marxist terms such as "scientific socialism" only indicated all the more that the new order would be "a highly despotic rule of the masses by a new and highly restricted aristocracy of real or pretended scholars." Since the people lacked learning, they would be relieved of the difficult burdens of government.[56]

Up to this point, Bakunin had painted a picture of the Marxists imposing their dictatorial will on the masses in order to realize their abstract schemes of social reorganization. Now he added to his prophecy the vision of a technological elite taking firm control of the economic forces of society, militarizing the workers, and concentrating on the development of the national economy as well as the consolidation of its own privileged position. According to Marx's theory, Bakunin wrote, the proletariat must seize the state and then hand it over to its guardians and teachers, "the communist party chiefs, in a word, Mr. Marx and his friends."

41

The latter would then proceed to "liberate" the workers in their own fashion.

They will gather up the reins of government in a strong hand because the ignorant people need strong guardians; they will establish a single state bank, concentrating in their own hands all commercial and industrial, agricultural, and even scientific production; and they will divide the mass of the people into two armies, one industrial and one agrarian, under the direct command of state engineers, who will form a new privileged scientific-political caste.[57]

In typical fashion, Bakunin failed to pursue this particular line of criticism of the Marxists, and his book veered off in another direction. In linking the "men of science" with "state engineers," however, Bakunin foreshadowed the connection Machajski was to draw between the socialists and the "intellectual workers." Machajski by no means adopted the whole of Bakunin's position. Most important, he did not share the anarchist conviction that immediate abolition of the state would be sufficient to prevent the rise of a new form of oppression. But much of what Bakunin had hinted at, implied, and touched upon fleetingly, reappeared in Makhaevism, now placed within the framework of a Marxian class analysis. The result was the first systematic theory of socialism as the ideology not of the proletariat but of a new class of aspiring rulers.

Throughout his attack on the new class, Machajski used the terms *intelligentsia* and *intellectual workers* interchangeably. In the Russian context, however, such usage was fraught with contradiction and confusion. The subject of the intelligentsia was of enormous importance in Russia because of its crucial position in the country's cultural and social life as well as in the revolutionary movement. For all its importance, however, there was great uncertainty about how to define it or even whom to include among its members. This uncertainty could be measured in sheer bibliographical terms, for the question "What is the intelligentsia?" generated a distinct literature of ever-expanding magnitude.[58] Machajski entered the discussion at a time when both the concept and the social reality of the Russian intelligentsia were undergoing far-reaching changes. Makhaevism did not resolve the ambiguities of this term; rather, it embodied them and sought to exploit them. Machajski's usage, therefore, needs to be set against the broader background of the intelligentsia's role in early twentieth-century Russian life.

By the turn of the century, the term *intelligentsia* had come to be used in at least three major ways that are of relevance here (though they by no means exhaust contemporary applications of the word). The broadest connotation was a cultural one, referring loosely to Russia's Western-educated minority. In this sense the intelligentsia traced its origins at least as far back as Peter the Great and his imposition of Westernizing reforms on a backward — or, as we would term it today, underdeveloped — Russia. Under Russian conditions, the result was the emergence of "two cultures," an elite which had more or less assimilated Western culture and modern habits of life and thought, and the bulk of the population which still lived in many respects according to the precepts and practices of medieval Muscovy.[59] The term *intelligentsia* came to designate the Russian "public," or "public opinion" (*obshchestvo*), the "conscious," more or less culturally Westernized segment of the population. It is in this way that an Okhrana official, reporting on the political atmosphere in the Russian countryside on the eve of the 1917 revolution, employs the term: "According to insurance agents, teachers, tradesmen and other representatives of the village intelligentsia, everybody is impatiently awaiting the end of this 'accursed war.'"[60]

Used in this way, the word inevitably carried an association with social privilege. Throughout the eighteenth century and the first half of the nineteenth, Western education and cultural exposure was virtually the monopoly of the court and the nobility. Even as educational opportunities began to open up to segments of the population lower down the social scale after the emancipation of the serfs, a university or even secondary-school education was still enough to place its recipient worlds apart from the ordinary Russian peasant or worker. To the latter, the educated individual was simply another *beloruchka*, or "white-hand," a representative of the privileged classes. Strikingly, however, it was *intelligenty* themselves who decried in the most vehement terms the privileged status of the educated. Over and over again, Russia's foremost writers and molders of public opinion gave vent to eloquent outbursts of guilt that the higher consciousness and cultural development they enjoyed had been achieved in an exploitative, parasitic fashion, wrung from the labor and sufferings of the downtrodden. As early as 1848, Alexander Herzen wrote: "All our education, our literary and scientific development, our love of beauty, our occupations, presuppose an environment constantly swept and tended by *others*, prepared by *others; somebody's* labor is essential in order to provide us with the leisure necessary for our mental development."[61] Another example, which had an enormous impact on the young populists of the 1870s, was Peter Lavrov's *Historical Letters (Istoricheskie pis'ma)*, which referred to "the long line of generations who have toiled" to support the members of the educated minority, and "the capital in blood and labor which has been lavished on their cultivation."[62] The "repentant nobleman" who became a familiar figure in the nineteenth century was at the same time, and even more so, a "repentant *intelligent*," more conscience-stricken over his cultural and intellectual advantages than his material privileges.

A second, somewhat narrower definition of the intelligentsia viewed it more in ideological than in cultural terms. In this sense the intelligentsia consisted of those people who were haunted by the contradiction between the ideals and models their Western education offered them and the Russian conditions in which they lived, and demanded that those conditions be changed — whether the change be liberal, radical, or, ultimately, revolutionary. Beginning with individuals such as Alexander Radishchev at the end of the eighteenth century, through the Decembrists who attempted the rebellion of 1825, to the intellectual circles of Moscow and Petersburg in the reign of Nicholas I, the tension between Western ideals and Russian reality generated an increasingly frustrated and radicalized set of individuals steeped in various Western-inspired ideological systems. By the second half of the nineteenth century, this intelligentsia had come to regard itself as the essential impetus to change and betterment against a selfish and stagnant establishment; to use Lavrov's popular term, they were the "critically thinking individuals" who were essential for progress and enlightenment. This phrase was particularly associated with the populist movement, and the populist revolutionaries of the sixties and seventies saw their mission in precisely these terms.

The "New Class"

It was the populist critic and historian Ivanov-Razumnik who provided one of the most influential, albeit idealized, formulations of the intelligentsia's role in Russian life, in the introduction to his *History of Russian Social Thought (Istoriia russkoi obshchest-vennoi mysli)*. He asserted the disinterested, nonclass character of the intelligentsia: since the eighteenth century it had stood outside of any estate or class "in its tasks, objectives, and ideals," and, he maintained, since the 1860s, in its social origins as well.[63] Ideologically, it was dedicated to the emancipation and development of the individual personality. Sociologically classless and ethically a defender of individualism, the intelligentsia was "the organ of national consciousness and aggregate of the people's vital forces."[64] It was as the selfless defenders of progress, enlightenment, and liberation against the forces of injustice and obscurantism that most *intelligenty* saw themselves and their mission in Russian life.

Toward the end of the nineteenth century, two developments occurred which began to alter this image of the intelligentsia. One was the rise of Marxism, which was now challenging populism as the dominant form of socialism in Russia, and, as part of that challenge, rejected the populist conception of the intelligentsia. With their economic definition of classes, Russian Marxists denied the independent significance of the intelligentsia as a special ideological or "spiritual" force transcending the class divisions of society. Like Kautsky, they held that economic classes alone had social significance, and the intelligentsia was merely a subordinate element of the class structure. Peter Struve, one of the foremost "legal Marxists" of the 1890s, succinctly expressed the Marxist view of the intelligentsia: "If social classes are the expression of the economic differentiation of a given social milieu, and if all social groups represent a real force only to the extent that they have such a character, i.e., either they coincide with social classes or belong to them, then it is obvious that a 'classless intelligentsia' is not a real social force."[65] Referring to the populist faith in ethical individualism, Struve in a phrase that became famous declared that "idealists," from a sociological point of view, were a *quantité négligeable:* for all their intellectual and moral significance, their actions could "create nothing solid in defiance of what is being advanced by the elemental historical process."[66]

45

Although the phenomenon of *intelligenty* who defended the interests of classes other than their own might seem to contradict the economic determinism of their doctrines, Marxists attached little theoretical importance to it. These were merely individual exceptions, like Marx and Engels themselves, not evidence of a classless intelligentsia espousing transcendent ideals. Following Marx, the Russian Marxists used the term "ideologists" *(ideologi)* to designate such individuals, maintaining that the ideals they adopted were class ideals determined by the class structure of society. If they had abandoned the ideals of their own class and adopted those of the proletariat, it was because they had perceived that the latter were the wave of the future.[67]

A second development, the evolution of Russian society in the latter nineteenth century, seemed to support the Marxist view of the intelligentsia's significance (or lack thereof). This period saw the rapid growth of professional, technical, and managerial personnel, a product of the social reforms and industrial growth that followed the emancipation of the serfs.[68] Whatever the Russian intelligentsia might have been in the past, increasingly, it appeared, it was being drawn into the economic structure of a modernizing country and was turning into the kind of new middle class Kautsky had described as a feature of capitalist development. As a result, Russian Marxists anticipated that with further economic progress the intelligentsia would be fully absorbed into the primary classes of the capitalist system, its upper strata assimilated into the bourgeoisie and its lower ranks falling into the proletariat.[69]

The elusive Russian intelligentsia, however, continued to evade the various theoretical formulations that attempted to pin it down. In their debates with each other — and, as Makhaevism began to make its contribution to the question "What is the intelligentsia?", with the Makhaevists as well — neither populists nor Marxists were able to maintain their position with much consistency. The problem the populists faced was that the intelligentsia as a social force was no longer confined to the narrow stratum of disaffected intellectuals that it had been in the sixties and seventies; to continue to identify it as a disinterested, "critically thinking" element of Russian society seemed increasingly obsolete and remote from reality. Vasilii Vorontsov, one of the leading populist writers of the latter nineteenth century, provides an example of the contradictions that could result.

As early as 1884, Vorontsov recognized the growing importance of the professions in Russia and devoted an entire article
to the "representatives of intellectual labor." Entitled "Capitalism
and the Russian Intelligentsia" ("Kapitalizm i russkaia intelligentsiia"), it took as its subject "the fate of those persons who
belong to the so-called free professions, i.e., those persons who
derive their means of subsistence from their work in the fields
of medicine, law, teaching, engineering, etc."[70] For the purposes
of this article, at least, these were the people Vorontsov meant
when he referred to the intelligentsia, sometimes modifying it to
the "working intelligentsia."

Vorontsov's purpose was to persuade Russia's professional
men that their own economic interest, even apart from moral
considerations, should impel them to support the populist program of national development. Reflecting the familiar populist
position that capitalism was an artificial implant in Russia which
could not thrive on such alien soil, he argued that improvement
of the peasant economy offered the intelligentsia greater opportunities for employment than capitalism could generate. Now that
the major governmental reforms of the postemancipation period
had been completed, he predicted that the state's demand for professional personnel would decline. "Two competitors remain —
the zemstvo and capitalism, or, rather, the people and the bourgeoisie. . . . Which of the two will be the Russian intelligentsia's
breadwinner?"[71] Maintaining that Russian industry was progres-
sively reducing its need for the services of professional specialists, Vorontsov tried to convince them that the growth of peasant prosperity offered them better job prospects and economic
security.

Although Marxists drew precisely the opposite conclusion in
regard to Russia's economic future, they could hardly have objected to Vorontsov's discussion of the intelligentsia as a group
of persons with definite economic interests and motivations. Elsewhere, however, this same author reverted to the more traditional,
but quite different, conception of the intelligentsia as selfless idealists moved by ethical considerations. He allowed that an intelligentsia is the product of a definite class, and a privileged one at
that, and that its social thought may therefore reflect its class
origins. In contrast to developments in the West, however, the
Russian intelligentsia was notably free of this disability. The class

47

from which it sprang, the service nobility, was a servant of the state and had neither political and economic independence nor an independent ideology. It was unable to represent the aspirations of the nation, and therefore the educated Russian had quickly abandoned the class which produced him. "As soon as enlightenment began to take root in Russian soil and the intelligentsia became differentiated into an independent social stratum, it immediately came in conflict with some of the existing forms, not in defense of the interests of some privileged minority but in the name of the ideas of justice and humanism."[72] Vorontsov presented the intelligentsia here not as a socioeconomic group but as an intellectual and moral entity. Its impact on society stemmed from its role as a teacher, as the bearer of enlightened and progressive ideas.[73]

Marxist-inspired efforts to reduce the intelligentsia to a strictly socioeconomic category were even less consistent. Inevitably, they had to confront the fact that the Russian intelligentsia had played, and continued to play, an ideological role distinct from, and even in contradiction to, its economic position. An example is the article "The Intelligentsia As a Social Group" ("Intelligentsiia, kak sotsial'naia gruppa"), published in 1904 by A. S. Izgoev, a legal Marxist in the nineties and now a liberal journalist. Izgoev began by rejecting as "subjective" and sentimental Mikhailovskii's definition of the intelligentsia as those whose "hearts and minds" were "with the people."[74] For an objective sociological definition of the intelligentsia, one must turn to the material foundations of society, to the sphere of socioeconomic relations. Its spiritual life aside, the intelligentsia consisted of people who must engage in economic activity in order to make a living. This raised the question of whether the intelligentsia constituted a distinct class; to answer it, a precise understanding of the term *class* was required.

Turning to Marx, Izgoev (like Machajski) found his division of classes inadequate for resolving the issue. At the end of the third volume of *Capital*, he wrote, Marx had set out to define the concept of class, but there the manuscript broke off. Among other things, Marx had failed to clarify the position of such individuals as doctors and officials within the threefold class division of landowners, capitalists, and proletarians. Were they members of these classes, or something separate? Marx's confusion,

Izgoev decided, stemmed from the fact that he had identified the entire fabric of social life with the process of material production alone. A broader view of socioeconomic life was needed in order to yield an adequate definition of class.[75]

Izgoev identified four ways in which people enter into economic relations with each other: landowning, the possession of capital, physical labor, and intellectual work. Corresponding to these functions were four distinct classes. "Contemporary society, in contrast to what Marx supposed, is divided into not three but four great classes: landowners, capitalists, physical laborers, and intellectual workers."[76]

But in fact the class of "intellectual workers" was not the intelligentsia. Izgoev now proceeded to distinguish from the intellectual workers "that social group which can be called the 'intelligentsia.'"

The feature which allows us to differentiate a certain number of individuals from the class of intellectual workers and unite them into a special social group, the intelligentsia, is *the element of the didactic [uchitel'stva], in the broad sense of the word, which is inherent in the professional activities of these persons,* the transmission of information and accumulated knowledge with the goal of instruction. It is a fully objective feature, which explains the material bases of the "intelligentsia's" existence without including such subjective requirements as the demand that the "heart and mind" of a representative of the intelligentsia be "with the people."[77]

It was not the transmission of information or expertise that Izgoev had in mind as the intelligentsia's most important function, however, but the struggle for individual and social freedom. In order to pursue its task of spreading knowledge, the intelligentsia came to demand self-respect and conditions of spiritual freedom. "The intelligentsia's feeling of its own dignity forces it to demand freedom, to defend its own independence and, even more, to defend freedom for hostile opinions, for its own opponents."[78] Hence, Izgoev concluded, under conditions of political repression the intelligentsia comes to play a leading role in society, representing the nation's demand for emancipation of the individual and freedom of the human spirit.[79] For all Izgoev's efforts to apply a precise socioeconomic class analysis, by the end of his article the protean intelligentsia had once again turned into something suspiciously resembling the classless "critically thinking individuals" who marched through populist literature.

After the 1905 revolution, as Machajski's views became better known, both Marxists and populists tried to clarify their own positions on the question of the intelligentsia by criticizing Makhaevism. At this point it is necessary to introduce another contributor to the history of Makhaevism, Evgenii Lozinskii. He was instrumental in making Machajski's views a subject of discussion in the Russian press. A prolific writer and intellectual dilettante, Lozinskii mirrored a number of the political and cultural fads of the Russian extreme left in the years before 1917. He had some ties to the revolutionary underground, but he also turned out an array of nonpolitical works on subjects ranging from educational theory to vegetarianism. Most important, he served as what might be termed the chief "legal Makhaevist"; like the so-called legal populists and legal Marxists of the 1890s, he popularized Machajski's views in legally published books and articles. Their publication was underwritten by the same banker's daughter who had financed the printing of Machajski's works in Geneva.[80] Although Lozinskii was Machajski's best-known disciple, relations between them were frosty. Machajski, in fact, barely acknowledged Lozinskii's existence — perhaps because Lozinskii scarcely mentioned Machajski in his major writings and failed to give him proper credit for the views he was elaborating. Most of Lozinskii's readers, however, seem to have been well aware of the source of his views. Lozinskii added little to Makhaevism and toned down its revolutionary rhetoric for purposes of publication, but he conveyed its main doctrines accurately and succeeded in disseminating them to a wider readership than they had reached previously. Although the first two parts of Machajski's The Intellectual Worker and one of his shorter works were reprinted in St. Petersburg in 1906, most of his writings were available in printed form only in obscure émigré editions. In the years between the 1905 and 1917 revolutions, therefore, Makhaevism as discussed in Russian publications often meant Machajski's basic positions as they had been reformulated and spelled out in Lozinskii's writings.

Lozinskii's principal Makhaevist work was a book entitled What, Then, Is the Intelligentsia? (Chto zhe takoe, nakonets, in-

telligentsiia?), which appeared in 1907.[81] Dissatisfied with what he considered to be Machajski's lack of precision in defining the intelligentsia as a class, Lozinskii tried to work out a more rigorous "scientific" definition. Accepting, like Machajski, the Marxist doctrine of class struggle — class interest was "the lever that moves and makes history"[82] — he distinguished five economic classes in contemporary society: landowners, capitalists, petty proprietors, intellectual workers, and manual workers.[83] This was very close to Izgoev's fourfold class division, which may well have been Lozinskii's starting point — he even used Izgoev's term *umstvennye rabotniki* for "intellectual workers" rather than Machajski's *umstvennye rabochie*. (Perhaps he felt that *rabotnik* had less of a proletarian connotation than did *rabochii*.) He acknowledged that Izgoev, unlike other Marxists, distinguished the intellectual workers as a separate class but complained that he had then proceeded "despite all logic" to single out the intelligentsia as a special group and surround it with "a halo of ideological holiness."[84] To Lozinskii, the intellectual workers *were* the intelligentsia, at the basis of whose existence lay "intellectual labor, knowledge, the arts and sciences, accumulated over the centuries and concentrated in its hands."[85] The salary or fee received by the intellectual worker constituted a return on the "capital" which he had invested in his long years of education and practical training. That "capital," in turn, was a product of the exploitation of the manual workers, despite the contention of the Social Democrats that the *intelligent*, like the proletarian, lived solely by his own labor.[86] Thus the intelligentsia constituted a class, owning property of a special kind (knowledge, diplomas) which provided its owners with a privileged and parasitic economic status.[87]

In the following year, a critique of Makhaevism in traditional Marxist terms appeared, D. Zaitsev's "Marxism and Makhaevism." Admitting that there was some disagreement among the Marxists themselves on the question of the intelligentsia, Zaitsev held that this did not invalidate the Marxist concept of class but merely demonstrated the failure of some Marxists to understand it correctly. He pointed out that Marx's definition of class was based on the principle of production, not distribution. Hence there could be only two classes in capitalist society: the proletariat, consisting of both manual and intellectual workers, and the bourgeoisie, including both landowners and capitalists. Lozinskii, however, had distinguished classes according to source of income, that is, on the principle of distribution rather than production of goods; therefore his conclusions, in Zaitsev's opinion, were scientifically unsound.[88]

⸱ Furthermore, it was impossible to draw a firm dividing line, as the Makhaevists tried to do, between physical and intellectual work, between transport workers and telegraphers, on the one hand, and, say, teachers and nurses on the other. The latter often received less pay than the average factory worker, and their working day was no shorter. Like those proletarians who continued to own plots of land in the villages, highly skilled workers occupied two class positions at the same time: they were both sellers of labor and owners of means of production. (Zaitsev here seemed to imply acceptance of Machajski's contention that knowledge was a form of capital.) Their role in the contemporary class structure did present analytical difficulties, but the Makhaevists' way of resolving them was in no way justified.[89]

The intelligentsia was not a separate class, Zaitsev maintained, but a heterogeneous collection of representatives of the existing social classes. It consisted of the conscious strata of the various groups which belonged to the bourgeoisie and the proletariat respectively, and it was therefore divided into a "bourgeois intelligentsia" and a "proletarian intelligentsia."[90] The *intelligent* was simply a "conscious" member, a spokesman, of the group or class to which he belonged by virtue of his relationship to the means of production.

But how was one to classify the *intelligent* who defended the interests of a class or group to which he did *not* belong, in particular the revolutionary socialist? Zaitsev reverted to the familiar concept of the "ideologist." Both *intelligenty* and ideologists were characterized by a consciousness of certain class interests. But not all *intelligenty* were ideologists. The *intelligent* belonged to a definite social group and served as a spokesman for it. The ideologist, however, had abandoned his own social group and identified himself with another one; he was a man who had forgotten his origins.[91] The rise of ideologists followed the same laws as the rise of geniuses — but unfortunately, Zaitsev conceded, contemporary science was as yet unable to explain these laws. Nevertheless, Russia had witnessed numerous examples of people who had renounced the interests of their own class to take up those of another. And foremost among them were the adherents of Marxism, the ideology of the proletariat.[92]

It was precisely at this point, the populist Ivanov-Razumnik objected, that *any* socioeconomic analysis of the intelligentsia severely contradicted itself. In his study of Makhaevism, he investigated the efforts of the Marxists and the Makhaevists to define the Russian intelligentsia in class terms and concluded that both were futile. In trying to take the Marxist approach to the intelligentsia to its logical conclusion, Makhaevism had succeeded only in reducing it to a logical absurdity.

This approach broke down whenever those *intelligenty* who applied it to the rest of the intelligentsia came to speak about themselves. They were forced to regard themselves as exceptions to the rule, as the sole *intelligenty* who had managed to surmount their class background and sincerely adopt the interests of the workers. There were Marxists who maintained that the intelligentsia on the whole belonged to the bourgeoisie, but then exempted from this dictum the "ideologists of the protelariat."[93] Now the Makhaevists came along, claiming that the intelligentsia constituted a separate class of exploiters. But what of the Makhaevists themselves? According to Lozinskii, they were a "rare exception," the very few *intelligenty* who were able to overcome their "wolf-like nature" and become the true friends of the proletariat. Like the Marxists, the Makhaevists tried to escape from the logical implications of their socioeconomic definition of the intelligentsia by making a "dizzy leap" to an ethical, or ideological definition.[94]

Ivanov-Razumnik concluded that the intelligentsia had always been, and remained, an ideological group to which the criteria of an economic class did not apply. Even if everything else the Makhaevists said were irrefutable, they would have proved only that the "intellectual workers" — but not the intelligentsia — formed a separate class. Anyone could belong to the intelligentsia, he affirmed, both the manual worker and the intellectual worker, the half-literate laborer and the professor, as long as he held certain views and shared a certain outlook.[95]

The debate over the nature of the intelligentsia had now come full circle. Despite the quantities of ink and intellectual energy expended on the issue, no satisfactory resolution proved forthcoming. The intelligentsia itself, whether populist, Marxist, or Makhaevist, typically sought a single "scientific" key that would unlock the puzzle of the intelligentsia's place in Russian history and resolve its contradictions. To borrow Isaiah Berlin's well-known characterization of Tolstoy in *The Hedgehog and the Fox*, the intelligentsia knew many things about itself but wanted to know one big thing. This eluded its grasp, for the question of the intelligentsia would not admit of a single, unambiguous answer. It was not merely a semantic debate over definitions, although the highly elastic usage of the term certainly contributed to the problem. It was the actual historical role of the intelligentsia in Russia that was so contradictory and open to such a broad range of evaluations. Under the conditions of relative backwardness that characterized Russia in the modern era, the intelligentsia (whether identified as the Western-educated stratum or as a certain part of it) played a number of different historical roles; it had no direct counterpart in the countries of Western Europe. Depending on how those roles were perceived, the intelligentsia could mean very different things to different people. It was the cutting edge of Western influence, which some viewed as a beneficent source of progress and others as a menacing force; it was the creator and mainstay of the socialist parties and the revolutionary movement against the autocracy, though, as such, it seemed to be acting contrary to its own material interests; it had sprung originally from the privileged, serf-owning segments of prereform Russia and was now becoming a well-paid instrument of Russia's industrial development — thus serving as an agent of economic progress or as a "tool of capitalism," depending on one's point of view.

Because the intelligentsia was such a distinctively Russian phenomenon, at the risk of irritating the reader with the repeated use of a foreign word this study consistently refers to members of the intelligentsia by the Russian term *intelligenty* (singular: *intelligent*) rather than as "intellectuals," the usual English translation. The term *intellectuals* is misleading in the Russian context in two respects. First, it is much more restricted in its English meaning than the term *intelligenty* is in Russian, for it refers to "thinkers," people who spend their time engaged in creative thought and writing about intellectual matters. A modicum of Western education and a more or less radical perspective, which generally suffeced to qualify Russians as *intelligenty*, hardly made them intellectuals (although, of course, some of them were). Secondly, the anti-intelligentsia sentiment which was so widespread in the lower reaches of Russian society, and which gave Makhaevism much of its social and political resonance, did not stem from hostility to intellectuals. Few Russian workers, much less peasants, had enough contact with intellectuals or their work to dislike or resent them *as* intellectuals. Their anti-intelligentsia sentiment stemmed from the broader associations which the word *intelligentsia* carried in Russia and which *intellectuals* cannot convey: association with a foreign, or at least alien and perhaps threatening culture; social and economic privilege; a sense of superiority to the masses and perhaps a desire to dominate them. These were the associations that brought teachers and university students, doctors, lawyers, and engineers, revolutionary propagandists and labor organizers together under the rubric of intelligentsia.

- This was the context within which Machajski formulated his answer to the question "What is the intelligentsia?" He denied that there were any contradictions or ambiguities in the intelligentsia's social role: the intelligentsia was a rising new class of "intellectual workers" which enjoyed a privileged position under capitalism. Furthermore, and of crucial significance, the intelligentsia was not merely a socioeconomic phenomenon whose role in the class structure of capitalism could be endlessly debated, but a growing political force, manipulating the socialist movement not to liberate the workers from economic bondage but to secure and perpetuate its own advantages.

Chapter 3

The Intelligentsia and Socialism

$\mathbf{H}$AVING TURNED his attention to the intellectual workers, Machajski became convinced that Social Democracy's shift from revolutionism to evolutionism reflected not the changing circumstances of the proletariat under capitalism, as the Marxists claimed, but the changing position of the educated classes. Therefore, the critique of socialism embodied in his second essay ("Scientific Socialism," which became part 2 of *The Intellectual Worker*) and all of his subsequent writings differed radically from the approach he had taken in his first essay. He noted in his preface to part 2 that in the previous year (1899) a French Social Democrat, Alexandre Millerand, had accepted a ministerial post in the French government. Here was good evidence that a movement which not long ago had promised to abolish the class system was beginning to help run it.[1] He now proceeded to rewrite the history of socialism, in Western Europe and in Russia, with the purpose of revealing how socialism served the intelligentsia as an instrument for enhancing its own position in the bourgeois economic and political system. In Lozinskii's more colorful language, there existed "a conspiracy of the contemporary socialist intelligentsia throughout the world," and the purpose of Makhaevism was to unmask the intelligentsia, "to lay bare to everyone its diabolically clever tricks, to reveal its exploitative class interest in the contemporary socialist movement."[2]

Socialism as Machajski perceived it was in essence the product of a family quarrel between the "educated bourgeoisie" and the "bourgeois aristocracy," the latter being the big capitalists under the protection of the absolutist state.

The Intelligentsia and Socialism

Socialism of the past century was created by those middle strata of capitalist society who can hope for their own emancipation even without the destruction of the workers' bondage, who can hope to attain a master's position for themselves in the bourgeois order. They are primarily the educated part of the bourgeoisie, and chiefly the professional intelligentsia. They are that part of privileged, ruling society which hopes to achieve its full sway if only absolutism be destroyed, i.e., the old, strong, centralized regime which usurps the growing national wealth; if only a sufficient degree of representative government be developed, with the help of which these future masters hope to restrain and limit the magnates to their own advantage.[3]

As long as the educated bourgeoisie saw the possibility of achieving political reforms through its own efforts, its objectives remained democratic rather than socialist. It promised only "liberty, equality, and fraternity" after the overthrow of the monarchy and the establishment of a democratic republic. Only when the old regime refused to give way sufficiently, and, at the same time, the manual workers had grown into a significant social force, did the intelligentsia become anticapitalist and turn to socialism. It now sought to draw the workers into its struggle by promising them the expropriation of the rich and the reorganization of the economy once full democratic freedom was achieved.[4]

As evidence that nineteenth-century socialism was basically a demand for political power by the educated bourgeoisie, Machajski cited the American case. In the United States, socialism had not developed because it had been unnecessary to combat absolutism.

In America, socialism did not manifest itself during the [nineteenth] century because absolutism had never existed there. The bourgeoisie, consisting of immigrants from the Old World, from the very start built its own state on a foundation of political liberty. But in each of the European countries where centralized state power had formed and concentrated over the centuries, there was a point at which it became obligatory for bourgeois educated society to declare itself socialist. This occurred when it became necessary to draw the working masses into the struggle with the absolute monarchical regime or with the remnants of the old sway of the nobility.[5]

In England, he believed, this point had been reached with the Chartist movement.[6] To a greater degree than in England, however, the intelligentsia of France and Germany began to profess socialism. In Germany particularly, "the intelligentsia declared itself the implacable enemy of the capitalists and their economy."[7] Moving further east, Machajski saw the political activity of the Polish nobility of Galicia before 1848 as an attempt to restore its undivided possession of the riches of Poland by upholding democracy and even socialism against the rule of the Austrian emperor. "Thus, by means of socialism, by means of socialist promises of full property equality among men, educated bourgeois society in all these Western European countries inveigled the working class into a struggle with the old regime, which offended these liberal gentlemen."[8]

But their promises to the workers evaporated as soon as the absolutist state and capitalism began to open their doors to the intelligentsia. Once it was admitted to the spoils of capitalism, the intelligentsia shed its revolutionism and became a staunch supporter of the existing order.

As absolutism was destroyed or limited, and along with it the sway of the crudest and most ignorant magnates, the learned people of Western Europe increasingly secured and multiplied the fat incomes of masters, both in state service and in the whole capitalist economy. From the socialist enemy of the capitalists the intelligentsia turned into their best friend, a learned counsellor, the director of all bourgeois life. This unchanging history of the intelligentsia has been repeated in all the Western European countries in turn: a rosy socialist youth and then, once it has received a sufficient salary for a parasitic existence, a full and equal bourgeois life.[9]

Machajski regarded 1848 as the turning point in this process, and specifically the June Days of Paris. He returned to this episode again and again in his writings, for he considered it the great watershed in the relations between the intelligentsia and the workers, and in the development of socialism. The suppression of the workers by the forces of the newly proclaimed republic proved conclusively that the class struggle within capitalist society was deeper than the antagonism between capitalists and workers which the *Communist Manifesto* had depicted.[10]

The aim of the "educated French bourgeoisie," whom Machajski identified as the instigators of the February Revolution, had been to wrest power and the wealth of France from Louis Philippe, "the king of the plutocrats." The bourgeoisie won the support of the workers by convincing them that universal suffrage would solve the problems of the proletariat. As in Russia later, the students and intellectuals fraternized with the workers and admitted them to their secret societies, which had as their goal the attainment of a democratic republic. Once the republic had been achieved, the bourgeoisie, to pacify the workers, "as a joke" created the national workshops to provide jobs for the unemployed. But then the chamber of deputies, elected by universal suffrage, assembled in Paris and voted to close the national workshops. The suppression of the workers' insurrection that followed the closing of the workshops showed once and for all the hollowness of the principles of political democracy. The June Days demonstrated that "democracy, the democratic republic, is just a reinforced prison for the workers, and the struggle for universal freedom is a bourgeois deception."[11]

Machajski laid the blame for the June Days squarely on the intelligentsia, and particularly the socialists. The workers "were demanding only a very simple thing—security henceforth from hunger, from unemployment."[12] But the socialists were no more prepared than the republicans to support this demand, for their plans called for the fulfillment of such goals only in the distant future, on the first day of the socialist order. The steadfast insistence of the workers on an *immediate* guarantee against starvation terrified not only the government and the liberal parties, but even the hitherto revolutionary circles of the socialists. As a result, the workers found arrayed against them not just the National Guard but "all of their allies of yesterday—the students, the intelligentsia, the parties and organizations in which the workers had so recently participated."[13] "'Woe to June!' cried the revolutionary socialist intelligentsia, the students, as well as Cavaignac."[14]

The June Days completely transformed the attitude of the intelligentsia toward the workers and ushered in a new phase of the history of socialism. Before 1848 the socialist intelligentsia of France, Germany, and Austria, in its struggle against the "feudals and plutocrats," had promised the workers an immediate end to capitalist tyranny. But the threat of an independent uprising of the workers, with its immediate, concrete economic demands, now came to haunt the consciousness of all revolutionary intellectuals.

The delicate task of utilizing the workers' movement to elevate the intelligentsia to a more advantageous position within the bourgeois order, while at the same time restraining the workers' demand for the total destruction of that order, now devolved on Marxism.

Marxism became the predominant brand of socialism after 1848, Machajski explained, because it was best suited to defend the interests of the intelligentsia under the conditions of the later nineteenth century. Unlike those who renounced their socialist dreams, satisfied with the democratization introduced in 1848, the Marxists demanded more and more concessions for the intelligentsia from the existing order. But two things had happened in 1848. First, the workers had indicated that they were not interested in the construction of a "new society" — the matter that was of central concern to the intelligentsia, which would rule it. Instead, the workers had shown their "unpreparedness" for socialism by demanding concrete and immediate improvement of their position. From that time on the socialists realized that they had to abandon their call for the immediate revolutionary transformation of society and concentrate on the long-term education of the workers to support the socialists' demands.

Secondly, the triumphant bourgeoisie after 1848 began to display a more generous attitude toward the intelligentsia. It realized that the reason for the latter's revolt was the concentration in a few hands of the wealth of the whole bourgeoisie, and that the intelligentsia's appetite for communism could be satisfied by admitting the intelligentsia into the ruling circles. Taking the "learned world" into its midst, the bourgeoisie made the further development of capitalism highly attractive, a prospect which rendered meaningless the old revolutionary plans of the socialists. Why destroy the capitalist order now? the socialists reasoned. Instead of eliminating the old middle classes, capitalism had created a huge new middle class in the form of the intelligentsia and had given it a privileged position. Not the overthrow of capitalism but its further development now became the task of the socialists.[15]

The doctrines of Marxism proved flexible enough to take these circumstances into account. For Marxism taught that capitalism did not just rob the workers but performed a great historical mission as well: it inevitably prepared the way for socialism. Original "revolutionary" Marxism was able to transform itself without difficulty into the more modern "evolutionary" Marxism by stressing the positive side of capitalism, capitalism as a necessary stage in the development of socialism. Now it became the first duty of the socialist — and of the workers he schooled — to wait patiently for the fruit of socialism to ripen, for any attempt to pluck it too soon might damage it. With the benefits of capitalism now accruing steadily to the intellectual workers, who were growing richer and more numerous, capitalism itself was increasingly fulfilling the original "communist" aspirations of the intelligentsia. Socialism, Machajski charged, had become a screen behind which "the class of intelligentsia and its defenders, the socialists" promoted the further development of capitalism.[16]

In this fashion Machajski "unmasked" socialism as a campaign to emancipate not the proletariat but the intelligentsia. Socialism was the protest movement of the "army of privileged 'employees' of capital and the capitalist state, who find themselves in antagonism with the latter over the sale of their knowledge and therefore appear, at certain moments of their struggle, as part of the anticapitalist proletarian army, as a socialist detachment."[17] Political democratization was the means by which the intelligentsia made its peace with capitalism. As soon as it had achieved that goal it abandoned the economic protest of the workers, for the exploitation of the manual workers was as vital to the "owners of culture and civilization" as it was to the owners of the land and factories. Western European Social Democracy was the ideological vehicle of the intelligentsia's accommodation to the existing order. "Science receives an honored place and an appropriate salary, and the bourgeoisie rules the minds of the proletarians with the aid of science. This result is expressed in the determined aspiration of Social Democracy in the nineties to become 'the one party of order!'"[18] Hence the evolution of Social Democracy to its present emphasis on legal tactics and the acquisition of political power reflected not the changing nature of capitalism or the improved position of the workers within it, but the evolving class interests of socialism's creator, the intelligentsia.

When he turned his attention to Russia, Machajski found the pattern of development he had discerned in Western European socialism recapitulated precisely in the history of the Russian socialist movement. In Russia, also, socialism had been generated by the friction between the intellectual workers, on the one hand, and the capitalist magnates and the absolutist state on the other. The conflict came to a head in the early 1870s. In this era of nascent Russian capitalism, "educated society," swollen by increasing numbers of intellectual workers and disappointed by the failure of the reforms accompanying the emancipation of the serfs to democratize the political order, turned to the idea of using socialist revolution as an instrument against the big industrialists.

Russian educated society in the sixties dreamed of emancipating itself from the Asiatic regime in the same way that this was being done in the advanced countries of Western Europe: by means of a simple democratization of the state in defense of the "rights of man," leaving the "social question" completely untouched. But in this period the antagonism between educated society and its plenipotentiaries, the capitalists, had already reached a high degree of intensity in the civilized world. Within a few years after the abolition of serfdom, this antagonism, this "capitalist contradiction," made itself felt in Russia, too. With the aid and protection of a strong government, the phase of "primitive accumulation" occurred here more rapidly than anywhere else, and innumerable *kulaks* arose. At the same time, the progress of capitalism was accompanied by the rise of numerous cadres of intelligentsia, of intellectual workers. Progressive society could not be content with the Asiatic regime and the sway of the *kulak:* too plain were the viands it was offered, and the *kulak* only inflicted insults on the *intelligent.* In the seventies, the progressive Russian intelligentsia in large numbers began to adopt Western European socialism.[19]

In Machajski's view of Russian history, populism corresponded to the pre-1848 phase of Western socialism, the effort to achieve an immediate socialist transformation of the existing order. Western European socialism provided the Russian intelligentsia with a revolutionary device that might enable it to draw the people into its own struggle. "Western European socialism, which had reduced the proletariat's task from *seizing the property* of the possessing classes to *transforming the mode of production,* inspired the Russian socialists with the thought that all the West's misfortunes stemmed from the fact that people there labored separately and not in associations."[20] It became a cardinal tenet of populism that backward Russia had the opportunity to proceed immediately to the construction of an agrarian form of socialism based on the peasant commune, without having to endure the horrors that industrialization was inflicting on the West. Therefore the populists argued that capitalism should not be allowed to develop in Russia, and later they maintained that because of the structure of the Russian economy it *could* not develop. As Machajski noted, Alexander Herzen had been deeply affected by the June Days of Paris, which he witnessed, and had determined that Russia must avoid the rise of a proletariat. But Machajski interpreted the populists' program of agrarian socialism as a desire to avoid not the spectacle of proletarian *suffering*, as the populists themselves claimed, but the specter of proletarian *revolution*, the only kind of revolution that threatened to expropriate the entire bourgeoisie, including the intelligentsia. A nonproletarian socialist revolution in the name of the peasant commune would permit the intelligentsia safely to mobilize a mass force for its own purposes.[21]

The failure of the "going to the people" movement in the 1870s represented the negative response of the masses to the intelligentsia's plans, a Russian analogue of the June Days. When it became clear that the peasants were not attracted to the vision of a socialist transformation, the populists realized that they would have to be indoctrinated over a long period of time.[22] At this point, however, the Russian socialist movement entered a new, Marxist phase. The Russian intelligentsia reached the same conclusion that Machajski had imputed to its Western counterpart: the fruits of Russian capitalism proved so tasty that the intelligentsia outgrew the fancies of its youth. Abandoning its plans for the immediate introduction of socialism, the intelligentsia realized, with the assistance of Marxism, that its real task was a political, or bourgeois revolution, and the further development of capitalism in Russia.[23] The Russian Social-Democratic movement, which arose in the 1880s and 1890s, undertook precisely this task.

While the populists tried to hold back the proletarian movement by claiming the impossibility of capitalist development in Russia, the Marxists did the same on the pretext of Russian capitalism's underdevelopment. The Russian Social Democrats contended that because Russian capitalism was backward, further economic and political progress was necessary before socialism could be achieved. Marxism brought up to date and "European-ized" the populists' attempt to ward off the occurrence of a pro-letarian revolution. Therefore it became the new ideology of the social force which had earlier clothed itself in populism: the in-tellectual workers, whose aim was to distribute the profits of capitalism more equitably among the various strata of bourgeois society.[24]

The Russian Social Democrats realized that the proletariat of-fered the intelligentsia a more effective instrument for freeing it-self from the tsarist yoke than did the peasantry. They believed that if they helped the workers wring some concessions from their employers, the workers in gratitude would help their edu-cated mentors attain a constitution. The Russian Social Demo-crats hoped to profit from the successful experience of their coun-terparts in the West, where "all sorts of liberal parties of offended gentlemen in precisely this way have been rising to power on the backs of the workers for a hundred years."[25] Two developments persuaded the Russian intelligentsia that the Marxists' calcula-tions were well founded: the evolution of European Social De-mocracy, with its insistence that an armed uprising of the prole-tariat was unthinkable and that Social Democracy must be the "one party of order," and the growing success of the Russian So-cial Democrats in convincing the workers to turn against the au-tocracy and demand political reforms. In the 1890s, therefore, Marxism grew steadily within the Russian intelligentsia, for it now felt the proletariat could be counted on to accomplish the bour-geois revolution — which was to be "the direct result of half a cen-tury of the socialist movement!"[26] Thus the intelligentsia's long search for a revolutionary force that would enable it to "tear the incalculable and incalculably growing wealth of the huge empire out of the hands of a few tsarist generals, bureaucrats, dignitaries, and *kulaks*, and use it to nurture educated society as freely as in the West" seemed to have been crowned with success.[27]

Although the Marxists were Machajski's principal object of criticism, he attacked all other schools of socialism in much the same terms. Like the Marxists, he regarded the landowning peas-antry as part of the bourgeoisie, and he interpreted the peasant-oriented programs of the Socialist-Revolutionary party and the anarchist followers of Peter Kropotkin as evidence that these groups wished merely to ensure the continued existence of the bourgeois order. They maintained that if the Russian peasants were supported in their desire to take over the nobility's land, their communal traditions would lay the foundations for a socialist order. Machajski had no faith at all in those traditions. The peasants' ambition to acquire property bound them firmly to the existing order instead of turning them into its enemies. The very possession of land, which was a form of property, led to exploitation, whether the land be held by an individual peasant, an entire household, or a commune. The end result of any program of peasant socialism would be the creation of a strong rural bourgeoisie, while the plight of the landless rural proletariat would remain unchanged.[28]

Machajski shared with the anarchists their repudiation of politics, but he felt that they had wilfully abandoned their own principles. He dismissed the French anarchosyndicalist movement as little more than a variety of legal trade-unionism.[29] He found a similar tendency toward reformist accommodation with the existing order in the ideas of Kropotkin, who had expressed a positive attitude to political freedom as a means of educating the masses and encouraging cooperative principles.[30] The anarchist movement was betraying its revolutionism and becoming merely another reformist current. "There is not a single anarchist theoretician who would firmly take the position that the emancipation of the working class is conceivable only as a violent act of revolt, the preparation of which requires a conspiracy hidden from the eyes of the law throughout the civilized world."[31] There were some anarchist groups and individuals, he conceded, who, "when sudden major outbursts of the worker masses do occur, try to broaden them as much as possible and in this way achieve a workers' revolution," but they were only isolated instances.[32]

In the end, Machajski found in the anarchists' hostility to the state merely an indication that they too, like the Social Democrats, represented a new ruling class seeking its own emancipation from the old regime. "The anarchists," he wrote, "declare war only on the oppression from the state which privileged society itself undergoes, which the Greek slaveowners suffered from the Macedonian emperors, the Roman patricians from their own emperors, the bourgeoisie and nobility of the Middle Ages from the

absolute monarchs who began to infringe on their 'golden freedom.'"[33] They were little more than extreme liberals, their real
goal being a check on the powers of the bureaucratic state over
them. "The limitation of the old bureaucracy is a necessary task
for all liberals, for all new masters, and every bourgeois revolution has its 'antistate' slogans."[34]

The socialist parties of the non-Russian peoples of the empire
fared no better at Machajski's hands. Adjusting the criticism of
these parties that he had begun in his first essay, he no longer
charged them merely with pursuing a misguided policy, the attainment of political freedom within national boundaries. The
Polish Socialist party, with its goal of national independence for
Poland, was really seeking the political emancipation of the Polish educated classes. Meanwhile, the Bund, the Jewish Social-
Democratic party, was "drawing the Jewish workers into the
struggle for the masters' rights of the Jewish intelligentsia." The
educated strata of the minority nationalities had their individual
quarrels with the tsar, but they all agreed that they would receive
their own right to rule when the Russian intelligentsia had succeeded in curbing the tsarist government.[35]

It was in these terms that Machajski analyzed the 1905 revolution, which illustrated the difficulty of exploiting the workers'
movement without permitting it to get out of hand. The intelligentsia needed the workers to exert pressure on the tsarist regime
for political liberties, but at the same time it had to restrain the
workers' own economic demands, the full satisfaction of which
would undermine the privileges of the intelligentsia itself. The inability of the socialists to carry out this delicate managerial task,
Machajski believed, accounted for the ultimate failure of this attempt at a "bourgeois revolution."

Writing in 1905, Machajski viewed the developing revolution
as the culmination of the long conflict between the intelligentsia
and the old regime. The tsar had refused to renovate his obsolete
system of government, and instead of allowing "learned people"
into the administration he had left everything in the hands of "ignorant generals, gendarmes, and priests." As a result, more and
more of the educated bourgeoisie had in recent years gone over
to the side of the revolutionaries. Now they hoped that the military defeat in the Far East and a nationwide uprising would force

the tsar to stop "insulting" the educated and call on them to help him rule.[36]

Bloody Sunday (January 9, 1905), when the workers of St. Petersburg came to the Winter Palace to petition the tsar, seemed to be evidence that the socialists could mobilize the working class to demand political reform. Bloody Sunday, he wrote, persuaded the educated bourgeoisie that the workers had at last ceased to believe in their old masters and were seeking new ones, new leaders and governors. Now even the most pacific "learned people" favored an insurrection.

Since the ninth of January the whole educated bourgeoisie has been calling the workers to arms and to a violent revolution against the government. Not just the students of the secondary schools, not just the university students, but the most respectable gentlemen, professors, writers, engineers; not just that part of the bourgeoisie which constitutes the so-called professional intelligentsia, but the enlightened strata of the various small capitalists; not just this petty bourgeoisie but some of the large proprietors, *zemstvo* gentry, even real counts and princes.[37]

Only the most naive individuals could maintain that all these groups were struggling for the emancipation of the workers. This was indeed a bourgeois revolution, he concluded, a revolution of the "white-hands" who were trying to establish their own rule over the Russian Empire.[38]

At the end of 1907, Machajski took up the question of why the revolution had failed to overthrow the monarchy. In essence, he held that the promise which the intelligentsia saw in Bloody Sunday had not been fulfilled; in the end, the socialists had proved unable to muster the popular forces necessary for a successful political revolution. In part, it was because the working class as a whole had remained indifferent to the revolution's political objectives. The workers had not been tempted by the prospect of political freedom, "which promised them the free chatter of the *intelligenty* instead of bread."[39] Only a revolution which promised them the satisfaction of their economic demands could have aroused their enthusiasm.

That, however, was precisely what the socialists wished to avoid, for they feared a workers' uprising for economic goals even more than a continuation of absolutism. In the midst of the revolution the intelligentsia had been seized with terror at the thought that its own position might be jeopardized by the complete destruction of the old order within which it had developed. There was no guarantee that the rebellious workers, having overthrown the autocracy, would then leave the "white-hands" in peace. Therefore in large part the revolution had failed because the autocracy found support not only in the classes closely tied to the old regime but in the educated bourgeoisie. Unpleasant as it might be to the "freedom-lovers," it turned out that the intelligentsia itself needed the autocracy.[40] The Russian socialists had demonstrated that they were much too faithful and avaricious guardians of the existing order to want to submit it to a fundamental risk. Only a general economic strike that would have mobilized the workers in town and countryside alike, "the hungry millions of Russia," could have accomplished the complete overthrow of the old regime.[41] The socialists themselves had helped to avert such a development, however, for any real threat to the stability of the bourgeois order threatened the economic interests of the class they represented.

The crucial step that Machajski took in the formation of Makhaevism was to claim that socialism embodied the interests not of the laboring classes whom it claimed to defend, but of the intelligentsia which had created it and propagated it. Did his theory have validity, and, if so, in what sense and to what degree? Machajski's analysis was seriously flawed by his search for strict Marxist answers to the questions he raised. Even after he had rejected Marxism as a political movement he continued to view the world through Marxist glasses. He looked only for the ideologically masked interests of economic classes, and this led him to conclude that socialism both in Western Europe and in Russia was merely a campaign by the class of intellectual workers, themselves a product of modern industry, for a larger share in the profits of capitalism through political democratization. The most serious weakness in his theory was that the flowering of socialism in the nineteenth century did not coincide exactly with the rise of industrial capitalism and hence of the intellectual workers, either geographically or chronologically. Instead, the two phenomena overlapped and intertwined, but remained distinct — most of all, in Russia.

~ Machajski himself pointed this out in his account of the origins of socialism, though without acknowledging it as a problem that required explanation. First, he conceded the absence of socialism in the United States, a country where capitalism was well developed. Secondly, he discussed the rise of Russian socialism mainly as a phenomenon of the 1870s, failing to explain the growing impact of socialism (of which he was well aware) as early as the 1840s, on such individuals as Herzen and Bakunin — well before the postemancipation industrial boom began. Capitalism, and with it the intellectual workers, flourished in the United States while socialism did not, and socialism arose in Russia in the absence of either one. Machajski perceived the increasing commitment of the intelligentsia to socialism as one moved from west to east in mid–nineteenth-century Europe. Capitalism, however, did not grow in strength in this direction but, on the contrary, became relatively weaker.

At least one of Makhaevism's critics, Ivanov-Razumnik, perceived that Machajski's presentation of the American case involved a serious contradiction. If socialism was a revolt of the "intellectual workers" against "capitalist robbery," as Machajski claimed, then how could he attribute the absence of socialism in that capitalist land to America's freedom from *absolutism?*[42] This is in fact the key to Machajski's theory of socialism. In his analysis the primary condition for the appearance of socialism is not really capitalism but absolutism. He cited a number of movements which, to one degree or another, partook of socialist ideas: English Chartism, French and German communism, the activity of the Galician Poles, and Russian populism. He attributed these movements to the more or less educated elements of European society who were dissatisfied with the hardships imposed on them by the regimes under which they lived. By no stretch of the imagination can capitalism be numbered among those hardships in all cases, nor can the supporters of these movements be considered intellectual workers in Machajski's sense of the term. The "hardship" they all endured was political or civil, not economic; it was a lack of political freedom and participation, not an overdose of capitalism.

Nowhere was this more striking than in the Russian intelligentsia's opposition to autocracy. Some of Machajski's own statements suggest that he realized this. He referred, for example, to "the hundred-year search of the liberal intelligentsia" in Russia for an effective weapon against the established order, a search culminating in the socialists' program for a "bourgeois revolution."[43] What the intelligentsia had been seeking for a hundred years, from Radishchev and the Decembrists to the Social Democrats and Socialist-Revolutionaries was, to use Machajski's words, liberation from the "tsarist generals, bureaucrats, and dignitaries"[44] — in short, from the oppressiveness of autocracy. In this sense Russian socialism was but the latest expression, though a highly radicalized one, of a campaign the Western-educated elite (or at least a segment of it) had been waging since the latter eighteenth century.

The contradictions and inconsistencies in Machajski's theory of socialism arose from his insistence on identifying the intelligentsia with the intellectual workers. In Russia these were two separate groups, and only toward the end of the nineteenth century were they beginning to overlap to any significant degree. An appreciable body of disaffected intellectuals with a growing interest in socialist ideas had emerged in the 1840s, and a revolutionary movement adhering to some of these ideas began to take shape in the 1860s; neither these developments nor the populists of the 1870s and the first Russian Marxists of the 1880s, for all their hostility to capitalism, were the products of a capitalist economy. It was only in the 1890s that a professional and managerial class in sizeable numbers began to appear on the Russian scene — and when it did, its members were not necessarily socialists, much less revolutionaries.[45]

Machajski's analysis suffered from his effort to fit the Russian intelligentsia and Russian socialism into the Procrustean bed of economic materialism. At the same time, this effort obscured the real value and originality of his theory: the realization that the ultimate objectives of revolutionary socialism — the overthrow of autocracy and the socialist transformation of the economic order — precisely because they were objectives devised by the intelligentsia, might in fact diverge from the interests of the workers themselves. The potential divergence was not a narrowly economic one, however, as Machajski unquestioningly assumed. Under the old regime the educated elite, including even its wealthiest members, suffered from a lack of personal autonomy, freedom of expression, influence over the most vital decisions affecting its society. The ideals of socialism, reflecting the consciousness of their intelligentsia creators, who felt these frustrations most keenly, tended to be cast in sweeping terms of human liberation. In the words of Martin Malia, whose excellent biography of Alexander Herzen helps us to clarify Machajski's insight, "socialism, when stripped of all programmatic contingencies, is quintessential democratic protest against an old regime."[46] Socialism represents the most extreme expression of such generalized protest, "of which the proletarian reaction against early industrialism, where it existed, is only a part."[47] Allan Wildman, referring to a later period, also sees Russian socialism as essentially a reflection of the intelligentsia's own sense of alienation.

> The primary commitment of the Social Democratic intellectual, like that of his Populist counterpart, had always been to the mystique of revolution itself, to the vision of a faultless society purged of the anomalies of the existing order in which the "intelligentsia" had no place. The workers' movement had always served him as a vehicle through which the world of values he rejected could be overthrown.[48]

The proletariat's grievances against the harsh conditions of early industrial life could serve as one mode of expression of socialist values, but they were only an element of the broader and deeper rejection of the established order that socialism represented. Therefore socialism could appear in Russia long before either industrialization or the proletariat, among gentry intellectuals like Herzen who bore no resemblance to Machajski's intellectual workers.

Machajski's theory implied, then, that socialism originated as an extreme form of liberalism, appearing with the greatest intensity in those countries where liberalism was an insufficient battering ram against the old regime. And it suggested that the evolution of socialism followed the course of political liberalization more closely than the course of capitalism (although the two were intricately related). As Machajski observed, to his great displeasure, by the turn of the century the process of moderation was well under way in the West. With socialists occupying ministerial posts in France and leading a large and respectable parliamentary party in Germany, the Social Democrats were increasingly disinclined to raze to the ground a system which now offered them considerable scope and influence. (What Machajski refused to consider, of course, was that democratization might be moderating the outlook of the workers as well, by granting them increasingly effective legal methods of improving their position.) The political reforms stemming from the 1905 revolution would help to determine whether Russian socialism was to follow the same path.

But what of the laboring classes, in whose name the socialists spoke? The early industrial workers, and in Russia the peasants as well, had no fewer or less severe complaints against the existing order than the intelligentsia did, and the stated objective of socialism was to satisfy those grievances once and for all. Machajski insisted, however, that the achievement of socialism would satisfy only the complaints of the intelligentsia, not those of the laboring classes. But it was not simply material interests that might diverge in the future (although Bakunin had pointed out that intellectuals were not inherently immune to the temptations of power and privilege). As Malia argues, while socialism embodied a quest for liberation, personal, social, and political, through a total remaking of the existing order, the masses were necessarily more concerned with the struggle for material survival and immediate, concrete improvement in their circumstances. They "want primarily to live, to achieve security, and ultimately to advance in terms of the situation in which they find themselves." Unlike the intelligentsia, "they are most vitally concerned with their own lot rather than with that of *all* mankind."[49] The intelligentsia sought the creation of a new world in which the alienation it experienced so acutely could be resolved, one in which every individual would have the means and the freedom to develop his consciousness, to lead a fully human existence. The intelligentsia craved the definitive liberation of suffering man; the workers wanted improvements in the conditions of the deprived proletarian. These two sets of aspirations might come together long enough to bring down the old regime. Ultimately, however, the intelligentsia, on the one hand, and the workers and peasants on the other, might prove to have very different, and fundamentally incompatible, images in mind of the new order that was to arise with the overthrow of autocracy and capitalism.

Interestingly enough, the one Russian Social Democrat who was able to break out of the confines of Marxist dogma and realistically evaluate the intelligentsia's role in the history of socialism was Vladimir Il'ich Lenin. In doing so, Lenin articulated a theory of socialism that was remarkably similar to Machajski's, though he drew precisely the opposite conclusion from it. In perhaps the most famous passage in all his writings, Lenin in *What Is to Be Done? (Chto delat'?)* asserted that socialism originated not with the workers but with the intelligentsia, and that the workers, on their own, could never rise above a reformist, or "trade-union" level. It is worth quoting these familiar words against the background of Machajski's theory.

We said that *there could not be* Social-Democratic consciousness among the workers [in the Russian strikes of the nineties]. That consciousness could only be brought to them from outside. The history of all countries shows that the working class, exclusively by its own efforts, is capable of developing only trade-union consciousness, i.e., a realization of the necessity of joining together in unions, fighting against the employers, striving for passage by the government of necessary labor legislation, etc. The doctrines of socialism, however, grew out of the philosophical, historical, and economic theories that were elaborated by the educated representatives of the propertied classes, the intelligentsia. The founders of contemporary scientific socialism, Marx and Engels, by their social status themselves belonged to the bourgeois intelligentsia. Similarly, in Russia, the theoretical doctrines of Social Democracy arose entirely independently of the spontaneous growth of the labor movement; they arose as a natural and inevitable outcome of the development of ideas within the revolutionary socialist intelligentsia.[50]

With these words, Lenin took a subtle but significant step beyond the usual Marxist conception of the intelligentsia's relationship to the working class. It is not simply that the intelligentsia, by virtue of its education, is able to articulate the proletariat's own consciousness of the historical necessity of socialism, casting it in precise "scientific" language and thereby serving, to use Marx's term, as the proletariat's "ideologists." In Lenin's formulation, so-

73

cialism is a product of the intelligentsia's consciousness, not that of the workers, and the intelligentsia has to instill it in the working class, which otherwise would fail to understand the need for carrying out to the end the revolutionary transformation of the existing order and the attainment of socialism. To be sure, *What Is to Be Done?* goes on to urge the creation of a party *of* workers, not just of *intelligenty*, but these are to be carefully schooled workers who have been raised to the intelligentsia's level of "socialist consciousness." For good reason, the passage quoted above is often considered to be the very foundation of "Leninism," for it asserts the principle of the leadership role of the "vanguard party," Lenin's most distinctive contribution to Marxism as well as the core of the future Soviet political system.

Needless to say, Lenin believed that only with the fulfillment of the socialist program would the true interests of the working class be realized, something which the workers' economic struggle by itself could never hope to achieve. Machajski, by contrast, believed that the goals of socialism served the interests only of the intelligentsia by deflecting the workers' direct attack on economic inequality, which alone could alter the inferior position of the working class. In short, Lenin placed his revolutionary hopes on the "consciousness" of the intelligentsia, while Machajski placed his on the "spontaneity" of the workers. Both, however, perceived the critical difference — along with the possibility of tension, and even of conflict — between them.

This inevitably raises the question of whether Lenin might have been familiar with Machajski's views, the earliest expression of which antedates the composition of *What Is to Be Done?* by at least a year or two. The answer, to the extent that it can be determined, appears to be no. To be sure, Lenin *could* have learned of Machajski's views by this time. Lenin had been exiled to Siberia from 1897 to January 1900, returning then to European Russia until he went abroad in July 1900. This was just about the time Machajski's Siberian essays were beginning to circulate. Although Lenin's place of exile was considerably to the west and south of Machajski's location, he had extensive contacts with other exiles,[51] and we have seen how quickly Machajski's hectographed pamphlets spread through the far-flung exile colonies. It is possible that through these contacts the pamphlets could have reached Lenin either before or after he went abroad.

There is no evidence in Lenin's writings, however, that such was the case. We know that Trotsky told Lenin about Machajski's essays upon reaching London after his escape from Siberia (see above, p. 22), but that was not until the autumn of 1902, and *What Is to Be Done?* was published in March of that year. The first mention of Machajski in Lenin's writings dates from December 1902–January 1903. In a preparatory document for the upcoming Second Congress of the Russian Social-Democratic Party, Lenin listed a number of issues that he felt should be reported on at the congress, including relations with non–Social-Democratic opposition groups; among the groups whose views and whose attitude toward the Social Democrats ought to be discussed he listed, without further comment, the *makhaevtsy*.[52] It is of interest that Makhaevism at this early point in its history had already gained sufficient recognition for Lenin to feel it merited a going-over at the Second Congress — but aside from putting the Makhaevists on his list, he says not another word about them. The second — and last — reference to Makhaevism in the fifty-five volumes of Lenin's collected works does not occur until 1921, when Lenin uses the term as an epithet against the Workers' Opposition.[53] These two passing mentions indicate that although Lenin had heard about Makhaevism by late 1902, either from Trotsky or from some other source, he attached little importance to it. Given Lenin's tendency to attack, defame, and, if possible, destroy those with whom he disagreed, it would have been out of character for him to maintain silence about someone he considered to be a serious ideological opponent or rival. For his part, Machajski ignored Lenin as completely as Lenin ignored him. He scarcely mentioned Lenin in his writings before the 1917 revolution, and when he did it was clear that he saw little to distinguish him from other Russian Social Democrats — a serious misperception, to be sure, but one that he shared with a great many of his contemporaries.

The striking similarity of Machajski's and Lenin's views on the origins of socialism, therefore, seems to have been a case of parallel but independent development. This in itself, however, is worthy of note. That both a leading proponent of Russian Marxism and one of its most vehement critics felt it necessary to assign such importance to the intelligentsia affirms once again the intelligentsia's crucial role in Russian socialism, in the Russian revolutionary movement, in Russian life.

Chapter 4

The "Socialization of Knowledge"

MACHAJSKI'S REJECTION of Marxism as a revolutionary movement went deeper than just a repudiation of its political tactics and its immediate objectives of parliamentary power in the West and a "bourgeois revolution" in Russia. He accused it of defending the interests of the intelligentsia even in its basic philosophical assumptions and psychological outlook. Those interests would find their realization with the achievement of Marxism's ultimate objective, the "socialization of the means of production," which, far from satisfying the aspirations of the proletariat, would consolidate the economic power of the new ruling class of intellectual workers. Using Marxism, and to some extent anarchism, as a foil, Machajski worked out an alternative revolutionary theory and program. Instead of socialization of the means of production, it would result in what he called the "socialization of knowledge."

Machajski attacked Marxism for the very reason that so many intellectuals were attracted to it: because it formed an entire philosophical world-view, a comprehensive explanation of the nature of society and the historical process. Although Marxism declared that it wanted to change the world, it also wanted to understand it, and to do so it had to stand back intellectually from the class struggle and its moral claims, to view it from the philosophical vantage point of society as a whole, or of universal human history. Thereby, Machajski believed, it rendered itself incapable of representing and defending the specific economic interests of the working class. It was not possible to achieve an objective comprehension of the class struggle and at the same time to embrace the subjective sentiments of one of the parties to it, to be both a dispassionate social scientist and a passionate spokesman for society's victims. These were two very different perspectives which created mutually exclusive loyalties and commitments. For Marxists, the interests of society as a whole — and, therefore, of its rulers and guardians — inevitably took precedence over the interests of the working class.

This aspect of Makhaevism displays not only anti-intelligentsia sentiment, that is, hostility to the presumed economic and political designs of the intelligentsia, but also an element of anti-intellectualism, hostility to the kind of thinking associated with intellectuals. This was an important component of Machajski's critique of other revolutionary currents, closely resembling Bakunin's earlier strictures against Comte and Marx. It marks out yet another area in which Bakuninism may have served as a source of inspiration, or at least as a precursor, of Makhaevism.

In 1906, Machajski published in St. Petersburg a Russian translation of selected passages from Marx's *The Holy Family*. The notes he supplied to this translation — actually, Makhaevist glosses on certain key phrases — go to the heart of his opposition to the Marxist world-view. In *The Holy Family*, he argued, Marx and Engels had started out on the right foot to develop a truly materialist view of history. For example, in criticizing Bruno Bauer and his idea of "progress," Marx declared that the concept of progress was "completely empty and abstract," that historical development had hitherto proceeded against the great mass of humanity and had reduced it to "an ever more dehumanized predicament."[1] Machajski regarded this passage as a precise expression of the proletariat's class consciousness. But instead of adhering to this position, he complained, Marx had gone on to construct a theory designed to show that there *was* absolute progress in history. The theory of mature Marxism, that history is the ceaseless development of mankind's productive forces, contradicted what the young Marx had correctly suggested. The Marxist doctrine that society arose to meet the productive needs of man stemmed not from a materialist point of view but from idealism, "from the idealist fiction that civilized society is a single economic cooperative, an involuntary collaboration."[2]

The rest of Machajski's notes elaborated the same point. "Scientific socialism" had by no means surmounted the utopianism of earlier socialist theories, as it claimed, but had incorporated it, camouflaging it with a facade of objectivism. Instead of recognizing that history is in fact "exclusively a matter of human hands, exclusively a result of human will," Marxism, in its attempt to marry German philosophy to the labor movement, placed its emphasis on "historical necessity," objective economic forces, laws of social development that were independent of human will.[3] Like any idealist or even religious system, Marxism began to pay superstitious homage to historical necessity, turning it into a kind of socialist providence which over the centuries has been preparing paradise on earth. As a result, it obscured what those few phrases of *The Holy Family* had momentarily made clear, that history over the centuries had created "not collaboration but slavery," that the historical process had no other meaning than the progressive enslavement of the majority of men.[4] To perceive the true class position of the workers, a Marxist would have to renounce the Hegelian notion of "an historical, objective, economic justification for every historical era." He would have to acknowledge instead that "the Marxist doctrine of the productive *needs of society*, the productive requirements of mankind, contains not economic *materialism* . . . but the old utopian viewpoint of a *single* society, a *single* mankind."[5]

From Machajski's point of view, human history began with conquest and had never been anything other than the succession of one ruling class by another over the toilers of the world. From antique slavery to medieval serfdom to modern industrial capitalism, the position of the laborers had remained unchanged.[6] Civilization had been built not on force alone, however, but on force supplemented and reinforced by the superior knowledge of the rulers. Throughout history, knowledge had been the monopoly of the ruling class, and "the intellectual workers of every age, of every country, have been the masters and the manual workers their slaves."[7] Even at the dawn of history, the more advanced tribes had been able to subjugate the backward ones through greater mastery of the secrets of nature. The fruits of civilization had always fallen to the masters, while the vast majority of men were condemned to lifelong ignorance and turned into beasts of

79

burden. "The capture of civilization by robbers — this is the essence of the workers' bondage."[8]

If history was entirely the product of force, deceit, and calculation, then it was a case of every class for itself. If economic oppression stemmed entirely from the conscious will of the oppressors, then it could be cast off by an act of will on the part of the oppressed, galvanized by their suffering and resentment. Any doctrine which tried to transcend these raw feelings and concern itself with the interests of society as a whole inevitably stifled the rebelliousness of the workers, and this was precisely the course Marxism had taken.

Marxism proudly proclaimed itself a "social science." But a social science, by its very nature, cannot be the enemy of historical development and the system of bondage it has produced. Instead of rebelling against the existing order, Marxism tried to understand and explain it. It is impossible, Machajski maintained, to interpret social development and at the same time speak for the masses who are revolting against it. In its effort to be dispassionately scientific, Marxism preoccupied itself with the "laws" of historical progress. But "it is impossible simultaneously to perform this philosophical, scientific function of the guardians of history and to assert that 'the whole of past historical development contradicts' the great majority of mankind," as Marx and Engels stated in *The Holy Family*.[9] The workers' revolution, as Machajski conceived it, was not the final step in the orderly march of history, but a revolt *against* history as it had hitherto unfolded. "The workers' revolution is a revolt of the slaves of contemporary society against historical laws, which to this day have turned the whole earth into their prison."[10]

Not only historical and sociological constructs but ethical and social ideals served to curb the resentment of the workers. All such ideals merely sanctified the conduct of the ruling classes and condemned those who rebelled against them. By its very nature, no ideal can promote the emancipation of the "slave class," for an ideal is universal; it concerns itself with the welfare of all humanity, and to consider the interests of just one class would violate it. Neither Christian, socialist, communist, nor even anarchist ideals could adequately represent the needs of the underdog, for they were cast in terms of "society" or "mankind" as a whole. In a lengthy critique of Kropotkin's ideas, Machajski determined that the anarchist world-view differed little from that of Marxism. To the extent that the anarchist adhered to such sentiments as "solidarity" and the inherent socialism of the Russian peasants, drew on contemporary science to substantiate his ideals, and sought to adjust anarchist goals to the relative level of development of different societies, he fell prey to "a special anarchist objectivism." Like Marxism, anarchism "establishes the same laws of historical development and historical continuity emanating from the historical conditions of existence of each 'country' that are independent of the will of contemporaries," leading the anarchists to agree with the Marxists that the impending revolution in Russia would be limited to the establishment of bourgeois democracy.[11] Inexorably, therefore, anarchism helped to undermine and restrict the revolutionary energies of the working class. "Anarchist science . . . paralyzes the tendency of the contemporary labor movement to a world-wide conspiracy, to a universal uprising of the workers with a single goal. Science, in both its Marxist and its anarchist application, proves to be a force that does not assist but hinders the uprising of the slaves of the civilized world."[12]

Regarding the existing order as the womb of the future, a necessary, and therefore justifiable, stage that mankind must pass through on the way to a better life, Marxism, far from the science it claimed to be, had actually become a new religious faith. Machajski in fact entitled one of the two essays that formed part 3 of *The Intellectual Worker* "Socialist Science As a New Religion." Instead of demanding the immediate alleviation of the plight of the workers here and now, Marxism, like Christianity before it, persuaded them to accept the trials of the present as the promise of future happiness. The believing socialist no longer viewed the existing order as a modern form of robbery — he began to cherish it as a preparation for the workers' ultimate emancipation. He had no doubt that bondage and exploitation were the roads leading humanity to the fraternal community of the future. "Socialism is a homily on happiness, on the just life, on the universal equality of future generations of humanity. It is a homily which forces those who believe it to broaden and strengthen the age-old system of robbery so as to attain this future happiness in the fast-

81

est way."[13] Just like priests, Machajski charged, the socialists consoled their listeners with the hope that future generations would inherit the earth. Socialism served as a religion for the slaves of the bourgeois order.[14]

It is in this context that Machajski's critique of Marx's economics can best be understood, for it stemmed directly from his rejection of Marxism as a "scientific" world-view. Machajski devoted much of part 2 of *The Intellectual Worker* to Marx's analysis of the capitalist system and to the consequences that would follow from Marx's objective of the "socialization of the means of production." Machajski's discussion took the form of an exegesis of volume 2 of *Capital*, accompanied by arcane formulas, equations, and terminology. Max Nomad wrote that aside from the rigors of imprisonment, reading part 2 of *The Intellectual Worker* was the most difficult experience Machajski's adherents had to undergo.[15] That can be believed, for in places it is almost impenetrable. Machajski himself, in his introductory note to the Geneva edition of the work, expressed regret that he had been unable to revise it instead of reprinting it as originally written in Siberia, for, as he acknowledged in a rare understatement, it was "insufficiently comprehensible and popularized."[16] Though the argument itself is complex and far from clear, the conclusion to which it led is perfectly plain: the Marxist goal of socialization of the means of production would produce not economic equality for the proletariat but a system of state socialism administered by, and for the benefit of, the intellectual workers.

Toward the end of volume 2 of *Capital*, Marx set out to investigate the economic process by which "social constant capital," i.e., the means of production of the capitalist system as a whole, is accumulated and replenished. According to Marx, a large part of the yearly product is not new value produced in the current year but represents the value of means of production handed down from the previous year and embodied in the current year's production. In the numerical example which Marx used, 9,000 units represents the total annual product, of which only 3,000 constitutes the new value of the year's production.

The sum of the product in values of this year is . . . 3,000. All other portions of value in the products of this year are merely transferred values, derived from the value of means of production previously produced and consumed in the annual production. Aside from the value of 3,000, the current annual labor has not produced anything in the way of values. That 3,000 represents its entire annual production in values.[17]

These 3,000 units are the "social revenue" from the year's production, and they alone form the consumable income of society, to be divided between the capitalists and the workers.[18] (In Marx's example, the workers receive 1,500 units as wages and the capitalists appropriate 1,500 units of surplus value as profits.) Marx recognized that an additional 6,000 units, which he called "constant capital-value," are produced in the current year in the form of replacements for the used-up means of production. Means of production, obviously, are not only handed down from the previous year and embodied in the current year's production, but, since they are used up, they must be created anew and passed on to provide for next year's production. They do not, however, constitute part of the "social revenue." Only one-third of the annual product, or 3,000 units, is the consumable income of society, while two-thirds, or 6,000, is in the form of means of production which cannot be consumed.[19]

Machajski refused to accept the category of "social constant capital," because he rejected the idea of a strict separation between means of production and articles of consumption in the economy as a whole. He maintained that Marx had illegitimately projected the economy of a single enterprise — the subject of the first volume of *Capital* — onto the capitalist economy as a whole. Only for an individual factory was there such a thing as "constant capital," means of production used up by the factory's workers to create "only" 3,000 new units of value. In the economy at large, these distinctions were erased.[20] Factory owners producing means of production for other factories make a profit from them (by exploiting their workers) just as the producers of consumer goods do; that profit takes the form of money, which can be used to buy articles of consumption. The means of production, sold to other factories, are then worked on by exploited labor to produce monetary profits for *their* owners. "Thus, labor power, operating in the area of preparation of means of production, creates, nonetheless, means of consumption. . . . The whole value of the yearly product produced by the working class over and above the share allotted to it for the preservation of its labor power is handed over to ruling educated society *in the form of articles of personal consumption.*"[21] Each year, therefore, the labor of the working class created a full 9,000 units of new value. Marxism claimed for the workers only that part of it (in Marx's model, one-sixth) pocketed by the capitalists as profit. Machajski maintained that the much larger portion which Marx tried to set aside as "constant capital" was also available to the rulers of society for consumption — whether those rulers be capitalists or intellectual workers. As the ideology of the latter, Marxism was neither able nor willing to reveal this fundamental economic truth.

What was at stake, then, was much more than capitalist profit as Marx had defined it. The much larger portion of social wealth that Marxism tried to withhold as nonconsumable capital goods had been produced by the labor of the workers, and they were entitled to all of it. Just how that was to be accomplished without destroying the productive capacity of the economy remained unclear. Evgenii Lozinskii suggested a clarification of Machajski's position: what was being demanded for the workers, he claimed, was not the right to divide up or "eat" the factories and machines, but an equivalent for the labor they had expended to produce them in the form of equal access to all articles of consumption.[22] This makes a fair amount of sense, and it may well have been what Machajski meant — but it is not exactly what he himself wrote.

Marx as an economist had little to fear from Machajski, because Machajski rejected the very enterprise of objective economic analysis. Marx recognized that the industrial system itself, and not just the way it was run by the capitalists, required that a large share of the annual product be used for investment purposes in order to keep the system running. He acknowledged, without regret, that this would be the case even when the means of production were socialized.[23] Machajski refused to view capitalism as a "system" at all. Adopting the perspective of the average worker, he reasoned that if all social wealth was the product of the proletariat's labor, as the Marxists themselves affirmed, then it should be placed at the immediate disposal of the workers. To provide support for this demand, and to demonstrate how the Marxists sought to deflect it, was the primary purpose of his digression into economic theory.

Marxism's economic analysis, like its philosophical and historical outlook, testified to its attachment to the existing order. Viewing society as an economic organism, concentrating on the forces and relationships of economic production, the Marxists did not wish to destroy the capitalist system but to take it over intact in order to ensure its further development. The Marxists, Machajski charged, declared war on the capitalist system not because it plundered the workers but because the rule of the "plutocrats" had led to its degeneration. In the Marxist view of history the successive ruling classes — nobility, capitalists, even ancient slave-owners — had been progressive forces when they first appeared. Only toward the end of their era of domination did they degenerate and become superfluous. The socialist revolution would ensue from the crisis of capitalism, the inability of the capitalists to continue running the economy and ruling society. They had to be swept away not because they were exploitative but because they had lost their vitality and usefulness. Marxism was determined not to overthrow the existing order but to cure it of its crises. [24]

"More than once in history," Machajski warned, "have 'senile' ruling classes been overthrown by revolutions in order to make way for new ones. But where is the guarantee that ruling classes will cease to exist altogether?"[25] The Marxists would consider their mission fulfilled once they had chased out the capitalists, once they had replaced the present "obsolete" rulers with new and more competent ones.

Anyone who rebels, like the socialists, only because the degenerate, idle masters are no longer capable of governing, demands only new, more capable masters; he breaks the trail for these new masters and thus does not weaken but strengthens oppression. This is what results from all the activity of the socialists. They force the crude, ignorant *kulaks*, the puffed-up magnates, and the untalented governors to call on the whole learned world of masters for help, to admit the intelligentsia, educated society, to power. [26]

That day would come with the realization of Marxism's ultimate goal, the "socialization of the means of production."

To help demonstrate that Marxism's objective was not to regain for the workers the full value of their labor, Machajski interlaced his analysis of Marx's economic theory with a comparison between Marx and Johann Karl Rodbertus — thereby making

85

life even more difficult for the hard-pressed readers of his second essay. Rodbertus (also known as Rodbertus-Jagetzow, 1805–1875), a lawyer, landowner, and, for a brief time in 1848, Prussian minister of education, was one of the creators of the concept of state socialism. Almost forgotten today, Rodbertus's economic ideas had stirred a flurry of interest in German socialist circles in the 1880s. The subject was therefore of greater immediacy and familiarity to Machajski's intended readers than it would seem today. Rodbertus was a critic of capitalism and, like Marx, an adherent of the labor theory of value, as well as a devoted monarchist and conservative. He therefore proposed a system that amounted to state regulation of the economy by a socially enlightened monarchy. In the early 1880s, Rodbertus's "conservative socialism" was rediscovered by German intellectuals who saw in it a nonrevolutionary alternative to Social Democracy as well as a justification for acceptance of the Bismarckian state and its social legislation. The new interest in Rodbertus and the publication of some of his works (which Machajski had at his disposal in Siberia) revived earlier charges that Marx had borrowed his fundamental ideas from Rodbertus, whose first work dated to 1842. This prompted a spirited defense of Marx, and critique of Rodbertus, by both Kautsky and Engels, a task which they considered important enough to devote much of 1884 and 1885 to fulfilling.[27]

Machajski did not charge Marx with plagiarizing from Rodbertus, but the accusation he did level against him was no less damaging: that Marx's economic theory would lead to a form of state socialism little different from the one Rodbertus had proposed. Like Marx, Rodbertus had wished to eliminate private ownership of land and capital while preserving "national capital," the economy's means of production which cannot be distributed to the workers; this, however, is precisely the source of profit.

Rodbertus recommends eliminating private capital in order to guarantee the perpetual existence of national capital. This means that he prefers to transform the process of the collection of profit by private entrepreneurs, the representatives of bourgeois society, into one perpetual national enterprise, run directly by the state, which distributes national profit to all its constituent parts, i.e., to the whole of ruling and governing educated society.

The task of volume 2 of *Capital* had been to lend the weight of "pure science" to Rodbertus's basic position.[28]

Essentially, Machajski was using Rodbertus to establish Marx's guilt by association: as far as the workers were concerned, the theories of Rodbertus, the conservative monarchist, and Marx, the defender of the proletariat, would amount to much the same thing. The major difference between them concerned the exploiters of the workers. A system of state socialism in an undemocratic state, such as Rodbertus had proposed, would mean the distribution of national profit only to the highest ranks of the ruling class. The objective of Marxism was to broaden that distribution to all the intellectual workers. Therefore, "the socialism of Social Democracy is *state socialism* implemented in a *democracy*," a "'socialist' distribution of national profit to the whole of educated society, the army of intellectual workers."[29]

The rights of ownership of the means of production pass into the hands of the state. The latter, in the guise of "replacing" the ever-growing "social constant capital," takes from the working class all the fruits of the increasing productivity of labor and hands them over to all the ranks of the army of "intellectual workers" as a reward for their "special talents and abilities."[30]

Machajski found in the writings of the Social Democrats no indication that the coming of socialism would result in equality of incomes. All the socialists' indictments of the capitalist order would lose their force as soon as the parasitical capitalist was replaced by an individual "with a diploma from a higher educational institution" certifying that he was versed in some specialty. A high income would be regarded purely as the reward for intellectual labor, and only if it reached scandalous proportions would there be any thought of limiting it.[31]

Thus the rewards of socialization of the means of production would go entirely to the intellectual workers, who would be able to pass on their monopoly of education to their children. As long as the technical knowledge necessary to run the economy and the government remained unattainable for the ordinary workers, then "regardless of the formal ownership of all material wealth, their bondage will remain unshaken."[32]

Machajski's critique of Marxism as an outlook on the world,

whatever it may tell us about Marxism itself, reveals a great deal about Makhaevism. The refusal to accept the possibility of evolution, development, peaceful accommodation in human affairs; the adherence to an unchanging truth which needs only to be repeated and instilled; the accusatory rhetoric, with its litany of formulaic epithets — all this gave Makhaevism a distinctly sectarian cast. Machajski's old friend, Stefan Żeromski, hit the mark when he wrote that if Machajski had lived in the Middle Ages he would have founded a religious sect; living in modern times, he founded a social sect.[33] The analytical, "scientific" side of Marxism was suspect to Machajski (though he himself was enough of an intellectual to comprehend it and even to emulate it when he chose); too great an interest in understanding the world diminished the passions required for changing it. This attitude imposed a certain intellectual rigidity and narrowness on Makhaevism and helped to limit its effectiveness as a revolutionary movement.

For all that, however, Makhaevism was not devoid of insight into the limitations of Marxism and its economic program. Machajski perceived — and with prophetic clarity, as Stalin's Russia was to demonstrate only too well — that socialization of the means of production would not necessarily alter the living standards of the workers. This may seem a commonplace today, but it was a perception rarely encountered among early twentieth-century revolutionaries. Social ownership of the means of production promised the end of private capitalism; it would not immediately signify the end of a hierarchical division of labor, wide inequality of incomes, and low rewards for the workers' labor — the primary sources of the workers' discontent. Whatever the moral and psychological satisfactions of liberation from the constraints of the old order, it might prove to be of little *economic* significance to the individual worker that the means of production were now in the hands of the state rather than of private entrepreneurs: he could still find himself in the position of reproducing and even expanding them without adequate compensation for his labor. As Adam Ulam has put it, "The chains felt by the proletariat are the chains of the industrial system. The chains Marx urges them to throw off are those of capitalism. Will the workers understand the difference?"[34] Machajski perceived a very great difference, and this perception underlay the revolutionary theory he formulated as an alternative to socialism.

As we have seen, the intellectual and ideological sources of Makhaevism were Marxism and anarchism, the latter specifically of the Bakuninist variety. Viewed more broadly, however, Makhaevism was part of that sea-change in European social thought at the end of the nineteenth century which has been called the "revolt against positivism." The term *positivism* here refers to the general tendency of late nineteenth-century thought to apply natural-science concepts to social behavior. Marxism became a major target of this critique, for, in the words of H. Stuart Hughes, Marxism was considered "an aberrant, and peculiarly insidious, form of the reigning cult of positivism . . . the last and most ambitious of the abstract and pseudoscientific ideologies that had bewitched European intellectuals since the early eighteenth century."[35]

Different conclusions could be drawn from a critique of the "scientific" character of Marxism. Those interested in the formulation of a more solidly grounded social theory sought to distinguish what seemed of general validity in Marxist theory from its political commitments, thus using the critique of Marxism to construct a modern social science. Others, like Machajski, moved in the opposite direction, their insight into the subjective character of Marxism leading them to a rejection of the validity of social thought itself. Hence the elements of anti-intellectualism and irrationalism which came to mark many of the new currents of thought arising at this time: on the one hand, a disenchantment with prevailing democratic and socialist political ideals, including Marxism, accompanied by a growing suspicion of the motivations of their spokesmen; and, on the other, a tendency to emphasize will, instinct, and intuition rather than reason as the true wellsprings of social action.[36]

In this context, of direct relevance to Makhaevism are the ideas of three figures who have been dubbed the "modern Machiavellians": Gaetano Mosca, Vilfredo Pareto, and Robert Michels.[37] Mosca, Pareto, and Michels are appreciated today for their contributions to the modern theory of social and political elites. They were "Machiavellians" in the sense that all three believed that men were moved by their needs and interests, especially the desire for power, and not by ideals or a sense of justice. This led them to probe beneath the formal rhetoric and explicit principles of contemporary political doctrines, where they found an ineluctable tendency to perpetuate the division of society into a dominant elite and a subordinate mass. Whether expressed as Mosca's "theory of the ruling class," Pareto's "circulation of elites," or Michels's "iron law of oligarchy," it was a constant and universal law of political, social, and economic organization, and neither parliamentary democracy nor Marxism was exempt from it. While generally sympathetic to Marx's critique of capitalism they asserted that even its replacement by some form of socialism would merely introduce a new variety of economic inequality and class division. They phrased this conclusion in pithy statements with which Machajski could readily have agreed. Mosca, for example, declared that even if capitalism were abolished "there would still be those who would manage the public wealth and then the great mass of those who are managed."[38] According to Pareto, even if the conflict between capital and labor were abolished, "conflicts would arise between the different kinds of workers of the socialist state, between the 'intellectuals' and the 'nonintellectuals,' between different kinds of politicians, between the latter and those they administer, between innovators and conservatives."[39] Michels pointed out the oligarchical tendencies of the workers themselves, claiming that working-class leaders of proletarian origin were simply "lifted out of the working class into a new class" of salaried party employees.[40]

However similar some of their criticisms of Marxism were to those voiced by Makhaevism, these social theorists had no fundamental affinity with Machajski. As a revolutionary activist rather than a sociologist, Machajski had little interest in social theory in and for itself. Indeed, with its claim to scientific objectivity and its sense of society as an organic structure or unity, social theory seemed to him merely a device of the ruling elite to deflect the demands of the laboring classes. Furthermore, Machajski's identification of socialism as the ideology of the intellectual workers, and the latter as the new ruling class that would succeed the capitalists, was more specific — and, whatever its validity, perhaps more original — than anything to be found in the general theories of elite circulation of Mosca, Pareto, and Michels.

Another turn-of-the-century figure, Georges Sorel, at first glance seems to stand even closer to Machajski. Inspired by syndicalism, Sorel too attacked parliamentarism and the political practices of contemporary socialism as serving merely the interests and ambitions of a new elite, the socialist party leaders. In his best-known work, *Reflections on Violence*, he warned, much as Machajski did, that a political general strike of the kind the socialists advocated would result in the transferral of power "from one privileged class to another," while "the mass of the producers would merely change masters."[41] Again like Machajski, what he appreciated in Marxism was its most militant element, its articulation of irreconcilable class war and of the proletariat's "stubborn, increasing, and passionate resistance to the present order of things."[42] Beyond that, however, Sorel's mystical conception of the economic general strike as a "social myth" and of proletarian violence as a way of reviving the flagging energies of a decadent civilization, reflecting the strong overtones of Bergson and Nietzsche in his thinking, sharply demarcate him from Machajski. For the latter, there was nothing mystical about the general strike. He perceived it as the most effective device for rallying the laboring classes and wresting economic concessions from the existing order. His image of working-class militancy derived not from *fin de siècle* philosophy but from his Polish experience and the impact on him of the 1892 Lodz strike.

Although Mosca, Pareto, Michels, and Sorel knew each other's work and drew upon it in various ways, there is no indication that any of them had ever heard of Machajski. Nor does Machajski appear to have been familiar with their writings, with the possible exception of Sorel. What is more significant than the possibility of any mutual influence, however, is the extent to which the anarchist critique of Marxism reverberated in the ideas of all these individuals. Sorel obviously drew part of his inspiration from syndicalism and anarchism, but even Michels, himself a socialist, refers frquently to Bakunin in *Political Parties* and quotes with approval Bakunin's warning about "bourgeois intellectuals" in *L'Empire Knouto-Germanique*.[43] If disillusionment with the "scientific" claims of Marxism and the disinterested objectivity of its practitioners contributed to the reorientation of European thought at the turn of the century, this development owed a certain intellectual debt to premises anarchism had been advancing since the time of Bakunin (though none of the figures discussed, any more than Machajski himself, believed the anarchists were immune to their own criticism). Those premises would be reformulated yet again in the next stage of the history of the "new class" theory, the post-1917 critique of the new Bolshevik rulers of Soviet Russia.

In the course of his analysis of Marxism, Machajski worked out his own revolutionary program, and it was essentially complete by the time of the 1905 revolution.[44] It breathed the spirit of implacable hostility to the existing order which had characterized him since his student days and which he found so sorely lacking in other revolutionary parties and currents. His image of the workers' revolution was a "slave revolt," a term he used repeatedly in his writings, an explosive mutiny against the existing order by those who had no share in its rewards and privileges and therefore no vested interest in its preservation. The driving force of this revolt was to be not "class consciousness," social ideals, or awareness of historical forces, but the resentment of the "have-nots" and their demand for immediate economic improvement. Of particular interest is his effort to identify and mobilize the social elements that seemed to harbor that resentment to the greatest degree.

As his criticism of Social Democracy indicated, Machajski believed that not only parliamentary institutions but even civil freedoms were irrelevant to the worker as long as his economic disabilities endured. It was only the intelligentsia that could profit from freedom of speech, assembly, and association, freedom of the press, and freedom to elect the rulers of the country. The only personal autonomy the worker could exercise in the bourgeois order was the freedom to sell his labor to the capitalists, and the only objective that could possibly be of benefit to him was immediate economic improvement.[45]

Nor was trade-union activity any more useful. Machajski's rejection of trade unions distinguishes Makhaevism from syndicalism, even though he advocated the syndicalist tactic of the general strike. Revolutionary syndicalism in France "stood for revolutionary action by unions to establish a society based upon unions."[46] Unions were seen as the nuclei of the new society and as the essential mechanism for achieving it. To Machajski, however, trade unions, like parliaments, represented a dangerous compromise with the existing order, for they tended to reduce the rebelliousness of at least a part of the working class by satisfying its better-paid and better-trained elements. Although he clung to the assertion that within the existing order the manual workers could expect nothing more than the status of industrial helots, Machajski occasionally gave way in his writings to criticism of the workers' tendency to accept those improvements that did come their way. In one place he hinted that the workers might in fact be susceptible to the temptation of rising within the existing order: "the socialists have begun in the most brazen fashion to instill in people's souls all those robbers' plans and calculations which give rise to the hope that this slave or that one will leap into 'society,' the starving peasant will become a well-to-do *muzhik*, the skilled worker a white-handed parasitical boss."[47] He referred scornfully to those workers who belonged to trade unions and to socialist organizations as the "pacified" strata of the working class willing to settle for trifling concessions from the capitalists or hoping to receive them by renouncing uprisings and conspiracies. Such workers, he complained, had been corrupted by the bourgeois world and then further demoralized by the socialists, who encouraged them to look down on their unorganized, badly paid comrades as a "half-criminal Lumpenproletariat" too benighted to fight for socialism.[48] The main effect of trade unions, therefore, was to create "a deep breach between the better-paid workers and those who live in poverty."[49]

Makhaevism swore implacable hostility to the existing order on the grounds of the workers' desperate economic plight. Consequently, it faced the threat (which Lenin recognized in *What Is to Be Done?*) of a fatal slackening of revolutionary incentive if the workers improved their living standard before the definitive overthrow of the existing order could be accomplished. Machajski's solution was to turn to those elements of Russian society who seemed least likely to be exposed to such "corruption." The agents of the Makhaevist revolution were to be the most alien-

93

ated and disinherited offspring of the industrial revolution in Russia: the unemployed, the worker-peasant, even the outcasts of urban life.

Machajski accused the Social Democrats of revising Marx's attitude toward unemployment in their eagerness to avoid a proletarian revolution. Marx had maintained that the "growing army of the unemployed," an inevitable product of capitalist development, would make the further existence of the capitalist order impossible. Now the followers of Marx had come to regard the unemployed "dregs" of the population not as part of the "working proletariat" but as a Lumpenproletariat composed mainly of lazybones and semicriminals.[50] A doctrine which defined the proletarian not as "one who has no means of subsistence" but as "one who owns no means of production" could not truly be revolutionary. Its adherents could not even consider touching off "an explosion of that volcano on which the class structure of Russia rests."[51]

The resentment and anger that could lead to such an eruption were effectively brought to a boil among the unemployed. "The unemployed man feels what he has sometimes forgotten while working. Amidst the torments of hunger he feels that he was born a slave, born without any right to even the smallest share in the riches which surround him, which have been created by generations of labor through the centuries and which he has increased by the labor of his own life."[52] These, Machajski declared, were the only feelings harbored by the unemployed worker, and to talk to him of "freedom of personality" and the "inviolable rights of the citizen" was nothing but the cruellest mockery.[53] Here was a revolutionary force neglected by even the most radical socialists, for only a true revolutionary would go among the unemployed, "where the strongest dissatisfaction and despair exist," where "only one spark" would be enough to touch off an uprising.[54]

The unemployed were not the only dry social tinder Machajski saw waiting to be ignited. He devoted some attention to the "dark" elements of the Russian towns, those subterranean strata of the urban population whom a Marxist might have termed the "Lumpenproletariat" and an ordinary citizen might have regarded simply as hoodlums. For example, he chose to regard the Black Hundreds, the protofascist street gangs which appeared during the 1905 revolution, as representatives of the "hungry masses," protesting against a revolution which promised them meaningless political rights instead of relief from their economic distress. "Thus a political revolution inevitably, by its own hand, paved the way for the Black Hundreds from the starving Russian masses to arise against it. A bourgeois revolution could give these people nothing; at least in the Black Hundreds they sometimes had rich aliens' [Jewish? Machajski used the term *inorodcheskie*] shops at their disposal." For the same reason the "well-dressed preachers of the socialist ideal" were set upon by "people in rags," as Machajski chose to characterize the perpetrators of pogroms against *intelligenty*.[55]

He drew a curious analogy between the Black Hundreds and the Galician peasant uprising of 1846. A half century earlier, he wrote, the Polish nobility of Galicia had demanded political rights from the Austrian government, and the Austrians in response instigated an uprising of the Galician peasants against their "freedom-loving masters." That the Galician peasants were incited by a reactionary government did not change the fact that "the peasants were fiercely venting their anger on their own predators." Similarly, the Russian intelligentsia was struggling for political freedom while the Black Hundreds were set upon it by the tsarist authorities, but this did not alter the fact that "the Black Hundreds are killing their masters, who, not satisfied that they live by robbing the workers, use the struggle of the workers to intensify their parasitism."[56]

In light of such statements it is hardly surprising that Machajski was accused of "sympathizing" with the Black Hundreds,[57] but this charge requires considerable qualification. He probably had few qualms about their methods, and he could shed no tears at the thought of *intelligenty* and shopkeepers being victimized. Machajski was a revolutionary, however, and his aims could have little in common with those of the monarchist Black Hundreds. Nor is there any evidence in his writings of the anti-Semitism that inspired the Black Hundreds. Machajski's wife was a Russian Jew, and some of his followers were Jewish. Furthermore, recognizing that anti-Jewish pogroms were sometimes instigated by provocateurs, he claimed that the kind of general strike he advocated was actually the best way to avoid them, for it united people of all races and nationalities in an act of working-class solidarity.[58]

There was some foundation, therefore, to Machajski's complaint in a letter to Żeromski that "it was enough to say that hooliganism is a crude, elemental protest against the fraudulent intention of the socialists to feed the hungry millions with political freedom, to be proclaimed an apostle of hooliganism."[59] Machajski did not address the larger issue, however: that his treatment of the Black Hundreds reflected the broad streak of violence that ran throughout Makhaevism, finding expression not only in his revolutionary tactics but even in his incendiary prose style.

In passages such as those dealing with the Black Hundreds, Machajski did in fact sometimes refer approvingly to the "hooligan,"[60] but this was a theme elaborated by Evgenii Lozinskii rather than by Machajski himself. As Lozinskii depicted him, the hooligan was an unemployed vagrant whose home was the street and whose way of life, if not directly criminal, was generally shady. What most interested Lozinskii about him was his status as a social outcast, the outsider *par excellence:* he owed nothing to society and therefore was neither bound by its prejudices nor had any vested interest in its existing structure. Here was a fresh, vigorous force that might cleanse the Russian scene of its accumulated social litter:

Onto the historical stage has come the frenzied, dirty, outcast figure of the fighting "hooligan." Amid an ever growing chorus of timid or indignant "oh's" and "ah's" from all of educated society (including even the most revolutionary socialists), this "hooligan" is beginning little by little to occupy the main arena of the historical struggle, not — oh, horrors! — as an enemy or rival of his "employed," i.e., laboring comrades, but as an independent fighter against the whole exploiting world, who has decided to repay the latter savagely for his unnatural, wasted life.[61]

His appearance, Lozinskii wistfully suggested, "may be *the beginning of the end* of all our barbaric culture and civilization, all our hypocritical, cannibalistic progress." The vagrant, with his unbridled energies, might stiffen the backbone of the workers' movement.[62]

Lozinskii's romanticized vision of the criminal, or tramp, as social rebel, was in fact a recurrent theme in Russian letters of the early twentieth century. With the growth of urbanization, Russian literature had begun to turn its attention from the countryside to the town. Among others, Maxim Gorky, in his stories and in plays such as *The Lower Depths (Na dne)*, had popularized the image of the urban derelict and vagrant. At the same time, mystical and apocalyptic images came into vogue, especially in the wake of the 1905 revolution. Leonid Andreev's play *Tsar Hunger (Tsar' golod)*, for example, written in 1907 — and cited approvingly by Lozinskii — was a vision of an urban apocalypse, a frenzied revolt by the "hungry" against the privileged classes and their oppressive civilization. Meanwhile, Alexander Blok, in a celebrated metaphor, visualized "the people" as Gogol's *troika*, trampling under its hooves the intelligentsia and the culture it represented, and other Symbolist poets were giving voice to similar images.[63] Hatred of *meshchanstvo*, or "bourgeois" life and values, accompanied by apocalyptic visions of its destruction, was a prominent feature of Russian culture as well as Russian political radicalism in this period, and to some degree the two elements rubbed off on each other.

In his celebration of the "hooligan," therefore, Lozinskii linked Makhaevism to broader currents of Russian thought and culture. Machajski himself, it must be said, was alien to such interests. Lozinskii participated much more fully in the intellectual life of the Russian intelligentsia; Machajski remained a single-minded revolutionary, searching for real-life agents of social upheaval rather than literary images of apocalypse. Nevertheless, the fact that Makhaevism did echo some of the preoccupations of contemporary culture is a useful reminder that it must be interpreted and assessed in terms of its own historical context. The apocalyptic tone of Makhaevism, the sense of a new world to be gained by a mass act of galvanized will, arose, undoubtedly, from that sectarian cast of mind characteristic of Makhaevism in general. At the same time, however, it accorded with a larger cultural trend in early twentieth-century Russia, and, as a result, may have sounded less outlandish, and more persuasive, in its own time than it might today.

Like so many other features of Makhaevism, the primary inspiration for Machajski's revolutionary program seems to derive from Michael Bakunin. In *Statism and Anarchy*, Bakunin declared that in order to overthrow a social system which oppressed it, a people must reject it so thoroughly that all its values and institutional appurtenances seem to belong to another world. In search of an element of the population that displayed such a mentality in Russia, he turned to the peasants. Unlike most populists, he rejected the village commune (*mir*) on the grounds that it had become a conservative institution, its patriarchal structure and its submission to external authority drawing it into the established order. Instead, he singled out the *razboinik*, the bandit of the Russian countryside, who was an outsider even to the *mir* and therefore not constrained by its traditions: "there is one individual among the Russian people who dares to go against the *mir*: it is the bandit. That is why banditry is an important historical phenomenon in Russia — the first rebels, the first revolutionaries, Pugachev and Stenka Razin, were bandits." As the commune had been turned into an instrument of the government and the rich peasants, "banditry remained the sole recourse for the individual, and for the people as a whole a universal insurrection, a revolution."[64]

Sharing Bakunin's image of revolution as a "universal insurrection," Machajski, too, sought a mass force utterly alienated from the established order and its institutions. Makhaevism, however, was a thoroughly urban ideology, its attention focused on the industrial towns of Russia, not the countryside. What Machajski found was a social element that seemed to be bringing into the towns precisely the kind of mentality that Bakunin had ascribed to his romanticized rural bandit. New industrial workers, freshly arrived from the countryside, were providing Russian industry with raw and potentially volatile recruits to the labor force. These were the people whose outlook Machajski considered the most promising for carrying out a Makhaevist revolution.

He had first expressed interest in these new proletarians in *The Intellectual Worker*, where he berated the populists of the seventies for insisting that there was no proletariat in Russia. Even at that time, he wrote, there existed not only hired workers but millions of "migrant proletarians"[65] who set out from the Russian villages to search for work all over the country. It was this social link between countryside and town that he subsequently focused on in greater detail. Machajski had no sympathy for the peasants as long as they remained tillers of the soil, and he refused to support their efforts to acquire more land, but he very much appreciated their presence in the towns.

The rural poor will begin to struggle for themselves and for all the hungry only when they abandon once and for all their hopes for a "black repartition," when they separate themselves from those peasants who want to strengthen and extend peasant landholding. . . . They will flock into the rich towns and together with the urban unemployed will demand security from famines, from unemployment. They will raise a revolt of the slaves like the one the workers of Paris raised a half-century ago.[66]

Makhaevism's insistence on immediate economic gains as the sole objective of the workers' movement was expected to appeal particularly to this group.

All strata of the working population rally in a moment to a mass economic strike, even the most benighted, the most uneducated. The cause is understandable to each one, even to the illiterate fellow who arrived just yesterday from the backwoods village, who has heard no agitator and known no socialist ideas. Even such unorganized workers as domestic servants, it turns out, unite at such a moment.[67]

That "illiterate fellow" fresh from the village, undergoing the psychological stress and economic hardship of his new status and unspoiled by socialist ideas, appeared to be the ideal agent of the Makhaevist revolution. Arriving from the countryside ignorant and unskilled, the new worker had few defenses against the insecurities of early industrialization, and he was the most ready victim of low wages and frequent unemployment. Trade unions were usually of little assistance to him, for, as Machajski pointed out, they were primarily organizations of the skilled and steadily employed. It was not only the frustration engendered in such individuals that made them potential recruits to political extremism, but the means they might be expected to adopt in coping with it. The Russian peasant in large part stood outside the legal and institutional framework of Russian society. For generations the helpless object of constituted authority vested in the nobility and the bureaucracy, his traditional recourse had been to burn and pillage the manor. Cut off from his land, the proletarianized peasant lost even that shred of conservatism which attachment to his property had given him. The new industrial worker, therefore, brought with him to the town an essentially anarchistic approach to social and economic grievances.[68] Machajski's proletarian saw his enemies in a highly personal and immediate way: the cultured and the well-to-do were the visible possessors of wealth and comfort, and their expropriation was a matter not of long-term economic processes and institutional procedures but of direct seizure. Wearing overalls instead of a peasant blouse, Machajski's new industrial worker was Bakunin's rural bandit in modern dress.

For the tactical part of his revolutionary program — how to harness popular resentments and direct them against the existing order — Machajski adopted the revolutionary syndicalist, or anarchosyndicalist, device of the mass general strike. He first outlined his plan in a May Day manifesto to the workers of Irkutsk in 1902 (later republished as an appendix to the Geneva edition of *The Intellectual Worker*). The manifesto called for "a universal conspiracy of workers," a strike by the entire working class. Rebelling against their "slave status," the workers' sole demand would be immediate improvement in the conditions of labor. Stopping work in one factory they would proceed *en masse* to the next, until finally entire cities would arise and the movement would spread throughout the state. Machajski warned that the intelligentsia would condemn such an uprising as "the wild outbursts of the rabble" and hope that the tsar's guns would put it down. He urged the workers to repudiate the socialists and their political objectives, to refuse to serve as "cannon fodder" for a bourgeois revolution that would benefit only the intelligentsia, and to battle solely for their own cause.[69]

A year after Machajski composed his proclamation to the Irkutsk workers, a general strike broke out in the south of Russia. To Machajski, the South Russian strike of 1903 provided vivid proof of the gulf between the intelligentsia's interests and those of the workers. He viewed the strike movement in Baku and Odessa as an attempt by the workers to turn a general strike into a workers' insurrection — an attempt which encountered the adamant opposition of the socialists. The spontaneous development of the strike and its presentation of purely economic demands violated the socialists' principle that the aim of the revolution must be a constitution: "The great outburst of worker resentment . . . caught the Social Democrats completely unprepared. The working masses mounted the strike in defiance of everything the Russian socialists were telling them and were writing in their pamphlets and newspapers."[70] Thereafter, the South Russian strike served Machajski as a model for the initial phase of a workers' insurrection designed to complete the business left unfinished in 1903.

Essentially, the Makhaevist revolution was to begin as a resurrection of the 1903 general strike and end as a new Russian edition of the June Days of Paris. Machajski maintained that the 1903 strike, because of its economic nature, had begun to attract "all segments of the urban working population, even the most uneducated." Had it continued along its original path, it would surely have drawn in "the starving millions of the countryside."[71] To accomplish this, a new general strike must begin, its principal demand being the creation of public works for the unemployed, along the lines of the National Workshops established in Paris in 1848. As we have seen, the June Days played a prominent role in Machajski's reconstruction of the origins of socialism. It was the archetypal confrontation that revealed to the workers once and for all that their enemy was not just the big property owners but the whole of "educated society." The unadorned economic demands of the Paris workers had frightened the intelligentsia into adopting Marxism to deflect the workers into political struggle. Therefore a new version of the June Days seemed to Machajski the best way for the workers to sabotage the political plans of the socialist movement as well as to attack the economic position of the intelligentsia.

The demand for public works for the unemployed would tap a revolutionary force which the socialist parties habitually neglected. "Neither the June insurgents of '48 in Paris, who raised a revolt against the republic which condemned them to starvation, nor unemployed workers who rebelled later were lucky enough to have even one learned socialist or revolutionary in their midst."[72] The establishment of public works in the towns, like the National Workshops of 1848, would reinforce the ranks of the urban unemployed with hordes of distressed laborers from the surrounding countryside. Machajski gave this description of the course the 1903 strike would have taken had it followed his program:

[It] would have attracted all the unemployed, all the vagrants whom the socialists repulse, for in order to confirm and support the conquests of the employed workers it would have demanded bread for the hungry, security for them from unemployment. But as soon as such an uprising of the workers had succeeded in forcing the authorities of the provinces and the capital to establish public works for the unemployed, then the workers' uprising would have found on its side all the hungry millions of the countryside, who now would have seen at last the possibility of living, instead of dying in dreams of a "black repartition."[73]

In this way a general strike was to be transformed into a massive popular insurrection.

The ultimate objective of the workers' efforts was to be what Machajski called the "socialization of knowledge,"[74] one of the most distinctive, and remarkable, elements of Makhaevism. The fundamental reason for the proletariat's inferior status, Machajski maintained, was its ignorance. The workers could be truly emancipated only when they achieved equal educational opportunity through economic equality.

Before taking production into their own hands, the workers must obtain for themselves and for their children the right to acquire knowledge in the way Messrs. white-hands acquire it. The workers will obtain this right when they raise the price of their labor to the same level as that of the white-hands, a level which enables them to support their children during their long years of study.

Until the workers in this way tear knowledge from the hands of the learned world, they will remain as they are now, knowing only manual labor, brought up to be slaves, and they will always be under the command of their masters — *intelligenty*, white-hands — even in a Social-Democratic state, even in an anarchist commune.[75]

The workers could not prepare themselves to run the economy merely by studying in their spare time, as some socialists urged. It was nonsense, Machajski declared, to expect a worker to achieve the same level of education after a hard day's labor that the *intelligent* attained in years of full-time study.[76] Education, like wealth, was the product of robbery, not of concentrated effort or superior talent, and the *intelligenty* had a monopoly on knowledge only because the exploited workers were compelled to furnish them with food, clothing, and shelter while they studied. Economic inequality, not intellectual superiority, was the source of the intelligentsia's advantages.[77]

The workers would strike for higher and higher pay, until at last

the wages of the worker will equal the income of the *intelligent*. But then the children of the manual workers will have the same opportunity for education as the children of the white-hands. Equality of education will perforce be established, and the school will cease to educate some to be slaves and others to be masters, as it does now. All will become educated people on an equal basis; there will be no one to condemn to the latter-day penal servitude of lifelong manual work, there will be no one to rob.[78]

Once equality of incomes had been achieved, the manual workers, or at least their children, could become intellectual workers. At last, what Machajski held to be the true source of class division and exploitation in modern society would be erased.[79]

Machajski did not develop the idea of the "socialization of knowledge" any further, and he left his image of utopia quite vague. Nevertheless, it gave Makhaevism a unique character among the revolutionary ideologies competing for attention in Russia. Makhaevism was not an anti-industrial theory. It did not embody any nostalgic remembrance of the harmonious rural community, of the sort that found expression in the glorification of the peasant commune by the anarchist-communists and the Socialist-Revolutionaries. Machajski fully shared Marx's opinion of the "idiocy of rural life," and he dismissed any idealization of the peasants. He condemned the fruits of modern technology only to the extent that they could not be enjoyed by the workers. His stated purpose was to distribute the rewards of modern life more equitably; he did not disdain them.[80]

Unlike Marxism, however, Makhaevism did not seek to rehabilitate physical labor, the honest joys of which were celebrated by so many nineteenth-century intellectuals who had never been forced to experience them. Machajski rejected the Marxist ideal of humanizing factory labor by ending the worker's "alienation" from the means of production and restoring his pride and satisfaction in his work. The worker's bondage consisted not in the fact that he was forced to sell his labor, but in the type of labor he was forced to perform. "The essence of the workers' bondage is the fact that they are forced to hire themselves out to *slave* labor, that they are condemned for life to executing the mechanical, *manual labor of slaves*. . . . It is not the hiring that is terrible — it is all a matter of the kind of work and the kind of pay."[81] To be hired in the way that an engineer or manager was hired, he added, was for most workers an unrealizable dream.

Throughout his writings, Machajski insisted that manual labor was degrading; his favorite term for it was "penal servitude." Assiduously shunning all "ideals," he usually dealt with education and acquisition of knowledge on a purely material level, as the means to social and economic advantage. In one or two places, however, he voiced the idea that intellectual activity was the defining attribute of man: the workers' coarse physical labor not only degraded them socially and economically but robbed them of their essential humanity. "The productivity of labor," he wrote, "grows to the degree that the secrets of nature reveal themselves to mankind and its mastery of nature grows. He [*sic*] owes this mastery to his *human* organism, to intellectual activity." But under the present organization of society, only a small minority were able to use their minds, the organ of man, while the rest were allowed only the exercise of their animal organs in physical labor.[82]

This element of Makhaevism, to be sure, seems to contradict the streak of anti-intellectualism it contained. (Machajski might have replied that it was only "science" in its historical role as an instrument of class rule that he rejected.) And Marxism, too, had always proclaimed the goal of erasing the distinction between mental and manual labor. It may be suggested, however, that in stressing the importance of education for the workers, Machajski proposed a more effective way of humanizing labor than social ownership of the means of production by itself offered, and at the same time foresaw very accurately what would become the main road to social mobility in modern industrial and postindustrial society.

Even apart from the practical problem of creating a movement capable of implementing it, Machajski's program contained a number of internal contradictions and inconsistencies. Some were unique to Makhaevism, but some were shared by other currents in the Russian revolutionary movement. First, while based on implacable hatred of the existing order, Makhaevism could attain its ends only by preserving that order and even opposing any efforts to overthrow it. The equalization of incomes through the withholding of labor, and the subsequent educational revolution, could not occur overnight; they assumed the retention of the present economic and political structure for an indeterminate length of time. On the surface, at least, Makhaevism proposed not the seizure of power by the proletariat but merely the exertion of irresistible pressure on the established authorities.

It would appear from Machajski's writings that when he abandoned Social Democracy, that is, after writing part 1 of *The Intellectual Worker*, he also abandoned the notion of the "dictatorship of the proletariat." In part 1, he defined as the proletariat's objective the establishment of a "revolutionary dictatorship, the organization of the seizure of political power."[83] Later, however, when he composed the preface to the printed edition of part 1, he spoke only of "worldwide workers' conspiracies, dictating, by means of worldwide workers' strikes, the laws of state power."[84] Instead of taking political power into its own hands, the proletariat would present the state with "concrete demands capable of immediate realization."[85] This now became the declared objective of Makhaevism. Only once more in his writings, in part 2 of *The Intellectual Worker* (written, it will be remembered, in Siberia, the first statement of his mature views), did Machajski refer to a dictatorship.

By means of its worldwide conspiracy and dictatorship, the proletariat will attain domination over the state machine, but not in order to extricate from difficulty, anarchy, and bankruptcy an economic order unable to cope with productive forces which have outgrown its narrow property limits. It will strive for domination over the government in order to *seize the property* of ruling, educated society, the property of the learned world. . . . And, destroying hereditary family property and all private funds and means of education, it will force the use of confiscated property for the organization of social education, for the "socialization of knowledge."[86]

Here, the significance of the word "dictatorship" is unclear, for the remainder of the passage refers only to forcing radical economic reforms out of the existing government. The intention of mobilizing the unemployed in fact precluded any attempt to overthrow the government. Unlike the employed workers, the unemployed could not wrest concessions from the individual owners of their factories. As Machajski pointed out, they would have to turn to the government to demand the establishment of public works, as the unemployed of Paris had done in 1848.[87]

The difficulties in Machajski's program were not lost on contemporary critics. It was pointed out that the Makhaevists assumed extraordinary forbearance on the part of the upper classes, who were apparently expected to yield more and more of their income to the workers while placidly continuing to fulfill their duty of running the economy and the state.[88] One critic acutely observed that if the bourgeoisie decided to resist, the workers would be saved only in the event of their own defeat. For if they won, they would either have to renounce the fruits of their victory and restore the old state of affairs, or socialize the means of production — a step which Machajski maintained would leave them at the mercy of the intellectual workers.[89]

A second set of problems was related to the nature of the social forces Makhaevism relied on to implement its program. Machajski sought to recruit those groups and individuals whose frustration and capacity for violence might be expected to generate the most implacable attack on the existing order. The simple and single-minded objective of seizing the property of the rich might well tempt such elements of the population, but it was questionable whether the objective of the "socialization of knowledge" could have much appeal to them. To the unskilled, illiterate semi-peasant, the prospect of educating his child to be a doctor or an engineer was about as meaningful as the idea of turning him into a nobleman; he had more immediate needs and narrower horizons. The hope of improving one's socioeconomic position through education and finding greater personal fulfillment as an *intelligent* was more likely to reside in those individuals whom Machajski rejected as insufficiently revolutionary: the more skilled and relatively well-off workers. To educate one's children to be white-collar workers, to rise into the middle class, is the ambition not of the bewildered and angry "illiterate fellow from the back-woods village" but of the more secure worker whose social expectations have risen and bear some possibility of fulfillment.

Where was the guarantee, furthermore, that the "hungry masses" would go on struggling for full equality of incomes once their most pressing needs had been appeased? The Paris insurrection of 1848 was not as promising an historical precedent as Machajski thought. One careful study of the National Workshops concludes that at most only one-sixth of those in the pay of the workshops participated in the insurrection. The government's decision to continue paying the workshop employees when the insurrection began was apparently a major factor in neutralizing the great majority of them. The unemployed among the insurrectionists were largely workers who had been denied places in the workshops: the continued assurance of their daily wages was sufficient to pacify most of the actual members.[90]

Nor was it certain that the elements of the population Machajski sought to mobilize would prove as readily explosive a force as he assumed. Recent research in the social history of prerevolutionary Russian workers has begun to question the long-held view that peasant migrants from the countryside were necessarily alienated and disoriented, dry social tinder available to the most incendiary currents within the revolutionary movement. In at least some significant industrial centers, such as Moscow, peasant-workers brought much of their peasant culture with them. They retained strong family and economic ties to their villages, as well as local networks of organization and information that persisted over generations. As a result, their lives contained a good deal more structure and stability than has previously been thought.[91] This did not necessarily render them passive, for the solidarity and organization they derived from their peasant culture could at times be translated into collective action. It would appear, however, that the image of a reservoir of anarchic peasant-workers crowded into the industrial towns and hovering on the brink of insurrection may have been as romantic as the populists' image of a revolutionary peasantry back in the 1860s and 1870s. In any event, the social fuel for the Makhaevist revolution was more complex, and less easily kindled, than Machajski believed.

There was a serious discrepancy between means and ends in Machajski's revolutionary program. The forces on which he pinned his hopes were suited, at best, to outbursts of violence against the existing regime, not to the kind of sustained but limited pressure on it that the realization of Makhaevism's objectives required. To resolve the dilemma, Machajski resorted to the familiar device of a conscious revolutionary elite that would help to guide the workers' movement in the proper direction. Although he repudiated all existing forms of working-class organization, he urged the establishment of an underground party, a "workers' conspiracy" *(rabochii zagovor)*. Its purpose would be to coordinate the proletariat's separate outbursts into a regular, planned mass movement to present the workers' ever-growing demands. "The party of the workers' revolution, the party of the workers' insurrections, will not demand political liberty — it will live underground, both under absolutism and in a democracy. Its sole demands will be economic demands concerning manual labor. Its sole task will be a conspiracy with the goal of uniting mass workers' strikes into one general insurrection."[92] These underground conspirators would presumably be Machajski and his associates. As Ivanov-Razumnik pointed out, however, there was no provision in the logic of Makhaevism for leadership of the workers by such a group. Machajski himself never raised the point that he was in fact an *intelligent*, not a worker, and that his oversight of the workers' movement might be open to the same suspicions and accusations he was leveling against the socialists.

Max Nomad, for one, ultimately concluded that Machajski's renunciation of the seizure of power was only a facade, behind which lurked familiar political ambitions. Nomad suggested that perhaps Machajski stopped referring to a revolutionary dictatorship in order to attract former anarchists and syndicalists. Given the close affinities between Makhaevism and anarchism, this is possible; on the other hand, anarchist groups and organizations themselves faced much the same dilemma as the Makhaevists, and their solutions were often no more rigorously consistent than Machajski's. The contradictions in Machajski's revolutionary program were inherent in his very concept of a mass revolution and need not have stemmed from a conscious attempt at deception. As Nomad points out, however, a movement strong enough to "dictate the laws of state power" would presumably be capable of taking power into its own hands.[93] In any event, Machajski never had the opportunity to demonstrate what his ultimate ambitions really were. The immediate question he faced was whether Makhaevism could organize enough revolutionary activists, and attract enough of a following among the workers, to become a viable competitor to the existing Russian revolutionary parties and groups. By 1905 Machajski had completed the theoretical foundations of Makhaevism, and the outbreak of revolution gave him the opportunity to carry his message back to Russia and try to create a revolutionary movement.

Chapter 5

The "Workers' Conspiracy" and the Russian Revolutionary Movement

A T T H E B E G I N N I N G of 1906, Machajski arrived in St. Petersburg and proceeded to organize a small band of his followers in the capital. Their primary objective was to persuade the workers to repudiate the political program of the socialist parties — a "bourgeois revolution" to replace autocracy with a parliamentary democracy — and instead to insist on the immediate satisfaction of their economic demands. Briefly, at least, Makhaevism achieved a measure of visibility as an organized movement, although in fact a variety of groups and individuals professing Makhaevist ideas had been appearing on the Russian scene for several years before this.

Before tracing the activities of the Makhaevists themselves, we have to turn our attention to that aspect of Russian life with which they were primarily concerned: the relations between workers and intelligentsia in the labor and revolutionary movements. In the two decades or so before the 1905 revolution, both of these movements were preoccupied with this crucial issue. The workers, striving to organize so as to press their demands for improved wages and working conditions, often had to avail themselves of the organizational skills and communications resources the intelligentsia alone could provide, especially at a time when most forms of labor association were illegal and had to be conducted underground. The revolutionary intelligentsia needed a mass base to use as a lever for prying loose the tsarist autocracy. The populists having been rebuffed by the peasantry in the 1860s and 1870s, a sizeable part of the intelligentsia adopted Marxism in the 1880s and 1890s and sought to rally the industrial workers under the banner of Social Democracy. The two social elements were drawn to each other by mutual need and, so it seemed, mutual interest.

As their contacts grew, however, the social and cultural barrier that separated the Western-educated stratum from the mass of the population in the society at large replicated itself in the relations between *intelligenty* and workers in the underground organizations. This is not to say that reciprocal trust and cooperation were unattainable; representatives of the two groups did work together productively and harmoniously. Even at the best of times, however, relations between them were fraught with a considerable degree of underlying tension which could erupt in outbursts of anti-intelligentsia hostility. So insistently does anti-intelligentsia sentiment recur throughout this period, in fact, that any attempt to treat it exhaustively would not only go well beyond the scope of the present work but would amount to a virtual recapitulation of the history of the Russian labor movement and of the Russian Social-Democratic party. My purpose here will be to examine some of its principal manifestations and their relationship to Makhaevism. The Makhaevists were unique in placing anti-intelligentsia sentiment at the very center of their doctrines and agitation, but they were by no means alone in giving voice to it. Machajski's attack on the intelligentsia drew attention precisely because it probed at one of the most painful spots in the development of Russian socialism. Here, as in so many areas, Makhaevism focused on an issue of great importance, even if it could not itself provide an adequate resolution of it.

Anti-intelligentsia sentiment appeared at the very dawn of the Russian labor movement, even before Social Democracy arose. Beginning with the Chaikovskii Circle in 1872, populist students during the 1870s were organizing propaganda circles among the metalworkers and textile workers of St. Petersburg. Almost immediately, a series of frictions arose between the workers and their mentors. When the students, disappointed with the response of the workers to their revolutionary aspirations, went off to the countryside to propagandize the peasants, the workers felt that their immediate interests were being sacrificed to the larger social and political objectives of the *intelligenty*; they were repelled by the ideological bickering of the different *intelligent* factions; and, increasingly, they resented manipulation by domineering "generals," as they termed them, leading some workers to demand the exclusion of *intelligenty* from their organizations.[1] These same complaints and accusations, along with new ones, would be repeated again and again in subsequent decades.

The first conscious and systematic questioning of the intelligentsia's motivations and sense of commitment to the workers found expression in the Tochiskii Circle of St. Petersburg in the mid-1880s.[2] Pavel Varfolomeevich Tochiskii was born in 1864 (given in some sources as 1865) in Ekaterinburg. His father, a Russian Pole of noble origin, was an officer in the Russian army, and his mother was of French origin. Tochiskii attended a gymnasium in Ekaterinburg but dropped out and made his way to St. Petersburg in 1884. There he became a metalworker, both to make contact with other workers and to earn a living, having broken with his father. In late 1885 he began to form an underground circle based on an amalgam of socialist ideas, including, but not limited to, Marxism. Called at first the Society to Help Raise the Material, Moral, and Intellectual Level of the Working Class in Russia — an unwieldy but accurate reflection of Tochiskii's aims — it subsequently adopted the name Tovarishchestvo peterburgskikh masterovykh (Association of Petersburg Artisans), and, all told, operated for something over two years.

Tochiskii himself left no writings from this period of his life, but to judge from the account by his close associate Andrei Breitfus, his views foreshadowed Machajski's in a number of respects. Breitfus, at the time attracted to populism, made Tochiskii's acquaintance in 1885 and found him highly critical of the Narodnaia Volia organization's use of terror, which, he believed, "in the last analysis was only a means of gaining power for the growing class of bourgeoisie." The people were too backward to take advantage of the intelligentsia's efforts: "the latter, supposedly struggling in the name of the people, could only help new enemies of the people take power." Real change was possible only as a result of a social movement by the one truly revolutionary class — neither the peasantry nor the intelligentsia, but the proletariat.[3] According to Tochiskii's sister, who was a member of the circle, Tochiskii rejected political struggle entirely and sought to organize the workers solely on the basis of their economic interests.[4]

Given these principles, Tochiskii's attitude toward the intelligentsia was, at best, ambivalent. On the one hand, he felt that the intelligentsia's assistance was essential for organizing the proletariat and developing its class consciousness, but on the other "he considered the revolutionary intelligentsia in general to be ideologists of the bourgeoisie." Therefore the intelligentsia must be regarded as a "casual guest in the revolution," to be tolerated only as long as the proletariat needed it. "He often said: 'You are with us until the first turning point, the first constitution which you will obtain from the government and which you need, and then our paths will diverge sharply.'"[5] To protect the workers from being drawn into political struggle, which at this time meant terrorist activities, he tried his best to minimize direct contact between workers and *intelligenty* within the circle, considering it "superfluous," as his sister put it, "to let the intelligentsia get close to the workers" and even trying to avoid those workers who had already been exposed to revolutionary propaganda and thus "corrupted by revolutionary adventurism."[6] With the intelligentsia supplying funds, literature, and other practical assistance, the circle concentrated on worker education and consciousness-raising, building an impressive library of legal publications as well as a much smaller stock of illegal literature. When some *intelligent* members undertook a more vigorous distribution of illegal literature to the workers, Tochiskii objected, fearing that it would merely excite them and increase their chances of arrest. (Thanks to Tochiskii's precautions, in fact, the worker members of his organization were not discovered by the police, and only the intelligentsia leaders were eventually arrested.) He now attempted, in effect, to exclude the intelligentsia members from active participation in the work of the circle and to reduce them to "passive" or auxiliary members. He was opposed by other members of the organization who agreed, over his objections, to widen the intelligentsia's role, but the issue became moot when the police broke up the association in 1888.[7]

Conflicts between workers and *intelligenty* punctuated the his-

tory of the Jewish labor movement within the western Pale of Settlement. In the early 1890s, a vehement wave of protest arose over
the decision of the movement's leaders to shift from "propaganda,"
that is, worker education conducted in small study circles, to
"agitation," a program aimed at reaching a broader mass of workers by concentrating on their practical economic needs, through
strikes, demonstrations, and factory organization. The protest first
surfaced in Vilna in 1893, led by Avram Gordon, an engraver
and a member of a study circle. Gordon believed that the dis-
semination of knowledge to the people was the true source of historical progress, and such educational work was the proper function of the intelligentsia. The latter's abandonment of cultural
work was a deliberate act of treason to the labor movement. Historical events such as the French Revolution and the revolutions
of 1848 had demonstrated that the intelligentsia wanted to de-
lude the people and use them for its own selfish interests.[8] Keeping the workers ignorant and dependent was an important part
of this effort. The agitation campaign, Gordon declared in terms
that strikingly anticipate Machajski, was the intelligentsia's way
of preserving its monopoly on the precious commodity of knowledge.[9] Similar views were expressed in cities across the Pale. One
of the opposition groups generated by this wave of protest, the
Group of Worker Revolutionaries, active in Belostok in 1897, was
headed by another engraver named Moisei Lur'e, who, as we shall
see, subsequently espoused Makhaevism. The antagonism between
workers and intelligentsia that erupted in the nineties never entirely disappeared from the Russian Jewish labor movement.[10]

A second wave of anti-intelligentsia sentiment broke over the
movement after the organization in 1897 of the Bund, the Marxist socialist party that spoke for the interests of the Jewish working class in Russia. The Bund soon began to place a greater emphasis on political action than on economic activity, and it sought
to impose a more centralized organizational structure on the labor
movement. Both endeavors generated new worker-*intelligent* frictions. By the early years of the twentieth century, workers were
accusing *intelligenty* of behaving in a dictatorial, undemocratic
manner, and were attacking the "despotism of the intellectuals."
Hostility to political action, which to many workers seemed both
overly abstract and overly dangerous, and hostility to those who

advocated it, also began to be voiced. Demands arose that the movement be led solely by workers, and in some cities the latter excluded the intelligentsia from the local committees.[11] Under these circumstances, it is not surprising that the Zubatov experiment (discussed below) received its first application in the Jewish labor movement of the Pale. In its effort to separate the workers from the revolutionary propagandists who sought to lead them, Zubatovism exploited precisely the kinds of tensions that existed in this region, and it found a fertile field for its activity within the jurisdiction of the Bund.

The question of the intelligentsia's relationship to the labor movement was a major theme in the first great "heresy" within the Russian Social-Democratic movement, the current that arose at the end of the 1890s and came to be known as Economism. This label was applied to several groups and shades of thought which were in fact quite distinct and not necessarily in agreement. In general terms, however, and with varying degrees of emphasis, those of the Economist persuasion held two basic positions: the priority of economic improvement for the workers over large-scale political change (although the necessity of political change was generally recognized), and the need for vigorous organizational development of the labor movement.[12] The most "radical" expression of Economism was the clandestine newspaper *Rabochaia mysl'* (*Workers' Thought*), issued from 1897 to 1902. The newspaper itself was the product of a conflict between workers and intelligentsia within the St. Petersburg Union of Struggle for the Emancipation of the Working Class, the Social-Democratic organization formed in 1895. The workers of the city, aroused by the great textile strikes of 1896 and 1897, had demanded a greater voice in the affairs of the union. They were supported by such labor-oriented *intelligenty* as Konstantin Takhtarev, who became one of the editors of *Rabochaia mysl'*, but were opposed by most of the other *intelligenty* in the Union of Struggle. The latter wanted to maintain the union's tightly knit conspiratorial character and felt that this precluded admission of workers into its inner circles, because the workers were not well versed in the ways of the underground.[13] From the thinking of the Takhtarev group came *Rabochaia mysl'*. Unlike most Social-Democratic publications, it was specifically intended to give expression to the workers' own views, and it devoted a large portion of its space to reports by workers on conditions in their factories.[14] It also gave voice to a broad streak of anti-intelligentsia sentiment, which, given the nature of the newspaper, must have reflected feelings widely held among the workers and not just by the editors.

In its first issue the newspaper proclaimed the independence of the labor movement from the *intelligenty* who had hitherto guided it, and the primacy of economic over political goals. The editorial asserted that the Russian labor movement owed its new vitality "to the fact that the worker himself is taking over the struggle, having wrested it from the hands of the leaders. . . . As long as the movement was merely a means of calming the suffering conscience of the repentant intellectual, it was alien to the worker himself."[15] The labor movement would now concentrate on the struggle to improve the workers' economic status, using strikes as its principal weapon, and political change would ultimately occur as a byproduct of the economic struggle.[16]

The paper was soon charged with harboring a distinctly unfriendly attitude toward the intelligentsia, and in a later issue the editors responded to this accusation. They declared that the primary task of *Rabochaia mysl'* was to give the worker a forum of his own. Since he could more easily understand the words of his fellow worker than "the abstract writings of the *intelligenty*," the paper gave preference to articles written by workers themselves. The editors, however, did admit to the charge that the paper was "against the intelligentsia," and described in highly unflattering terms those categories of *intelligenty* whose participation in the labor movement the paper opposed. They rejected as completely unreliable the members of the professions, such as lawyers, artists, writers, and priests. They were only slightly more favorably disposed to students. Like Tochiskii, they valued the services the students could provide, such as collecting funds and distributing literature, but considered them irrevocably part of the ruling classes by virtue of their education and social origins. "It must never be forgotten that while they are revolutionaries today, tomorrow they will be procurators, judges, engineers, factory inspectors, in short, officials of the Russian government."[17] Therefore, while their contributions to the labor movement might be useful, they must not be allowed any significant influence in the workers' affairs. The only *intelligenty* who would be warmly welcomed were those few "ideologists," or "white crows," who self-lessly devoted themselves to the struggle for liberty and equality.[18]

Rabochaia mysl' expressed the hope that the labor movement by itself, without the mediation of the revolutionary intelligen-tsia, could persuade the authorities through pressure and persua-sion to improve the conditions of industrial work. At least some of the editors were clearly thinking in terms of the legalization of the labor movement. The editors announced that they had been sending copies of the newspaper to the ministers of finance and internal affairs, the over-procurator of the Holy Synod, and all the factory inspectors of Petersburg, in order to acquaint them with the workers' views. Had they been sure it would reach him, they added, they would even have sent a copy to the tsar, for "it would be very useful for him, too, to acquaint himself with the life and thought of the workers."[19]

Machajski had the opportunity to learn about Economism from some of the exiles in Viliuisk, and he was familiar with *Rabochaia mysl'*. At one point in *The Intellectual Worker* he even seems to have borrowed its characterization of the students as future rul-ers of the proletariat.[20] His few references to the newspaper and to Economism in general, however, were ambivalent.[21] On the one hand, he could not but approve of the emphasis the Econo-mists placed on economic improvement over political objectives; on the other, Machajski could conceive of the labor movement only as an underground, revolutionary struggle, whereas the strand of Economism represented by *Rabochaia mysl'*, though critical of the intelligentsia, led toward legalization of the labor movement. Therefore he could not regard Economism as a sig-nificant exception to the efforts of the socialist intelligentsia as a whole to curb the true revolutionary spirit of the working class.

In the early years of the new century, what remained of the Economist tendency within the Social-Democratic party gave way before the forces grouped around the émigré newspaper *Iskra (The Spark)*, with Lenin in the forefront. The adherents of *Iskra* re-asserted the primacy of political goals, maintaining that the first task on Russia's historical agenda must be the overthrow of tsarist absolutism. At the same time, they placed renewed emphasis on the party as an underground, conspiratorial organization, requiring a centralized, hierarchical structure which would serve both to safeguard the party's doctrinal purity and to ensure the fulfillment of its revolutionary tasks. The imposition of these views was achieved only at the high cost of intensified discord between the *intelligenty* who staffed the party's local committees in the Russian towns and the workers among whom they operated. The frequently autocratic ways of the self-appointed committeemen provoked increasingly bitter resentment, and the "*Iskra* period" of the Social-Democratic party saw the rise of numerous "worker opposition" groups within its local organizations.

The most frequent demand of the workers was for a more democratic form of organization, one in which the workers themselves would elect their own leaders and have a voice in the determination of policy. In 1902, for example, the workers in Kremenchug rebelled against the attempt to reconstitute their party organization along the centralized lines advocated by *Iskra*. "The members of the committee were all newcomers whom the workers did not know personally. They declared themselves the committee without any sanction on the part of the workers, and in the latter's eyes they were like uninvited 'Varangians' who had come to 'rule and reign' over them."[22]

Similar discords arose in Ekaterinoslav and Odessa — two cities, significantly, where Makhaevist organizations made their appearance. The Ekaterinoslav committee had a long history of worker independence and worker control of the organization. The efforts of newly arrived *intelligenty* to assert control over the committee's activities nearly provoked an open breach with the workers, who insisted on maintaining their influence. A compromise was worked out under which the two groups maintained separate but cooperating committees, but at the beginning of 1903 the issue of centralization produced a new schism in the Ekaterinoslav organization.[23] The Odessa workers had also begun to express the opinion that "in a workers' movement, workers ought to be the leaders."[24] In 1901, a workers' opposition group formed, demanding that the members of all party organs be elected. Attempts by the *intelligenty* on the Odessa committee to justify the existing system of cooptation on the grounds of conspiratorial necessity were received as evidence that they distrusted the workers. Finally, in 1902, the workers' opposition withdrew from the

Social-Democratic organization and formed an independent group called the Workers' Will (Rabochaia volia), which lasted until 1903.[25] Descriptions of similar frictions in other cities, such as St. Petersburg and Tula, appear in the reports submitted by local committees to the Second Party Congress in 1903.[26] Worker dissidence and opposition cropped up also in Kharkov, Kiev, Tiflis, and Ivanovo-Voznesensk.[27] As previously mentioned, the Bund was experiencing a similar wave of worker opposition in its local organizations.[28]

Nor was it only intelligentsia high-handedness and worker independence that generated frictions between the two elements. The intelligentsia's preoccupation with doctrinal orthodoxy, which the workers often found incomprehensible, also created antagonism — a problem which the Bolshevik-Menshevik disputes would later exacerbate even further. On one occasion in Kharkov, for example, when a group of factory workers got together on their own initiative and asked the local Social-Democratic committee for propaganda literature and speakers, they were rebuffed on the grounds that they were "trade unionists." When asked if this was true, one worker replied: "We haven't gone into these questions; the devil only knows what we are."[29]

Into the breach between workers and intelligentsia stepped Sergei Zubatov, the creator of the experiment in so-called police socialism. (Like Makhaevism, Zubatov's effort was dubbed *zubatovshchina* by its critics and is frequently referred to by that pejorative term in the literature.) Zubatov became the chief of the Moscow Okhrana, the tsarist political police, in 1896, then served in St. Petersburg from 1902 until his dismissal from the government in 1903. A devoted monarchist, Zubatov was well aware of the gulf that existed between the industrial workers and the intelligentsia, and he set out to capitalize on it by persuading the workers that the autocracy, not the revolutionaries, understood their true interests. The themes sounded by Zubatov and his representatives are so close to those of Makhaevism that it is worth examining the rhetoric and aims of the Zubatov experiment in some detail.

The basic premises of Zubatovism were set forth in 1898 in a memorandum sent by General D. F. Trepov, then police chief of Moscow, to Grand Duke Sergei, the Moscow governor-general.

This memorandum was actually the work of Zubatov himself,[30] and it asserted that the intelligentsia regarded the labor movement primarily as an instrument for furthering its own political purposes.

> The history of the revolutionary movement has shown that the intelligentsia alone does not have the forces to struggle with the government, even when armed with explosives. With this in mind, all the opposition groups are now applauding the Social-Democratic movement, in the calculation that by drawing the workers into antigovernmental undertakings they will have at their disposal a mass force which the government will have to take into serious consideration.[31]

The German Social Democrats, the document contended, had originated the method of joining "their own ideal aspirations with the everyday, more vital demands of the workers," and their Russian counterparts were now adopting it by engaging in economic agitation and supporting strikes. "If the petty needs and demands of the workers are being exploited by the revolutionaries for such deeply antigovernment purposes, shouldn't the government as quickly as possible tear this . . . weapon from their hands?" In order to thwart the spread of revolutionary activities among the workers, the government must take the initiative in satisfying their economic grievances through legal channels, "keeping in mind that only the most youthful and energetic part of the crowd will follow an agitator, while the average worker always prefers a less glittering but more peaceful and legal solution." Problems arose not just from the unruliness of the workers but from the failure of the factory owners themselves to observe the laws and respect the workers' rights. The solution was for the police to supervise relations between workers and employers and to demonstrate to the worker that there was a better way out of his difficulties than that offered by the revolutionaries: "What occupies the revolutionary must necessarily interest the police."[32] The ideas set forth in the report won the firm support of both Trepov and Grand Duke Sergei, and Zubatov was able to proceed with their practical application.

Zubatov had been a radical in his student days, and he brought a first-hand knowledge of the revolutionary movement and the psychology of its participants to his work in the political police.[33]

The first object of his attention was the Bund. In the summer of 1898 a number of Bund leaders were arrested and brought to Moscow for questioning. In the course of the interrogations, Zubatov concluded that the situation among the Jewish workers of the Pale was favorable for his plans. When another group of arrested Bundists was brought to Moscow in 1900, Zubatov made a concerted effort to persuade them of his views. He treated them benevolently, engaged them in long discussions of the labor movement, and gave them books by judiciously selected authors, including Eduard Bernstein. (He referred to Bernstein as "our ally against the outrageous Russian Social Democracy."[34]) He described in the following terms the form his gentle brainwashing took when political prisoners came before him:

In the interrogations I am separating the antigovernment element from the mass with brilliant success, I can honestly say. In the Russian movement, and perhaps also in the Jewish movement, I am successfully persuading my public that the workers' movement is one thing while the Social Democratic movement is another. In the former the goal is a kopeck, in the latter it is an ideological theory. . . . the Social Democrats, ignoring [the worker's] immediate interests, call upon him to help the "privileged" classes achieve their interests (to carry out a revolution), promising him all kinds of benefits afterwards.[35]

Zubatov succeeded in winning some of the Bundists over to his ideas, perhaps aided by the fact that several members of his captive audience were quite young and impressionable. Mariia (Mania) Vil'bushevich, for instance, who became Zubatov's chief organizer in Minsk, was only nineteen or twenty at the time of her arrest, and some of the other activists were not much older.[36]

Zubatov's converts returned to Minsk and in 1901, having broken definitively with the Bund, formed their own organization, called the Jewish Independent Workers' party. The principal point of the manifesto the new party issued was the rejection of politics. It was criminal, the Independents declared, to sacrifice "the material interests of the working class for political goals which at present are alien to it," and they denounced the Bund for regarding economic demands primarily as an instrument for revolutionizing the workers. Their own objectives would be limited to material and cultural improvement of the Jewish workers, or, as they phrased it, to the attainment of "bread and knowledge." Their program called for the establishment of a variety of nonpolitical economic and cultural organizations open to workers of any political persuasion (or none at all), and promised that the party would be democratically organized and governed by the rank and file.[37]

The Zubatov organization in Minsk was perfectly calculated to appeal to both currents of opposition that had arisen previously in the development of the Jewish labor movement. On the one hand, it promised peaceful educational and cultural development, and on the other it championed legal economic activity over political action. At the same time, it offered a democratic form of organization responsive to the needs and wishes of the workers themselves.[38] Not surprisingly, it became immensely popular among the Jewish artisans of the city, especially when the Independents proved effective in promoting strikes. The factory owners, aware of the Independents' connection with the police, were often quick to grant concessions. In some cases the Minsk police acted as mediators in labor disputes or even actively sided with the workers.[39] In a report at the end of 1901, Zubatov claimed a membership of more than fifteen hundred in the organization.[40]

By the summer of 1903, however, the Independent Workers' party in Minsk had collapsed, undermined by the acute contradictions in the tsarist government's policies. The Zubatov organization existed in a kind of legal limbo; it operated with the sanction of the police but did not have full legal status. It was therefore subject to all the whims of the Petersburg bureaucracy and the opposition of some of the local authorities. When the gains which the workers had initially wrested from their employers proved ephemeral, they began to withdraw their support from the Independents.[41] At the same time, events occurred which made it increasingly difficult to represent the autocracy as the protector of the Jewish proletariat. The Kishinev pogrom in April 1903 was widely considered to have occurred with government complicity; and in June of that year Interior Minister Plehve, who was regarded as anti-Semitic to begin with, banned the further activity of Zionism in Russia, a movement with which a number of the Zubatovites in the Pale were closely identified.[42] Even before the general strike of 1903, which brought an abrupt end to the Zubatov experiment as a whole, the Minsk Independents had disbanded.

The same themes, with some variations, were repeated in Moscow and Odessa, the other two cities where Zubatov's agents succeeded in creating mass organizations. In Moscow, the organizers were mainly factory workers, members of the "worker-intelligentsia," rather than *intelligenty*, as in Minsk.[43] Their rhetoric, however, was similarly filled with anti-intelligentsia sentiment. They urged the workers to separate themselves from the "petty *intelligenty*," as they termed the revolutionary socialists. (They did, however, welcome the services of liberal intellectuals such as the Moscow academics who participated for a time in the Zubatovites' educational program, giving lectures which proved quite popular with the workers.) The revolutionaries, they maintained, were interested only in using the workers for their own political ends, deflecting them from their economic demands and bringing them only suffering and prison terms. In 1901, they formed a Society of Machine Workers, the first of several associations devoted to mutual aid, education, and peaceful organizational activity in allegiance to the autocracy.[44]

The high point of the Zubatov experiment in Moscow came on February 19, 1902, when Zubatov's agents demonstrated their influence over the workers by ushering a peaceful crowd estimated at some fifty thousand to Alexander II's monument in the Kremlin, to commemorate the anniversary of the emancipation of the serfs. Soon, however, thanks to pressure from the factory owners as well as apprehension on the part of some government authorities over the Zubatovites' involvement in strike actions, the character of the movement changed. It took on a more conservative cast, overtly religious and monarchist, thereby anticipating the Gapon organization that was to arise in St. Petersburg in 1904. The activities of the Zubatovites were curtailed and the organization lost most of its effectiveness, although remnants of it survived into 1905.[45]

The site of Zubatovism's greatest success — and spectacular collapse — was the city of Odessa. The chief Zubatov organizer in Odessa was Genrikh (Khunia) Shaevich, a young Zionist who claimed to hold a doctoral degree from the University of Berlin. He had met Mania Vil'bushevich at a Zionist congress in Minsk and then returned to Odessa to form a branch of the Independents.[46] In August 1902 the Independent Workers' Group of Odessa (soon renamed the Independent Workers' party) issued a manifesto to the Odessa workers.

Various parties have long been trying to organize us, but until now we have not had one purely workers' organization. Those parties which work among us set themselves very large but very distant goals. They are striving for a worldwide overturn, i.e., they want to change all of human life.

Setting themselves such enormous goals, which embrace all social life, those parties have neither the time nor the opportunity to pursue our *particular* workers' interests with sufficient attention, or to satisfy them.[47]

What labor really needed, the manifesto continued, was not lofty abstractions but trade unions. Although these were forbidden in Russia, the reason for the ban was the association between the labor movement and the revolutionary parties. If purely economic unions were organized, independent of any political parties, there was no doubt that the government would be persuaded to allow them.

The rejection of politics as the preoccupation of the intelligentsia pervaded the rhetoric of the Odessa Zubatovites. The manifesto of the Union of Odessa House-Painters, one of the constituent unions of the Independent Workers' party, contained the following statement:

The *purely economic* union of house-painters should be distinguished from the various *political* workers' parties. The union is completely independent of political parties. We do not yet know how the government will regard our union, but we can be sure that its members will not be exiled to Siberia as political criminals.[48]

Going somewhat beyond the bounds of strict loyalty to the throne, the Independents declared, in response to criticism from the Socialist-Revolutionary party, that it was irrelevant to the workers' needs whether they had a monarchy, a republic, or a constitutional state. Instead of inciting the workers against the autocracy, the socialists might inform them that "even in republics, socialist ministers deport strikers (Millerand)." The workers' welfare depended not on the system of government but on the strength of their organizations.[49] As they had elsewhere, the workers of Odessa responded enthusiastically to the formation of nonpolitical labor organizations, an official report putting the membership of the Independent Workers' Party in April 1903 at 2,000.[50] Remarkably, the Independents were able to transcend the national and religious cleavages of this polyglot city, bringing together Russian and Ukrainian as well as Jewish workers.[51]

Zubatov's agents in Odessa carried out their mission only too well, for their efforts generated a well organized and increasingly independent labor movement in Odessa. In the summer of 1903, this movement slipped from the grasp of its creators and produced Russia's first general strike—the South Russian strike of 1903, which so impressed Machajski. The strike began in Odessa in early July and lasted for several weeks; order was restored in Odessa with a minimum of violence, but the strike spread to other cities throughout the southern part of the empire. It was a spontaneous phenomenon, but there can be little doubt that the agitation of the Independents played a major role in provoking it.[52] In any case, it was too much for the authorities. Shaevich was arrested and sentenced to five years in Siberia, although his sentence was commuted the following year. Zubatov himself was dismissed from government service, and with the end of his career came the end of the experiment in "police socialism."

The enthusiastic response of the workers to the Zubatovites' message in three such disparate cities as Minsk, Moscow, and Odessa, indicates how shrewdly Zubatov had perceived the tensions between the workers and the intelligentsia. His enterprise failed to sustain itself for a number of reasons, not the least of which was the fact that most of his agents were sincerely devoted to the interests of the workers and were not mere tools of the police.[53] Therefore Zubatov could not always control the mechanism he had constructed or keep it on the course he had set for it. The major share of blame for Zubatovism's downfall, however, appears to lie with the tsarist government, which treated the Zubatov experiment with the utmost ambivalence and inconsistency. The ministry of the interior was opposed on the issue by Count Witte's ministry of finance, and the interior ministry itself was deeply divided at every level. The bureaucratic infighting that resulted was problem enough, but it was symptomatic of an even deeper flaw in the government's approach. Zubatov himself put his finger on it when he complained of the confusion displayed by some of the provincial authorities, a confusion stemming from "their inability to distinguish a *revolutionary* labor movement from a *peaceful* one."[54] It was a handicap that pervaded the entire autocracy. The intrinsic contradictions of Zubatovism could have been resolved only by some form of legalization of trade unions — a step which many of the participants, including Zubatov himself, anticipated as its logical outcome. But if the autocracy was deeply suspicious of "self-activity" even among the educated and property-owning segments of society, still less could it countenance organization by the working class — one which, despite impressive displays of self-discipline, was still raw and volatile and had to be dealt with very carefully. With the Zubatov episode the government in a sense did what some scholars believe Social Democracy had done: it helped to foster a labor movement which it was then unable to handle. As a result, the Zubatov organizations served to increase the sense of frustration with the government which they were intended to overcome.

As far as Makhaevism is concerned, it seems to have had no points of contact, either personal or ideological, with Zubatovism.[55] If Machajski could not approve of Economism because it led toward trade unionism rather than revolution, he could hardly have had any sympathy for a tendency that led in the same direction under the sponsorship of the tsarist police. He kept silent about the Zubatov phenomenon, however, and his writings contain only a few ironic but fleeting references to it.[56] Makhaevism and Zubatovism arose independently of each other and developed separately, but their attacks on the revolutionary intelligentsia, coming as they did from opposite ends of the Russian ideological spectrum, showed a remarkable similarity. This is additional evidence, if such be needed, of just how widespread and acute the "question of the intelligentsia" in its relationship to the working class had become.

The socialist parties had for the most part been powerless to counter the rise of the Zubatov organizations (although the Bund had some success on this score in Vilna), and they were in no position to capitalize on their collapse. The Social-Democratic leadership, after the party's second congress in 1903, became almost totally immersed in the factional dispute between Bolsheviks and Mensheviks which had rent the party. To many workers, the party schism was both incomprehensible and inexcusable. It seemed to them that the *intelligenty* were indulging in doctrinal hair-splitting at the expense of the workers' interests, and the squabbling reinforced anti-intelligentsia feelings. In a letter to the Bolshevik newspaper *Vpered (Forward)*, for example, a group of St. Petersburg metalworkers declared that the working class was impatiently awaiting the restoration of unity among the party leaders. "If it is not forthcoming, then [we will know that] we have no intelligentsia proletariat [*intelligentskii proletariat*], and if we did have one, then it no longer exists: they have sold the labor movement to the capitalists. Long live the worker proletariat!"[57] The breach between workers and *intelligenty* within the party remained unhealed, and the approach of the 1905 revolution caught the Social Democrats unprepared and unable to mobilize the working class under its banner.

The domination of the party by the intelligentsia generated worker apathy as well as worker hostility. Excluded from the inner councils of the local committees and unable to influence their decisions, the workers tended to lose interest in their operation. The lack of communication that had developed between the two elements became forcefully apparent in the events of 1905. Several witnesses testify to the shock the party experienced when the Petersburg workers failed to respond to the Social Democrats' call for a May Day demonstration. Despite the carefully laid plans of the local party organization, an embarrassingly insignificant number of workers actually appeared for the march.[58] According to S. I. Somov, a Menshevik active in the Petersburg organization, this episode dramatized the extent to which Russian Social Democracy had remained a party of revolutionary *intelligenty* rather than a party of workers. The latter had come to regard the party "not as their own business but someone else's, the intelligentsia's," and they felt little sense of personal responsibility for it. As a result, they left it to the party leaders to organize the May Day demonstration without deeming it necessary to take an active part in it themselves.[59] Although the party proclaimed itself a proletarian party, it was run by *intelligenty* at every level. As one worker complained, whenever workers succeeded in forming a district organization, an *"intelligent-*tsar" would inevitably arrive to supervise it. Some were benevolent tsars, perhaps, "but we need neither good nor evil tsars, we ourselves want to rule in our own party, and we must set up our own procedures in it."[60] Even in the heat of revolution the gulf between the two forces was not easily bridged, as in the case of a leader of the precious-metalworkers' union in Petersburg who attempted to address a meeting on November 13, 1905: the workmen allowed him to proceed only after they were assured that he was "neither an intellectual nor a student."[61] It was only under the impact of the 1905 revolution that the Social Democrats, and particularly the Mensheviks, began to address themselves seriously to the task of creating a party of the workers and not just for the workers.[62]

The prolonged effort by Russia's revolutionaries to bring together their own grievances against the tsarist autocracy and those of the industrial workers had not been crowned with success by the time the 1905 revolution erupted. Russian Marxists, for all their dedication to the "working class," all too often found themselves rebuked and rebuffed when it came to organizing actual workers. The sources of the tension that arose between them were numerous and complex: issues of leadership and subordination, exacerbated by underground conditions; the divergence between the political objectives of most *intelligenty* and the economic preoccupations of most of the workers; educational, cultural, and social differences. Some of these antagonisms were specific to the Social-Democratic movement, but others were more deeply rooted in the nature of the Russian intelligentsia and its relationship to the uneducated masses. All this provided fertile soil for Makhaevism, and as its doctrines circulated and became known, individuals and groups of various sorts found in it a persuasive explanation of their dissatisfaction with the intelligentsia.

The history of the Makhaevists twined in and around the anti-intelligentsia currents discussed above, intersecting with some, closely paralleling others.[63] A wide variety of individuals were drawn to Machajski's doctrines, whether they actually joined Makhaevist groups or merely expressed approval of his views. For some, Machajski's criticism of the intelligentsia provided sanction for a crude social resentment of the privileged classes. One example is the testimony of a Jewish worker named B. A. Breslav, whose brief memoir, published in 1928, begins as a tribute to Gorky and ends as a tribute to Machajski. When he was arrested for labor activity in 1901 Breslav was illiterate, and he learned to read only in prison and exile. Discovering Gorky's works, he was greatly impressed by their descriptions of life among the lower classes. He was particularly struck by a line in *The Lower Depths*, where one of the characters says of a nobleman he encounters that lordliness (*barstvo*) is like the smallpox — the disease may go away, but it leaves traces on the face.[64] This remark "on the impossibility of a complete regeneration and merger with the proletariat on the part of those who came from a class milieu alien to us" fell on fertile soil, for Breslav was already becoming disillusioned with the intelligentsia. At first he had idealized those *intelligenty* he had encountered in underground circles for their apparent selflessness and dedication, but "when I came into close contact with the intelligentsia in prison and exile, my initial idealization fast disappeared, and a strong reaction even set in against my original enthusiasm."[65]

These sentiments found confirmation when, in exile in eastern Siberia in 1902, he came across Machajski's two essays, "which literally called for a pogrom against the intelligentsia."[66] The essays showed him how the intelligentsia used the struggle of the workers for its own class interests — and, remembering the remark in Gorky about "lordliness," he felt that it underscored Machajski's views.[67]

A more sophisticated example of the kind of social envy to which Makhaevism could appeal appears in the reminiscences of M. Vetoshkin, a village schoolteacher who had been expelled from his post in 1903 for propagandizing his pupils. Having come across Machajski's *Intellectual Worker*, he arrived at the beginning of 1904 in Irkutsk — the city where Machajski had organized his first group, in 1902 — hoping to support himself by giving lessons and to pursue the interest in Marx which his reading of Machajski had aroused. "I was full of Makhaevist attitudes," he recalled. "*The Intellectual Worker* had made such a strong impression on me that I knew this book, which at the time passed from hand to hand in an illegal lithographed edition, almost by heart. The intelligentsia seemed to me almost the main enemy of the working class."[68] He hoped also to organize a Makhaevist circle in opposition to the local Social-Democratic committee, but this plan was cut short by his arrest. In prison he encountered Social Democrats who succeeded in reeducating him, and he renounced Makhaevism in favor of Marxism.[69]

In the second installment of his memoirs, however, he admits that he had not fully overcome his Makhaevist sentiments. While engaged in party work in Tomsk in 1905, he found himself envying the articulateness of the university-educated *intelligenty* in the party, especially their ability to use Latin and German words. "It must be said that along with some envy of the oratorical skills of the Tomsk *intelligenty*, I also harbored a certain degree of alienation in regard to them, which I had underscored from Machajski's book and of which, evidently, I had not been completely cured in prison, although it seemed to me that I had broken decisively with Makhaevism."[70] After a meeting, for example, he had thought to himself: "There they are, with a good education, while our brother, coming out of a worker's poverty, feeds on crumbs from the table of the educated gentlemen."[71] He himself had had only the meager education a teachers' seminary could offer, and his father, a laborer in a saltworks, had always scorned those who lived by "light work," including the intelligentsia. His father's influence had no doubt predisposed him to Makhaevism, he concluded, and although intellectually he had overcome it, some of it had remained within him.[72]

As Vetoshkin's memoir indicates, Makhaevism left a lasting legacy in Irkutsk even after the arrest of Machajski's group. As late as 1908, when an attempt was made to reconstitute the previously arrested Social-Democratic committee there, the workers insisted that no *intelligenty* be allowed as members. The Social-Democratic organizer, M. M. Konstantinov, later professed not to have been surprised at the mistrustful and even hostile attitude of the workers. Even before this time he had encountered among the workers "a distrust for [the intelligentsia's] commitment and sincerity" and a desire to run their own organizations: "'They can help us with advice and carry out the organization's decisions, but not direct us.'"[73] He hastens to add, however, that this attitude was not "what at this time was still fresh in the memory of many of us under the name of 'Makhaevism.'" He knew that Machajski had propagated his views in Irkutsk before the revolution but asserts, not convincingly, that they had enjoyed popularity not with the workers but with other *intelligenty*.[74]

Makhaevism's advocacy of worker independence of the intelligentsia was the main source of its appeal to individuals who were active in the labor movement. One example was the Jewish printer Moisei Lur'e, mentioned above. Born in Kovno gubernia in 1871 or 1872, he became a highly individualistic Social Democrat, retaining his early connections with the Polish Socialist party and sometimes collaborating with populist revolutionaries.[75] In the mid-1890s, he and his brother Mikhail organized the Group of Worker Revolutionaries, which operated in several cities of south Russia from a base in Belostok. By 1898, it had evolved into the Workers' Banner (Rabochee znamia), which issued an underground journal by that name. One of the continuities of Lur'e's political outlook was his hostility to the intelligentsia. He accused it of wanting to withhold "real knowledge" from the masses in order to be able to use them as a "blind tool," and in Kiev he and his followers made common cause with some *narodovol'tsy* in opposition to the Social Democrats' turn from propaganda to agitation.[76] According to one of his close associates in the Group of Worker Revolutionaries, he was deeply suspicious of what he regarded as the intelligentsia's "rightist tendency." In his opinion, "the intelligentsia in its majority latches onto the workers' movement to try to use the hands of the workers to pull the bourgeoisie's chestnuts out of the fire for it, or with its own group interests in mind."[77]

Given this attitude, it is not surprising that Lur'e was drawn to Makhaevism. Arrested in 1901, after twenty months in prison he was sent to Iakutsk to serve a term of exile. In Siberia, he encountered Machajski's doctrines and found himself very much impressed with them.[78] Even after his return to St. Petersburg in 1906, where he organized armed detachments for the Bolsheviks, he was still "raving over Machajski."[79] Lur'e himself never joined a Makhaevist group, but, according to one source, a worker who had belonged to his early group in Kiev turned up in the ranks of Machajski's adherents in 1905.[80]

Vera Davidovna Gurari, a revolutionary and labor organizer, did formally join the Makhaevists. A Jew converted to Orthodoxy, Gurari was born in Poltava in 1865 and had attended gymnasium.[81] She had a long and rather eclectic revolutionary career. We first hear of her in the 1880s as the organizer of several underground circles in St. Petersburg. In this period when the demarcation between populists and Marxists was still hazy, she is described as "a social democrat, terrorist, and narodovol'ka."[82] In 1897, upon returning to Petersburg from a term of administrative exile, she was drawn into Social-Democratic activities in the capital. From the fall of 1898 to her arrest in April 1899 she led a workers' circle called the Group for the Self-Emancipation of the Working Class. As its name suggests, the organization was critical of intelligentsia domination of the labor movement. Its manifesto complained of the *intelligenty*'s tendency to form an exclusive "areopagus," a "touching union of *intelligenty*" to which they refused to admit workers, and declared that the workers must take their cause into their own hands. It also asserted that political goals must be subordinated to, and grow out of, the economic struggle.[83] This position was very close to that of the Economists, and, in fact, one of the group's activities was to distribute the newspaper *Rabochaia mysl'* to its members. It also succeeded in issuing May Day proclamations to several of the factories of St. Petersburg, listing economic demands for which the workers should strive.[84]

With the arrest of her Petersburg group, Gurari was exiled to Siberia. There she became a convert to Makhaevism and was a member of Machajski's Irkutsk group.[85] She surfaces again in Ekaterinoslav in 1903. Ekaterinoslav, it will be remembered, was one of the towns where relations between workers and *intelligenty* in the Social-Democratic committee were most antagonistic. Apparently taking advantage of this friction, Gurari organized a Makhaevist group consisting of several dozen Jewish workers who had previously belonged to the Social-Democratic organization.[86] She soon found herself back in Siberia but retained her ties with Machajski: she reappears one last time as a Makhaevist in the Workers' Conspiracy in St. Petersburg.[87]

It was in Odessa that Makhaevism as an organized movement showed the greatest staying power. Odessa was particularly susceptible to the penetration of Machajski's doctrines. The "worker opposition" within the local Social-Democratic organization was so vehement that it generated an actual schism, and it was in

Odessa that Zubatovism had proved particularly popular. By 1902, a mimeographed copy of *The Intellectual Worker* was circulating in Odessa, and Machajski's views were beginning to make headway among both unemployed artisans and workers antagonized by the Social-Democratic committeemen.[88]

In 1903 or 1904, a group calling itself the Implacables (Neprimirimye), consisting of both Makhaevists and anarchists, arose in Odessa. Two of its members, Mitkevich and Chuprina, were alumni of Machajski's group in Irkutsk. The Makhaevist influence manifested itself in the group's rejection of utopian ideals, its emphasis on the economic goals of the labor movement, and its denunciation of the intelligentsia as a parasitical class. In addition, the Implacables circulated copies of *The Intellectual Worker*. The police soon put an end to their activities and seized the printing press they had established.[89] Before their dispersal, however, they had made their presence felt sufficiently for kindred groups to turn to them for support. At the beginning of 1904, a group of anarchists in Belostok, having heard that the Implacables were supplied both with funds and with literature, sent an emissary in quest of financial assistance, and he did not come back empty-handed.[90]

After another attempt at joint activity with the anarchists, the Makhaevists formed a group of their own, calling it The Workers' Conspiracy (Rabochii zagovor). It succeeded in issuing a hectographed pamphlet setting forth its views but then disappeared.[91]

The Odessa anarchists belonged to a third category of individuals to whom Makhaevism proved attractive: revolutionary militants. Rejecting the main socialist parties' program of achieving a "bourgeois revolution" as a stepping-stone to a classless society, such revolutionaries could find in Makhaevism a persuasive explanation of what they regarded as foot-dragging on the part of the socialists. One example is N. M. Erdelovskii, originally a Social Democrat, who became a Makhaevist briefly and ended up as an anarchist terrorist. Erdelovskii was a participant in the bombing of the Libman Café in Odessa in December 1905. This was one of the more notorious instances of what anarchists of a certain stripe called "unmotivated terror," that is, indiscriminate acts of terror directed not against specific individuals but against members of the ruling classes in general.[92]

Another revolutionary activist who stopped briefly at Makhaevism on his way to terrorism was Vladimir Lapidus, known as "Striga." Born into a comfortable Jewish family, Striga became a revolutionary animated by a burning hatred of the "bourgeois order" and a passionate desire to bring it down. Unable to accept the slow-moving strategy of the Social Democrats, he was attracted to Machajski's doctrine that the intelligentsia was pursuing its own class interest, and in Odessa he joined the Implacables. Subsequently, however, he became an anarchist terrorist, for the anarchist vision of the future society provided him with positive ideals to which he could commit himself. Ultimately he met a more dramatic end than Makhaevism could offer him: after engaging in terrorist activities in Belostok and Warsaw, he accidentally blew himself up in Paris with one of his own bombs.[93]

Thus, Makhaevism's field of operation was not only the labor movement, where it sought to challenge the Social Democrats for the loyalty of the industrial workers, but also the extremist fringe of the Russian revolutionary movement, where it interacted with both anarchist and Socialist-Revolutionary elements. As might be expected, given the similarity of many of their positions and especially their shared Bakuninist heritage, Makhaevism and anarchism had a particularly close relationship. Even when they did not explicitly voice approval of Makhaevism, anarchists often expressed views similar to Machajski's, for anti-intelligentsia attitudes were deeply rooted in Russian anarchism.[94] Daniil Novomirskii, for example, who headed a group of anarchosyndicalists in Odessa from 1905 to 1907, like Machajski branded Social Democracy the ideology of "a new middle class" consisting of the "bourgeois and petty-bourgeois intelligentsia." He accused the Social Democrats of wanting to maintain the state for the benefit of the managerial and technical elite, which would direct the socialist economy and govern the working class through its control of parliamentary institutions. In distinction to Machajski, however, Novomirskii adhered to the anarchosyndicalist program of replacing the state with a system of federated workers' associations to administer the economy.[95]

Even if they did not always go as far as Novomirskii in their charges against the intelligentsia, anarchists were receptive to criticism of it. As one anarchist critic of Makhaevism put it, the anarchists believed that the relationship between proletariat and intelligentsia should be "not sharply hostile, as Mr. Lozinskii preaches, but not overly intimate either, as Social Democracy would have it."[96] Given the many points in common between the Makhaevists and the anarchists, a considerable degree of interchange, both personal and ideological, took place between them, although Makhaevism always maintained its distinct identity.[97]

Besides its close relations with anarchism, Makhaevism may also have played a role in the emergence of Socialist-Revolutionary Maximalism. One of the forerunners of Maximalism was a dissident group called the *agrarniki,* or "agrarians," which arose in 1904 among the younger Socialist-Revolutionary émigrés in Geneva. These were proponents of agrarian terror, acts of terrorism directed against landowners. Their leading practitioner was M. I. Sokolov, but the group's theorist, who at the time called himself E. Ustinov, was none other than Evgenii Lozinskii. As a pamphleteer and journalist, Lozinskii was serving on the editorial board of the Socialist-Revolutionary newspaper *Revoliutsionnaia Rossiia (Revolutionary Russia).* It was Lozinskii who drafted a resolution embodying the young insurgents' position that was adopted at a Socialist-Revolutionary conference in Geneva in October 1904. As a result, these dissidents were sometimes known as Ustinovites.[98] In the spring and summer of 1905, the group published three issues of a newspaper called *Vol'nyi diskussionnyi listok (The Free Discussion Page),* which sharply criticized the official party program. In particular, the paper rejected parliamentary forms of struggle and political activity in general, and it opposed the party's distinction between "minimum" and "maximum" objectives. Instead of aiming merely for a "bourgeois" revolution which would establish a parliamentary order and socialize agricultural land but not industrial enterprises, the group called for the immediate establishment of a full-scale socialist order in both town and countryside through mass social action.[99] Most notably for a Socialist-Revolutionary group, the dissidents assigned a prominent role in the forthcoming revolution to the urban workers, taking the Paris Commune as their model in much the same way that Machajski had drawn inspiration from the June Days of 1848.[100]

The agitation of the Ustinov group was not well received by the party leadership; by the end of 1905, the party had not only officially repudiated the dissidents' positions but had forced them out of the party itself. The second issue of *Vol'nyi diskussionnyi listok* quoted a declaration in *Revoliutsionnaia Rossiia* that "the editorial group of *Vol'nyi diskussionnyi listok*, as such, stands outside the party of Socialist-Revolutionaries."[101] In December 1905 the group published one issue of a newspaper called *Kommuna (The Commune)*, in which it announced that it had withdrawn from the Socialist-Revolutionary party and joined the newly formed Union of Revolutionary Socialists, under whose imprint *Kommuna* appeared.[102] Even more than its predecessor, this publication looked to the urban workers as the revolutionary vanguard and even detailed a program for organizing a "dictatorship of the proletariat" in the towns.[103]

The Ustinov group was one of several left-wing currents within the Socialist-Revolutionary party which, under Sokolov's leadership, in 1906 came together to form a new Maximalist party. Lozinskii himself, however, seems to have played no further role in this development, having by now broken with the Socialist-Revolutionaries entirely and turned to Makhaevism. Between February and May 1907, three issues of a newspaper entitled *Protiv techeniia (Against the Current)* appeared in St. Petersburg under his guidance. It called itself a "journal of social satire and literary criticism," and it consisted of commentary on social and political issues of the day from the point of view of familiar Makhaevist positions on the intelligentsia and socialism. It was published legally, with Lozinskii as editor, and in it he explicitly repudiated Socialist-Revolutionary Maximalism.[104] It is uncertain who, besides Lozinskii himself, may have contributed to this little publication — if, indeed, there were any other contributors: all of the signed articles in the three issues bore either Lozinskii's name, his initials, or one of his pseudonyms. To the uninitiated reader, Lozinskii had transformed himself into an entire group.

Whether, and to what degree, Machajski's ideas actually contributed to the emergence of the Ustinovites, and ultimately of Maximalism, is unclear, for it is unclear whether Lozinskii or any of his fellow Socialist-Revolutionary militants adopted Makhaevism prior to 1907. Certainly, party dissidents had the opportunity to familiarize themselves with Machajski's doctrines much earlier. The main center of their émigré activity was Geneva, and this was where Machajski had settled in 1903 and where his writings were published in 1904–1905.[105] There is no mention of Machajski in *Vol'nyi diskussionnyi listok* or *Kommuna*, however, and neither publication displays the attitude toward the intelligentsia that was the hallmark of Makhaevism. It is more likely that the immediate influence on the Ustinovites was anarchism, as suggested not only by their antipolitical and antiparliamentary stance but also by the pains they took to distinguish themselves from the anarchists.[106] Lozinskii's ideological evolution, however, provides further evidence of the extent to which Makhaevism interacted with, and helped to fertilize, those currents that stood on the militant left-wing fringe of the Russian revolutionary spectrum.

The organized activities of the Makhaevists culminated with Machajski's St. Petersburg group in 1906 and 1907. The group called itself the party of the Workers' Conspiracy (Rabochii zagovor) and established an underground printing press in Finland.[107] The Makhaevists were also able to finance legal editions of *The Intellectual Worker*, parts 1 and 2, and *The Bourgeois Revolution and the Workers' Cause*, both of which appeared in 1906. They began issuing proclamations and agitating in the factories as well as among the unemployed. They also appeared at workers' meetings to criticize the representatives of the socialist parties and urge the workers to expel *intelligenty* from the labor movement. The socialists responded by accusing the Makhaevists of "provocation" and by sponsoring condemnations of them whenever possible. From the latter, some idea of the message the Makhaevists were trying to convey to the workers can be gleaned. In February 1907, for example, a meeting of the unemployed in one of the city's districts adopted the following resolution:

After listening to the representatives of the Workers' Conspiracy with indignation, the meeting rejects their proposals directed against a democratic republic, against the organizations of the working class, and against the socialists, and expresses its confidence that only by rallying around the socialist banner can the workers overthrow capitalism and thereby rid themselves of capitalism's inseparable companion, unemployment.[108]

This did not stop the Makhaevists, however. On April 18, the Marxist newspaper *Tovarishch (Comrade)* reported the appearance of representatives of the Workers' Conspiracy party at another meeting of the unemployed. Debates with the Social Democrats and the Socialist-Revolutionaries ensued, and the meeting adopted a resolution rejecting the Workers' Conspiracy's demands and tactics.[109]

A month later, *Tovarishch* reprinted an item from *Rech' (Speech)*, the newspaper of the liberal Constitutional-Democratic, or Kadet, party. It described the participation of Makhaevists in a workers' meeting called to hear a report on the recent Fifth Congress of the Social-Democratic party in London.

After the reading of the report, orators of the Workers' Conspiracy group ("Makhaevists") came forward and subjected the report on the congress to severe criticism. They tried to show that the congress had ignored the most burning issues of worker life, such as lockouts, the trade-union movement, etc. The orators attributed this to the influence of the intelligentsia on the congress. The Makhaevists called on the workers to form a new party. The meeting, however, adopted a resolution expressing confidence in the Social-Democratic Party.[110]

In August, *Tovarishch* reported the reappearance of Makhaevist agitators among the workers of Vasil'evskii Island and the Petersburg Side, commenting that "their influence is especially strong on the unemployed of these districts." To halt the spread of that influence, a workers' meeting had been held on August 24 at which the Socialist-Revolutionary speaker "pointed out that the Makhaevists say nothing about the ideal of the future, while the socialist parties advocate perfectly clear goals." The Social-Democratic representative concurred, and, the response of the Makhaevists having met with little sympathy, the meeting adopted the following resolution:

Taking into account the fact that the organization under the name of the Workers' Conspiracy propagates slogans among the workers which are fundamentally harmful and hinder the proper conduct of the class struggle; that the Workers' Conspiracy, in calling the workers to an armed uprising and a general political strike consciously engages in provocation of [*provotsiruet*] the worker masses; and that, finally, the Workers' Conspiracy, which does not acknowledge socialist doctrine, hampers the triumph of socialism, the meeting does not recognize the Workers' Conspiracy as a party of the working class and calls on all those who have fallen under its influence to return to the bosom of the socialist parties.[111]

The Makhaevists remained undaunted. At a meeting in the Vyborg district in September a representative of the Workers' Conspiracy declared that the political parties which claimed to represent the proletariat had led the labor movement onto a false path. He attributed this to the social composition of the parties, "more than three-quarters of which consist of half-proletarianized *intelligenty.*" Only labor organizations which excluded "the party intelligentsia element" could properly represent the workers.[112]

The socialists, in turn, kept up their attacks on the Makhaevists. At a meeting of factory workers in the Narva Gate district several weeks later, the Social-Democratic and Socialist-Revolutionary representatives, after a spirited debate with the Makhaevists, succeeded in passing a resolution branding their activity "extremely harmful and provocational," and recommending that their meetings be boycotted.[113] Such condemnations evidently did not prevent the Workers' Conspiracy from calling a "crowded meeting" of workers of the Vyborg Side on October 17. According to the report in *Tovarishch,* however, the speeches of the Makhaevists were met with a total lack of sympathy on the part of the workers, who dispersed shouting "provocateurs," "hooligans," and other epithets.[114]

Exactly what course of action the Makhaevists urged upon the workers of St. Petersburg remains unclear. Since the Makhaevists concentrated particularly on agitation among the unemployed, Vladimir Voitinskii, at the time a Bolshevik, encountered them frequently in his capacity as chairman of the Petersburg Council of the Unemployed. "They summoned the workers to 'direct action,'" he states in his memoirs, "understanding by this the forcible seizure of all of life's necessities and revenge on the enemies of the toilers. In practical terms it came down to expropriations and individual terror."[115] At one rally, Voitinskii claims, an offended Makhaevist drew a gun on him but backed down when Voitinskii produced a pistol of his own.[116]

Machajski himself, on the other hand, presented the activities of the Makhaevists in a very different light. In a letter to Żeromski in January of 1911, he stoutly denied that they had engaged in either terrorism or banditry. There was only one place in the whole of Russia, he maintained, evidently referring to St. Petersburg, where the Makhaevists for an extended period of time had been able to disseminate their literature, print a series of proclamations, and conduct agitation. To do so, they had had to concentrate all their forces on this organization during its two-year existence.[117] Even here, however, they had fielded no armed detachments, and, in fact, "no Makhaevist even carried a Browning, either his own or a borrowed one." As evidence of their nonviolent behavior he claimed that no Makhaevist had been brought before a military court (which tried terrorists), or had even been sentenced to hard labor, only to administrative exile. Charges and insinuations of banditry and expropriations had been the work of the socialist and liberal press. The sole objective of the Makhaevist organization had been "a mass strike with economic demands and the demand for the most comprehensive public works for the unemployed."[118]

Neither account can be accepted at face value. The Makhaevists, like the anarchists, did tend to attract a motley assortment of characters to their organizations, and it is possible that some of them engaged in unsavory activities. But Makhaevist propaganda caused the socialists a good deal of embarrassment, and it was convenient to try to dismiss the Makhaevists themselves as mere hoodlums. Even Voitinskii concedes that Makhaevism found a decided response among the workers. At times the Makhaevists succeeded in introducing resolutions expressing "distrust of the socialists," and even when the workers, after heated debate between the Makhaevists and Social Democrats, declared their continued faith in socialism, "even then the appeals of the Workers' Conspiracy left a certain trace."[119] Nor were the socialists above the use of smear tactics to discredit their opponents. According to Max Nomad, "the Socialists of the various schools spread leaflets among the workers and the unemployed warning them that the 'Makhayevtzy' . . . were agents of the tsarist police. (I myself saw one of these leaflets in the Museum of the Revolution in Moscow during my visit in 1930)."[120]

On the other hand, as we shall see in the next chapter, Machajski wrote his letter to Żeromski from a Galician prison at a time when he was trying to fend off rumors that he had engaged in banditry and possibly in terrorist activity as well. He therefore had every incentive to emphasize the peaceable nature of the organization he had headed in the Russian capital. There is no evidence that Machajski himself ever participated in terrorist acts or armed expropriations, or that he advocated them. Nevertheless, the highly militant tone of his writings, as well as the company the Makhaevists kept on the extremist fringe of the revolutionary movement, could not help but leave him and his followers open to such charges.

Outside of St. Petersburg, the only other site of Makhaevist activity during the period of the 1905 revolution was Warsaw. Upon his arrival in Petersburg, Machajski had despatched his Viliuisk disciple Porębski to the Polish capital in the hopes of creating a Makhaevist organization there.[121] The results, according to his 1911 letter to Żeromski, were very meager. There was "one Warsaw worker," he wrote without naming him, who, as "an old acquaintance," had some knowledge of Makhaevism and during the time of the revolution may have disseminated that knowledge. "He was the sole Warsaw Makhaevist." Lacking any literature to distribute, and unable to compose any himself, he was unable to create a movement or an organization. Therefore the Warsaw Makhaevists, Machajski claimed, were limited to a circle of a few sympathizers.[122] He acknowledged that a group calling itself the Workers' Conspiracy (Zmowa Robotnicza) had appeared in Warsaw and engaged in armed robbery in 1906–1907. He vehemently denied any connection with it, however: "the one authentic Warsaw Makhaevist and his closest associates of course had nothing to do with any assault" and were never accused of such a connection by the police. He himself, he maintained, had heard of the "Conspirators" only in the middle of 1907, half a year or so after their appearance. They only used the name of the Makhaevists, he insisted, and if the Makhaevists had not existed they would have carried out their attacks under some other label, perhaps that of anarchism.[123]

As already mentioned, the circumstances under which Machajski wrote this letter gave him every reason to dissociate himself from terrorist activities of any sort. Max Nomad's account of the Warsaw Workers' Conspiracy suggests the possibility of a somewhat closer connection between this group and the Makhaevists — though just how close cannot be determined.[124] In any event, the Warsaw Makhaevists accomplished little, and, aside from those groups which have already been discussed, there is no firm evidence that Makhaevist organizations operated anywhere else.[125] By the time the Petersburg Makhaevists established their presence, the revolutionary wave was already ebbing, and they soon had to carry on their efforts without their leader. At the end of 1906, some members of the Workers' Conspiracy were arrested, and Machajski himself fled to Finland and thence to Germany. By the spring of 1907 he was in Cracow.[126] By the end of 1907, Makhaevism as an organized movement, at least on the territory of the Russian Empire, had come to an end.

Two general themes stand out in the troubled history of intelligentsia-worker relations and Makhaevism's place in it. One is the depth and pervasiveness of anti-intelligentsia sentiment among Russia's workers, dating from the very beginnings of the labor movement. Such sentiment emanated from virtually every segment of the highly variegated industrial working class: from nonpolitical workers as well as active members of Social-Democratic organizations, from barely educated individuals and "conscious" members of the worker elite. At some point the *intelligent's* education, values, and way of life — what made him an *intelligent* — made him alien to the world of the worker and his outlook, and the workers themselves were acutely aware of the existence of a sharp dividing line. Depending on individual circumstances and personalities, the two worlds could be, and often were, effectively bridged. But hostility to the intelligentsia was never far beneath the surface, and even when clashes occurred over specific, practical matters, they were frequently nourished by a deeper resentment. The Menshevik B. I. Gorev put his finger on this emotional undercurrent when he attributed the workers' receptivity to Makhaevism to "animosity toward the 'committeemen'" on the one hand, and "the instinctive distrust of many workers for 'gentlemen' [*gospodam*]" on the other.[127] The deep social and cultural gulf that separated the Western-educated elite from the traditionalistic mass of the population found reflection in the labor and Social-Democratic movements as it did in other spheres of Russian life.

The second theme that permeates this history is the degree to which the intelligentsia itself endorsed this hostility. *Intelligenty* of various stripes voiced suspicion of the intelligentsia's motivations and doubts as to its selfless commitment to the workers' interests. Makhaevism was merely the most extreme and consistent expression of a deep ambivalence about itself which the intelligentsia harbored. Therefore ideas closely similar to Machajski's could emanate from *intelligenty* who had nothing to do with Makhaevism. Even while claiming, as the country's "critically thinking individuals," ideological and organizational leadership in the battle against the existing order, many *intelligenty*, afflicted by the intelligentsia's guilt-ridden sense of its own privileged place in the world of consciousness, undermined the intelligentsia's moral claim to such leadership. They were, in effect, "Makhaevists from above," as a journalistic wit termed the critics of the intelligentsia who contributed to the *Signposts* collection of 1909.[128] As such, they articulated the spontaneous anti-intelligentsia impulses that welled up from below, reinforcing them and lending them a degree of legitimacy. Some such sentiment was probably inevitable, given the fissures within the country's culture and social structure, but it was *intelligenty* themselves who gave it an ideology, nurturing the image of the intelligentsia as a parasitic and self-interested class.

If hostility to the intelligentsia was so significant among both workers and *intelligenty*, and Makhaevism was the sharpest and clearest expression of it, why did the Makhaevists have so little success as an organized revolutionary force? Aside from embarrassing the socialist parties and provoking the bitter attacks which the latter felt constrained to level against them, the Makhaevists were able to put forth only a few ephemeral groups in a few towns. Purely practical obstacles such as lack of resources and Machajski's forced emigration obviously had their effect, but inherent ideological limitations seem to have been the principal factor in Makhaevism's failure as a revolutionary current. Makhaevism was both too broad and too narrow to serve as an effective revolutionary ideology. Its criticism of the intelligentsia appealed to people of such divergent viewpoints and interests that it could not weld them together as a cohesive force; it might provide them with a gratifying explanation and justification of their frustrations, but those frustrations were so diverse that they had little in common besides a shared interest in Machajski's doctrines. At the same time, Makhaevism was too narrow in that it was an essentially negative standpoint. While criticizing and rejecting the ideals and programs of the other revolutionary movements, it offered in their place only the haziest vision of a new and better world and no prospect of achieving it in the near future. This was not enough to galvanize the energies or justify the commitment of those who were taking great risks to overthrow the existing order. As a result, Makhaevist groups could at best serve as temporary way stations on the road to some more positive and satisfying ideology; they could not compete with the other revolutionary parties. The Workers' Conspiracy petered out as the revolution of 1905 subsided, and it was to play very little role in the revolution of 1917. That revolution, however, while settling the fate of the autocracy and capitalism in Russia, did not resolve the question of the intelligentsia's role in the new order. Therefore the history of Makhaevism as an expression of anti-intelligentsia sentiment by no means came to an end in 1917.

Chapter 6

Cracow–Paris–Moscow

O NCE AGAIN an émigré in Western Europe, Machajski had not yet given up his quest to create a movement based on his doctrines. He published a detailed exposition of his revolutionary program in the form of a journal, *Rabochii zagovor (The Workers' Conspiracy)*, a single issue of which appeared in Geneva at the beginning of 1908, and settled in Cracow, part of the Austrian province of Galicia. As he had been expelled from the Austrian Empire in 1891, after his arrest for trying to smuggle illegal literature into Russian Poland, his residence in Cracow was illegal, and he assumed the name Jan Kiżło. In a letter to Żeromski in 1910, he claimed that he spent his two years in Cracow toiling as a lowly copyist "at a very respectable establishment," earning the meager sum of forty Austrian florins a month. Only with the financial assistance he received from a brother was he able to support himself and his wife.[1] The reality of his life in Cracow, however, was more complex.

Machajski's closest associate in Cracow was Max Nomad (who operated under the name of Czarny), and Nomad's account sheds a very different light on Machajski's activities at this time. According to Nomad, one of Machajski's adherents, whom he identifies only as "Kolya," worked in the imperial mint in St. Petersburg. Having "appropriated" the sum of 25,000 rubles, he forwarded it to Machajski to support the efforts of the Workers' Conspiracy. With these funds, Machajski was able to finance the printing of *Rabochii zagovor* as well as some Polish translations of his writings, and to establish a rudimentary propaganda apparatus.[2] (Whether he also held the job he described to Żeromski remains unclear.) Machajski supervised the activities of the Cracow organization, which consisted mainly of the young and energetic Nomad. The latter agitated among the unemployed and the unskilled, as well as among disgruntled *intelligenty*. Of the émigrés who had come from the Congress Kingdom in the wake of the 1905 revolution, members of the Polish Socialist party (PPS) must have seemed a particularly ripe target. The revolution had brought an influx of new members into the party, many of whom felt a strong sense of solidarity with the Russian revolutionary movement and were willing to subordinate the cause of Polish independence to the goal of social revolution. This brought them into increasing conflict with the "old guard" of the PPS, led by Piłsudski, which distrusted the Russian movement and gave national liberation priority over the class struggle. In November 1906, the party split. Piłsudski and the right wing broke away from what was now the majority of the party and formed the PPS "Revolutionary Fraction," while the left wing, which abandoned the slogan of independence, formed the Left PPS, now similar in orientation to the Social Democracy of the Kingdom of Poland and Lithuania (SDKPiL) with which it would eventually merge. The Polish Social Democrats of Galicia (PPSD), led by Ignacy Daszyński, supported the position of the PPS "old guard" and therefore were also the object of the Makhaevists' attentions.[3]

In these circumstances, the Makhaevists managed to win over some former members of the PPS as well as the PPSD and tried to disseminate Makhaevist literature in Warsaw.[4] The established parties became sufficiently alarmed at the inroads of the Makhaevists to begin attacking them and spreading unsavory rumors about them. According to Nomad, "We were called provocateurs, tsarist spies, and bandits."[5] Nomad's colorful account describes socialist meetings convened specifically to refute the Makhaevists and featuring Daszyński himself; one such meeting nearly turned into a riot.[6] Within two years, however, the Makhaevists' activities had come to an end: Nomad left Cracow at the end of 1909, and shortly thereafter Machajski, apparently fearful of growing attention from the police, resettled in the Tatra Mountain resort of Zakopane. A number of factors probably contributed to Machajski's withdrawal from active political combat: the slanders of his opponents, the exhaustion of his financial resources, per-haps his own exhaustion after so many years of crying in the wilderness. Most important, however, is the likelihood that Ma-chajski's ideas simply had little appeal to Polish socialists. For those who placed Polish national independence in the forefront, Machajski's consistent rejection of nationalism had nothing to offer. For those who found in the international socialist move-ment a substitute homeland worthy of their loyalties and total devotion, Machajski's antisocialist version of class struggle could not provide an attractive alternative. Makhaevism, therefore, found it impossible to make any real headway on Polish soil.

Unable to find work in Zakopane, Machajski again turned to Stefan Żeromski, with whom he had resumed his friendship in Cracow in 1907. On May 5, 1910, he wrote to Żeromski in Paris, asking him to recommend Machajski's wife for a job at a sana-torium in Zakopane run by Dr. Kazimierz Dłuski. Dłuski, a so-cialist of long standing, had been a prominent member of the Great Proletariat party and later was a supporter of the PPS. He was also a close acquaintance of Żeromski's. The faithful Żerom-ski sent the recommendation and also made other representa-tions on Machajski's behalf, but none of his efforts bore fruit. Machajski even devised a scheme to translate Żeromski's latest work into Russian and have it published in Russia, but nothing came of it.[7]

Instead, Żeromski's good offices had unintended consequences of a very different sort. Wacław Sieroszewski, also a friend of Dłuski and in Paris at the time, heard of Żeromski's advocacy of Machajski. A poet and novelist, Sieroszewski had been active in the early Polish socialist circles of the 1870s and had spent many years in Siberian banishment. On the basis of what he had heard about Machajski during his exile in Russia, and about the bandit activities of the supposed "Makhaevists" in Warsaw, Sieroszew-ski wrote to Dłuski urging him to exercise caution in his dealings with Machajski — who was still using the name Kiżło — lest he find himself the victim of some kind of "expropriation." The police in Zakopane learned of Sieroszewski's letter and arrested Machaj-ski. They found no evidence that an assault of any sort was being planned, but Machajski's real identity came to light, and he was threatened with expulsion from Galicia. Even worse, the investigation unearthed a totally unfounded rumor that at the time of his arrest at the Russian border on his way to Lodz in 1892, Machajski had attacked or even shot a Russian border guard. Now he faced not merely expulsion from Austrian territory but the possibility of being handed over to the Russian authorities for a capital offense![8]

It was at this point that Machajski wrote the long letter to Żeromski referred to in the previous chapter, in which he denied that he or any of his authentic followers had ever engaged in acts of terror or banditry, in Russia or in Poland. Machajski's wife had already written to Żeromski asking him to speak out in Machajski's defense, and Machajski's own letter, smuggled out of prison, naturally presented his political activities of previous years in the most defensible terms. In Zakopane, he wrote, he had done nothing but give lessons as a private tutor and try to make ends meet. All those acquainted with him there knew that "Kiźło, occupied exclusively with trying to assure his existence in Zakopane, in the entire year of his stay here has not opened his mouth to propagandize anyone, nor has anyone heard of any pamphlet of Machajski's whatsoever arriving in Zakopane."[9] As for his activities elsewhere in Poland, "No Makhaevist literature existed in the Polish language before 1909. Only then did two tiny pamphlets appear, and, so far as I have heard, scarcely a few score copies made their way to Warsaw, where, moreover, in view of the general present-day reaction, no one knows anything about them." Nor had any references to those pamphlets or to the Makhaevists in Cracow been made in the present case against him.[10] Thus did Machajski gloss over his two years of activity in Cracow, finding himself in the peculiar position, for a revolutionary, of seeking to minimize the impact his ideas and conspiratorial efforts had had.

On this occasion, Machajski did not have to rely on Żeromski alone for assistance. His troubles had come to public notice, and reports of his arrest appeared in a number of Polish newspapers in both Russia and Austria.[11] Machajski, who had always complained bitterly of slander and persecution at the hands of his political opponents, found a surprising number of defenders willing to take a public stand in his behalf. Roman Dmowski, for example, had been a leader of Zet, the Union of Polish Youth, to which Machajski had belonged at Warsaw University. Now head of the National Democratic party (Stronnictwo Demokratyczno-Narodowe, the successor to the Liga Narodowa), he espoused a brand of right-wing nationalism which was far removed from Machajski's views. Nonetheless, Dmowski published an article in a Warsaw newspaper praising Machajski's "noble character."[12] Even Sieroszewski, in a letter to the editor of a paper in Lwow, expressed regrets at the turn events had taken.[13] Żeromski's contribution to Machajski's defense was an eloquent article entitled "In the Matter of Machajski." It appeared in the Cracow newspaper *Nowa Reforma (New Reform)* and contained Żeromski's reminiscences of Machajski from their student days in Kielce and Warsaw. Describing him as someone who throughout his life had been "an anchorite, an exile, subject to continual persecution," Żeromski wrote in his concluding remarks: "However one may assess his social theories, it is beyond doubt that he himself is a man of high worth, Mickiewicz's 'suffering man, struggling man, a man free in spirit.'"[14]

These efforts proved successful. Machajski was sentenced to two weeks' imprisonment for illegal residence and registration under a false name, and then was allowed to leave Austria. In the spring of 1911, he and his wife settled in Paris.[15]

For the next six years, he lived a modest and totally nonpolitical existence in the French capital. His French was none too good, and his personal contacts were confined mostly to the local Polish colony. With Żeromski's help, he secured a modest job at the Bibliothèque Polonaise. He tried once again to supplement his income by translating some of Żeromski's works into Russian, but he was unable to find a publisher for his translations. He had to resort to giving lessons to the children of Polish and Russian émigrés — having thus come full circle back to his student days.[16] On the eve of the Russian Revolution, in addition to tutoring, he was working as an archivist in a bank; his wife was living in Moscow.[17]

As it did for so many of Russia's political émigrés, the outbreak of the revolution rescued him from his humdrum existence and held out the prospect of a new lease on political life. At the end of June 1917 he wrote to Max Nomad that he would long since have left for Russia, but ill health had delayed him. He had quit his bank job, however, and was now waiting to board a ship provided by the Provisional Government to take émigrés back to Russia.[18] "It is not yet my revolution," he told friends in Paris, "but it is a revolution, so I'm going to it."[19]

When he arrived in Petrograd, he found his old comrade Bronislav Mitkevich, who had been a member of his group in Irkutsk and had escaped from prison with him. Other former associates as well as new recruits joined them and formed a Makhaevist organization. The Makhaevists began to appear at public meetings, and Mitkevich achieved some success as a spokesman for the group's ideas. Material resources to support an organized group were lacking, however, and the Makhaevists had some difficulty orienting themselves in the midst of a revolution whose speedy radicalization tended to outflank even the most militant programs and positions. After the Bolshevik seizure of power in October, the Makhaevists dwindled away.[20]

The last concrete manifestation of Makhaevism was the appearance of a single issue of a journal entitled *Rabochaia revoliutsiia (The Workers' Revolution)*. It came out in Moscow, dated June–July 1918, although parts of it were written earlier; none of the articles were signed, but the editor was listed as "A. Vol'skii." The journal gave Machajski the opportunity for a final restatement of the basic tenets of Makhaevism in the light of the Russian Revolution, and it reflected his fundamentally ambivalent attitude toward the Bolsheviks.

In attempting to account for the Bolshevik seizure of power in Makhaevist terms, Machajski faced an acute theoretical dilemma. The new Bolshevik regime, established in the name of socialism by avowed socialists, was clearly much more radical than the "bourgeois revolution," with its parliamentary system and unfettered capitalism, which Machajski had always anticipated as the immediate outcome of socialist politics and the first step on the intelligentsia's road to power. Yet, it by no means measured up to Machajski's definition of a true "workers' revolution." In *Rabochaia revoliutsiia*, Machajski resolved the dilemma by arguing that the Bolsheviks were no more radical than the Jacobins of the French Revolution. At most, they were effecting a democratization of the bourgeois system that would extend the fruits of the revolution to the lower strata of the intelligentsia but would continue to withhold them from the workers.

Machajski's evidence for this position was Lenin's new program of economic moderation, to which *Rabochaia revoliutsiia* was a direct response. By the spring of 1918, Lenin was backing away from the initial Bolshevik policy of "workers' control" in industry in an effort to restore order in the factories and regularize production. A sweeping revision of Bolshevik industrial policy was announced, including the restoration of managerial authority, the tightening of labor discipline, and measures to retain and reward the so-called bourgeois specialists, the former managers and technical experts. (The grudging manner in which the specialists were to be rewarded for their services is reflected in Lenin's remark that the high salaries they would require constituted a "tribute" that had to be paid for Russia's backwardness.)[21] Lenin's term for the economic system these policies would create, a hybrid of capitalist and socialist elements, was *state capitalism* — a rather tactless choice of words which horrified revolutionary purists of every stripe. To Machajski, such backtracking on the part of the Bolsheviks served as confirmation of what he had been predicting for two decades: a socialist revolution, far from destroying the capitalist system, would merely set the stage for the intelligentsia to replace the capitalists as its new rulers.

The definitive overthrow of capitalism, Machajski insisted, could be achieved only through an immediate, universal expropriation of the bourgeoisie. This would entail not only the confiscation of all means of production, but also of all accumulated wealth — requiring the strict limitation of intelligentsia salaries.[22] The Bolsheviks, however, for all their initial hostility to capitalism and declared intention of dismantling it, were now willing to settle for a much more modest program; despite the nationalization of some enterprises, the managers and technical experts were still in charge and receiving high salaries, while the workers were being subjected to strict labor discipline. The Bolsheviks were once again referring to the construction of socialism as a gradual, long-term process, and Lenin's state capitalism offered little prospect of radical change in the position of the workers.[23]

Why had the Bolsheviks so disappointed the hopes the workers had placed in them? In part, Machajski attributed the Bolsheviks' retreat from their initial promises to what he called the "intelligentsia counterrevolution," strikes and sabotage by the *intelligenty* in protest against the equalization of wages and other measures that would have undermined the existing order.

Bolshevism represented a mortal threat to the bourgeoisie, but it was neither able nor willing to carry it out. It retreated before the will of the intelligentsia.

The Russian intelligentsia, famous for its rebelliousness, almost entirely socialist, led by recent revolutionaries with martyrs' haloes — the noble Russian intelligentsia saved the bourgeoisie from ruin, saved it from a workers' revolution.[24]

The Bolsheviks readily acceded to the intelligentsia's demands, however, because, like all socialist parties, they regarded the capitalists as the sole exploiters of the working class and had no desire to attack the privileges of the intelligentsia. Far from being enemies of the intelligentsia, the Bolsheviks were exponents of its interests.[25] "They are not fighters for the emancipation of the working class, but defenders of the lower strata of existing bourgeois society, and of the intelligentsia above all. As such, they simply do not *want* a universal expropriation of the bourgeoisie," one that would expropriate the intelligentsia along with the capitalists. Once in power, therefore, they had quickly reverted to the program socialists had always preferred, a program of gradual nationalization of the means of production, which preserved the high salaries of the intelligentsia.[26]

Like the Jacobins in the French Revolution, the Bolsheviks were effecting only an extreme democratic version of the "bourgeois revolution." They had destroyed the old political order but had not established economic equality, and without control over all social wealth the working class could not become the ruling class.[27] To whom, then, had power passed under the Bolsheviks?

Power, slipping out of the hands of the capitalists and landowners, can be seized only by the lower strata of bourgeois society, the petty bourgeoisie and the intelligentsia which, as the possessor of the knowledge needed for the organization and administration of the entire life of the country, acquired and firmly secured for itself the right to lordly incomes, the right to a share of plundered wealth, to a share of national profit.[28]

Much as Bakunin had predicted, some of these new rulers were former workers.

> In the Bolshevik dictatorship, "advanced" workers [*rabochie "peredoviki"*], from revolutionaries expressing the will of the masses turn into state functionaries. . . . They become the usual rulers, commanders, and supervisors, stepping out of the worker mass and joining the lower strata of bourgeois educated society.[29]

These individuals, Machajski claimed, were especially zealous in imposing the new measures of worker discipline. The masses now found themselves ruled by "a new bureaucracy," a "people's [*narodnaia*]" bureaucracy consisting of "*intelligenty* and of semi-*intelligenty* from among the workers," who "previously were revolutionaries but after the October revolution became state officials."[30]

For all his professed disappointment with the Bolshevik regime, however, Machajski did not advocate its overthrow. Despite their failings, the Bolsheviks were preferable to the Mensheviks and Socialist-Revolutionaries, and Bolshevik rule was a far better alternative than counterrevolution.[31] Instead, he reiterated his earlier strategy of the workers "dictating the laws of state power," exerting pressure on the government to carry out their economic demands.[32] The end result of this pressure would be, in effect, a second revolution, a real "workers' revolution." First of all, private property must be confiscated, and then the wages of the manual workers must be raised to the same level as the salaries of the intelligentsia. One last time, Machajski limned the Makhaevist utopia, where all would have equal access to education: "Full emancipation of the workers will ensue only with the appearance of a new generation of equally educated people, which will inevitably arise once equal payment for manual and intellectual labor has been won, once the *intelligent* and the worker possess identical means for the education of their children."[33]

Machajski was not alone in viewing the Bolsheviks as he did. At the time *Rabochaia revoliutsiia* appeared, a radical critique of Lenin's policies in terms very similar to Machajski's was being voiced by the anarchists, on the one hand, and by the left wing of the Communist party itself, on the other. (In his usual fashion, Machajski dismissed both sources of criticism as lacking in seriousness.[34]) By 1918, anarchist writers were already criticizing the Bolsheviks in terms reminiscent of Bakunin's critique of Marxism. One accused the Social Democrats of deeming it necessary to retain the state "so that, in a socialist society, so-called organizers of production can take the place of present-day entrepreneurs. These organizers will not receive profits, but they will be allotted special subsidies by their fellow administrators."[35] Another cast the rule of the Bolsheviks in more specifically Makhaevist terms, warning of the emergence of a "new class" of rulers from the intelligentsia:

The proletariat is gradually being enserfed by the state. The people are being transformed into servants over whom there has risen a new class of administrators — a new class born mainly from the womb of the so-called intelligentsia. Isn't this merely a new class system looming on the revolutionary horizon? Hasn't there occurred merely a regrouping of classes, a regrouping as in previous revolutions when, after the oppressed had evicted the landlords from power, the emergent middle class was able to direct the revolution toward a new class system in which power fell into its own hands?[36]

Such accusations did not remain confined to the Bolsheviks' political opponents, who were rapidly being stifled in any case. More ominously, they began to surface within the ranks of the Bolsheviks themselves. The Left Communists, who formed the ultraradical wing of the Bolshevik party, originated in opposition to the Treaty of Brest-Litovsk; they advocated revolutionary war against the Germans rather than Lenin's pragmatic peace settlement. They applied their revolutionary fervor to domestic policies as well, criticizing particularly what they considered to be the reimposition of bureaucratic hierarchy as the new regime consolidated itself. They were especially vociferous in their opposition to Lenin's policy of state capitalism, warning that it would lead to "bureaucratic centralization" and "the rule of various commissars."[37] As Stephen Cohen has written in his biography of Nikolai Bukharin, who at the time was one of the leaders of the Left Communists, underlying the controversy were "two enduring fears of idealistic Bolsheviks: the potential emergence of a new ruling class, and the 'bureaucratic degeneration' of the Soviet system."[38] The start of the civil war and the introduction of war communism soon rendered the issue of state capitalism moot (although some of its features would reappear in the New Economic Policy of 1921), but with the end of the civil war the apprehensions that had fueled the controversy of 1918 would come to the surface once again.

Machajski himself, however, now left such disputes to others. When it became apparent that the Workers' Conspiracy could not be resurrected, he made his peace with the Bolshevik order. In 1918, he took a job in Moscow as a copy editor for *Narodnoe khoziaistvo (National Economy*, subsequently renamed *Sotsialisticheskoe khoziaistvo, Socialist Economy*), the journal of the Supreme Council of National Economy.[39] As far as can be determined, he no longer played an active role in the political life of the new Soviet state. Makhaevism itself, however, lingered on, for the anti-intelligentsia sentiment it represented continued to fester within the Russian working class and continued to find articulate expression within the left wing of the Communist party.

At the Tenth Party Congress of March 1921, two ultra-left opposition currents that had crystallized within the Communist party made themselves heard. One was the Workers' Opposition, which advocated a greater role for the trade unions in the management of industry. The other was the Democratic Centralists, who drew their leadership from the ranks of the former Left Communists and urged a greater degree of democratization within the party. What the two currents had in common was concern over the growing centralization of power in the hands of the party's top leaders, at the expense of other organizations such as the trade unions and the Soviets, and of the rank-and-file party members. They expressed this concern in their repeated attacks on "bureaucratization" — attacks which included warnings of the rise of a new, nonproletarian ruling elite. The Workers' Opposition, for instance, proposed as one measure to combat bureaucratization a requirement that every party member spend three months annually doing physical labor and sharing the living conditions of the workers.[40]

Though three years had elapsed since Makhaevism had last found expression in print, it had not been forgotten, and the term, which had now become a synonym for hostility to the intelligentsia, figured in the debates of the congress. On the one hand, it was used to stigmatize the opposition forces. In a brief document written at the beginning of March, Lenin called for the congress to condemn "the syndicalist, anarchist, Makhaevist inclination of the Workers' Opposition."[41] Proposals to ensure the authentic proletarian character of party workers led Emel'ian Iaroslavskii, a former Left Communist but now a spokesman for the party leadership, to accuse the Workers' Opposition of "playing at Makhaevism."[42] Makhaevism was also employed by the opposition as a warning to the leadership to mend its ways. Calling for structural reforms within the party, the Democratic Centralists warned that popular discontent had affected even "advanced strata of the proletariat," where, among other disturbing signs, "an intensification of Makhaevist sentiments" could be detected.[43]

Such sentiments soon manifested themselves. The Tenth Party Congress duly condemned the Workers' Opposition and the Democratic Centralists. Left-wing discontent among party stalwarts persisted, however, and generated two small underground groups (the Tenth Congress having banned the organization of "factions" within the party), the Workers' Group (Rabochaia gruppa) and the Workers' Truth (Rabochaia pravda). In the pronouncements issued by these groups, anti-intelligentsia feelings received even more overt expression than previously, and in terms almost identical to Makhaevism.

The Workers' Group, an outgrowth of the Workers' Opposition, was led by Gavriil Miasnikov, a long-time Bolshevik of genuine proletarian origin: a metalworker from the Urals, he had joined the Bolsheviks in 1906.[44] His group's manifesto, issued in 1923, voiced a crude enmity to middle-class *intelligenty* in general: the best policy in regard to Kadets, professors, and lawyers, it declared, was to "bash their faces in."[45] More unusual was the extension of this enmity to the Bolsheviks. The manifesto characterized the Soviet government as "a high-handed bunch of *intelligenty*," "a bureaucratic fraternity which holds the country's wealth and the government in its hands." The right to speak in the proletariat's name had been usurped by "a little handful of *intelligenty*."[46] It is not surprising that the official Soviet account of the Workers' Group characterized it as a hotbed of Makhaevism.[47]

The Workers' Truth was more intellectual in its origins and

appears to have drawn some of its inspiration from the ideas of the former Bolshevik theorist Aleksandr Bogdanov, who had stressed the technical and organizational side of economic power and class differentiation, rather than ownership.[48] The real source of class division and exploitation, the Workers' Truth argued, was not ownership of the means of production but "the contradiction between organizers and organized." In the present period, the bourgeoisie had given way not to the proletariat but to "the technical intelligentsia under state capitalism."[49] According to the manifesto of the Workers' Truth, this technical intelligentsia formed the nucleus of a rising new bourgeoisie. "The working class drags out its miserable existence while a new bourgeoisie (i.e., workers in positions of responsibility, directors of factories, heads of trusts, chairmen of Soviet Executive Committees, etc.) and the NEPmen wallow in luxury and call to our minds the picture of the life of the bourgeoisie of all eras." Only the technical intelligentsia was capable of running industry, but "in its methods of work and its ideology this intelligentsia is bourgeois to the core, and it can build only a capitalist economy. A new bourgeoisie is being created from the fusion of the energetic elements of the old bourgeoisie and the increasingly prominent organizing intelligentsia." These technicians, managers, and bureaucrats constituted the new exploiters of the proletariat, and the Communist party had become "the party of the organizing intelligentsia."[50] The solution, in addition to a resurgence of proletarian consciousness and proletarian culture, was to end "the contradiction between organizers and organized" by making technical knowledge available to the whole proletariat.[51]

The existence of these two groups was brief. Miasnikov, who had previously drawn Lenin's ire, was arrested in May 1923 but was allowed to leave the country for Germany. The Workers' Group continued to operate, but when it began to step up its agitation in connection with a wave of strikes that broke out in Moscow and other cities in August and September 1923, the party authorities grew alarmed and ordered the GPU to suppress it. The Workers' Truth quietly withered away.[52]

The denunciation and repression of the ultra-left critics within the party, however, did not necessarily signify official repudiation of their anti-intelligentsia sentiment. Even while he was denouncing "Makhaevist attitudes" and authorizing police measures against those who allegedly propagated them, Lenin was sending out signals of a very different sort in regard to the intelligentsia. Throughout his political career, Lenin displayed the same ambivalence toward the intelligentsia that was shared by so many of its own members; in some respects Lenin manifested this ambivalence more sharply than most, and his attitudes as well as his rhetoric fluctuated violently. In *What Is to Be Done?* he had expressed the conviction that only the intelligentsia could be trusted to carry the socialist revolution to a successful conclusion. On other occasions, however, his hostility and contempt erupted in such phrases as "the intelligentsia scum," "the scoundrelly intellectuals," "that riffraff," which pepper his writings.[53] After 1917, he firmly maintained the position, unpopular with many other Bolsheviks, that Russia's economic development required the continued services of the "bourgeois specialists," and he insisted that they be retained and well paid, at least for the time being. But it was also Lenin who, in a letter to Maxim Gorky in 1919, referred to *intelligenty* as "lackeys of capital, who fancy themselves the nation's brain. In fact, they are not the brain but the shit."[54] And it was Lenin who, in 1922, formulated the policy that led to the expulsion from Russia of scores of the country's most prominent scholars and men of letters. On May 19 of that year he wrote to Feliks Dzerzhinskii, the head of the GPU, "concerning the exile abroad of writers and professors who are assisting the counterrevolution."[55] On August 31, the front page of *Pravda* announced the expulsion of "the most active counterrevolutionary elements among the professors, doctors, agronomists, and men of letters."[56] Those expelled included a number of prominent mathematicians, economists, historians, and philosophers; no specific charges were brought against them, and their only crime seems to have been a certain measure of intellectual independence. While Lenin himself would no doubt have been repelled by Stalin's later treatment of the intelligentsia, here, as in many other areas of state and party policy, he set a dangerous precedent for his successors and established few safeguards — legal, institutional, or even moral — to prevent it from being invoked. As *Pravda* ominously concluded the article that announced the expulsion, it was merely a "first warning" to counterrevolutionary elements of the bourgeois intelligentsia.[57]

At the very least, such currents as the Workers' Group and the Workers' Truth indicate that as stalwart Bolsheviks became increasingly apprehensive over the rise of stifling bureaucratism and a new privileged elite within the party, they began to employ terms and accusations strikingly reminiscent of Makhaevism. Whether they drew specifically on Machajski's ideas cannot be determined. According to Max Nomad, sometime after 1918 "a new edition of the first part of his *Intellectual Worker*, authorized by the somewhat tolerant censorship office, was seized and destroyed by the secret police as dangerous to the regime,"[58] but Nomad supplies no date as to when this occurred. Intriguingly, at the end of 1922 Machajski wrote to Nomad with an urgent request for a copy of his pamphlet *The Bankruptcy of Nineteenth-Century Socialism*. So anxious was he to receive it that he asked Nomad to have a typewritten copy made if a printed text could not be found. Regrettably, he did not explain what purpose he intended to make of it.[59] Certainly, none of the Bolshevik dissidents claimed to have derived any inspiration from Machajski, and, if there was any, it was most probably indirect. It is more likely that they drew on that much larger and long-standing reservoir of anti-intelligentsia feelings and ideas to which Makhaevism contributed and of which it was the most systematic expression.

In any case, Machajski was by now approaching sixty and in poor health, and he professed contentment with the nonpolitical nature of his editorial job. "My work earns me a decent living," one of his letters read. "I am satisfied with its 'neutrality,' for from the very start I have avoided all ideological guidance of the writing, and my editing is purely technical, purely literary (stylistic corrections, etc.)."[60] He died in Moscow on February 19, 1926, just three months after the death of his old friend Stefan Žeromski. Ironically, he ended his days as one of those very "intellectual workers" against whom his entire political thought had been directed.

Machajski's passing received a surprising amount of attention in the Soviet press. *Izvestiia's* obituary notice, which even included a photograph, consisted of a biographical sketch written by A. Shetlikh, who had been a fellow exile of Machajski's in Viliuisk and, for a time at least, an adherent of his views.[61] Two weeks after Machajski's death, *Pravda* ran a four-column-wide "obituary"—not of Machajski himself but of Makhaevism.

Written by N. Baturin, it was filled with contradictions but at the same time was quite informative. Baturin began by identifying Makhaevism as one of the varieties of anarchism, original only by virtue of its "particular absurdity and incoherence" — but then proceeded to give a fairly detailed and not inaccurate summary of its doctrines. He lumped Makhaevism together with the Economism of *Rabochaia mysl'*, with Zubatovism, and even with the Black Hundreds, claiming that it relied on the most backward, semipeasant strata of the working class and was confined mainly to such backwaters as Siberia. At the same time, however, as the more honest Social Democrats had conceded in the past, he admitted that even among the workers in industrial centers Makhaevism had "enjoyed great notoriety and sometimes even fleeting success," for it probed at the sore spot of the Social Democrats' underground organizations, the "abnormal relations" between the fiercely conspiratorial *intelligenty* and the workers.[62]

Machajski was buried in the Novodevichii Cemetery in Moscow, his grave topped by a monument that was the work of his associate of many years earlier, the French-born sculptor known as Pontiez. Stark and unadorned, the gravestone bore nothing but the name of the deceased, in Russian — and, at last, rendered correctly: Ian Vatslav Makhaiskii.[63] The brevity of the inscription proved more appropriate than anyone at the time of Machajski's demise could have known. Though Machajski himself was gone, *Pravda*'s report of Makhaevism's death was somewhat exaggerated and its epitaph was yet to be written. Very shortly the last, but by no means the least interesting chapter of the history of Makhaevism began to be played out.

Chapter 7

Makhaevism After Machajski

W

HAT MIGHT BE termed the posthumous history of Makhaevism unfolded on two distinct though related levels. One was the development of the theory of the "new class," the concept that arose in certain Marxist, or ex-Marxist circles to explain the tumultuous changes occurring within the Soviet Union in the 1930s. Although it had no direct connection with Machajski's doctrines, the "new class" theory as applied to Stalin's Russia in many ways represented an extension of Makhaevism. The other level was the transformation of the Soviet social and political elite that took place from the First Five-Year Plan to the Great Purge. While the "new class" theory failed to provide an adequate explanation of this phenomenon, other elements of Makhaevism shed some unexpected light on it — and may even, in fact, have made a modest contribution to its occurrence.[1]

The contention that under Stalin a "new class" had usurped power in the Soviet Union had two basic sources. On the one hand, it expressed the apprehension that the revolutionary overthrow of the existing order, instead of abolishing hierarchical authority for good and all, would create a new ruling elite emanating from the revolutionaries themselves. This apprehension tended to be felt most keenly by ultraradicals, those revolutionary purists who believed that a whole new order of human relations was possible on the very morrow of the revolution. Its first major expression was Michael Bakunin's critique of the Marxists: as an ultra-revolutionary, Bakunin deeply distrusted the Marxist view that a new order of things required a more or less gradual unfolding of an historical process. Through Bakunin, this critique, and the underlying outlook which had generated it, became an integral part of the anarchist tradition. The second source was, of course, Marxism itself. While Bakunin was content to use the term *new class* in the general sense of a new ruling elite of former revolutionaries, it was Machajski who gave it a more precise Marxist formulation, even while disavowing both anarchism and Marxism. Defining the "new class" as the "intellectual workers," he specified its relationship to the productive process, its ideology, namely, socialism, and its place in the Marxist scheme of history as the would-be successor to the capitalists. In doing so, he stretched Marxist categories to the breaking point, as subsequent applications of the "new class" theory to the Soviet Union were to demonstrate.

After 1917, the developments described above replicated themselves in microcosm within the Soviet Communist party. The ultra-left wing elements of the party, with their abhorrence of hierarchy and privilege, harbored a vision of revolution and its possibilities similar to that of the anarchists; and when that vision clashed with reality, they naturally tended to cast their criticism of those they held to blame in Marxist terms. By the time the "new class" theory came to be applied to Stalin's men, however, it had taken on a life of its own, and its exponents were for the most part unaware of how much it owed to Machajski.

The suppression of opposition groups within the party after the Tenth Congress of 1921 did not put an end to the various warnings that a new ruling elite might be in the making. One of the most notable expressions of such a viewpoint in the twenties emanated not from a dissident but from one of the top leaders of the Communist party, Nikolai Bukharin. Bukharin had at one time been a Left Communist, and even after his embrace of the NEP and the official policies of the party he continued to voice some of the concerns of the party's left wing. On several occasions he warned of the possible "internal degeneration" of the revolution and the rise of a "new class" of exploiters of the workers. The threat stemmed from the low level of the proletariat's cultural development under capitalism. Because of the bourgeoisie's monopoly of education, the working class was unable to develop ideological, administrative, or technical leadership from its own ranks. Therefore, during its struggle against capitalism it had had to rely on members of the bourgeois intelligentsia, and even after becoming the ruling class it must make use, during a transitional period, of bourgeois technical specialists.[2] From the necessity of depending on forces culturally more advanced than itself but socially hostile to it, the proletariat faced the possibility that the technical intelligentsia, the "new bourgeoisie" which had arisen under capitalism, along with a segment of the workers' own party, might turn into "some new class, . . . a new social formation."[3]

The danger, as Bukharin described it, came from two directions. On the one hand, "a new class may arise, standing at the top of the heap, while the working class is transformed into an exploited class; a new bourgeoisie will arise, in part from the NEPmen, to use the Russian expression, and in part from the intelligentsia whom we are utilizing."[4] On the other hand, even individuals of proletarian origin and with calloused hands, when separated from the mass of the workers by their position in organizational and administrative posts, might be assimilated by their more cultured colleagues and become part of "the embryo of a new ruling class."[5] These were essentially the two components of the "new bureaucracy" whose formation Machajski had warned of in 1918 and the dissident Bolsheviks had subsequently criticized. To ward off the first danger, Bukharin wrote, the workers must be educated in order to replace the old intelligentsia as quickly as possible. To prevent the second from materializing, this new workers' intelligentsia must be prevented from turning into a closed caste passing on its educational monopoly to its sons and grandsons. As Bukharin defined it, the problem was cultural and educational as much as economic: to preclude the rise of a "new class" it was necessary to erase "the contradiction between those who know and those who do not know."[6]

As Stalin consolidated his power in the late twenties, critics outside the party began to express the growing conviction that the party had failed to resolve the problem Bukharin had identified and that a new class had in fact taken power in the Soviet Union. Gavriil Miasnikov, now in Western European emigration, continued the criticism of the party leadership that he had begun earlier in the twenties. In contrast to his previous attacks on the intelligentsia, he now directed his anger specifically against the party bosses, demanding a multiparty system and freedom of expression and political organization for workers, peasants, *and* intelligentsia. In 1931, he published in Paris a booklet in which he contended that the Soviet Union represented a "state capitalist" order. By this, he meant something quite different from a socialist economy with capitalist elements, as Lenin had used the term in 1918. State capitalism signified "the bureaucracy organized into a ruling class, the bureaucracy standing at the head of production and the state." This bureaucracy disposed of all the resources of industry and, like the bourgeoisie before it, exploited the working class, which remained economically and politically enslaved. "The rule of the bourgeoisie has been replaced by the rule of the bureaucracy."[7]

Ironically, the individual most responsible for fostering the idea that the Stalinists represented a new ruling class was Leon Trotsky, who consistently *rejected* just such a contention. Trotsky, of course, was quite familiar with Machajski's views and had once even argued about them with their author. Throughout the thirties, however, he continued to express disagreement with any "new class" theory. In an article written in late 1933, he referred in passing to Machajski, and to Miasnikov as well (who had tried unsuccessfully to get Trotsky to write a preface for his booklet[8]), in order to dismiss the idea that the Soviet bureaucracy represented a new class of rulers and exploiters of the proletariat, comparable to the bourgeoisie before it. The bureaucracy, Trotsky insisted, lacked an independent position in economic production and distribution, and therefore could not constitute a class. Given the socialized nature of the Soviet economy, the proletariat remained the ruling class, as it had been since 1917, regardless of the political power and economic privileges enjoyed by the bureaucracy — privilege did not signify the existence of a class.[9]

Trotsky elaborated on this position in his book *The Revolution Betrayed*, which was published in 1936. He rejected the notion that the Soviet economy constituted a form of "state capitalism." Since the means of production remained socialized, and there had been no reversion to private capitalism, the Soviet state remained a workers' state, albeit a "degenerated" one, in which the "dictatorship of the proletariat" prevailed.[10] Hence, the bureaucracy which had usurped political control from the proletariat, primarily as a consequence of Russia's backwardness, did not constitute a class. It was merely a ruling stratum or caste, of which Stalin was the creature and the tool.

The attempt to represent the Soviet bureaucracy as a class of "state capitalists" will obviously not withstand criticism. The bureaucracy has neither stocks nor bonds. It is recruited, supplemented and renewed in the manner of an administrative hierarchy, independently of any special property relations of its own. The individual bureaucrat cannot transmit to his heirs his rights in the exploitation of the state apparatus. The bureaucracy enjoys its privileges under the form of an abuse of power. . . . Its appropriation of a vast share of the national income has the character of social parasitism.[11]

Trotsky was very vague about where this bureaucracy came from, or what its social origins might be, merely hinting at its bourgeois or petty-bourgeois roots.[12] It seemed to consist merely of faceless careerists, and Trotsky could therefore present it as a temporary or transitional phenomenon, a parasitic growth upon the socialist economy which a new proletarian revolution would sweep away.

Trotsky found himself on the horns of a cruel dilemma, both ideological and personal. To have denied that the Soviet Union, even under the aegis of the hated Stalin, remained a "dictatorship of the proletariat" would have called into question the validity of the October Revolution and the construction of the Soviet state, and thereby Trotsky's life work. But in order to uphold, in Marxist terms, the socialist character of the Soviet system under Stalin, Trotsky found himself depicting a ruling class (the proletariat) which did not rule, and a group of rulers (the "bureaucracy") who did not seem to belong to a class. It is difficult to refrain from accepting Robert McNeal's conclusion that "in a sense Trotsky struggled to *avoid* making a Marxist analysis of Stalinism."[13]

It was not Trotsky but some of his former adherents who cut this Gordian knot. Lacking the kind of commitment to the Soviet system that inhibited Trotsky, they began to argue that its rulers had in fact become a "new class" standing in the same exploitative relationship to the workers as the capitalist class it had replaced. The first was Bruno Rizzi, an Italian ex-Trotskyist whose book *La Bureaucratisation du monde* was published in 1939. Rizzi asserted flatly that the October Revolution had produced not the "dictatorship of the proletariat" but a new ruling class, the bureaucracy, a combination of state and party functionaries, technical experts, and intellectuals. According to Rizzi, the bureaucracy consisted of "officials, technicians, policemen, officers, journalists, writers, trade-union big-wigs, and the whole of the Communist party."[14] The Soviet Union was neither a capitalist nor a socialist, neither a bourgeois nor a proletarian state: it was a local manifestation of a new and unanticipated phase of world-historical development, what Rizzi called "bureaucratic collectivism." Private ownership of the means of production was being eliminated, but only to be replaced by state control. Hence the capitalists were being ejected but were giving way to a new ruling class, the bureaucrats who administered the state. The "new class" differed from the capitalist class only in that it owned the means of production collectively rather than individually. Through its monopoly of political power, the bureaucracy as a class was able to exploit the proletariat, appropriate surplus value, and enjoy a privileged standard of living. Not socialism but bureaucratic collectivism was the historical successor to capitalism, and while it was most fully developed in the Soviet Union its growth was discernible in the fascist and even the democratic states of the West.[15]

Max Shachtman and James Burnham, also ex-Trotskyists, were soon echoing Rizzi in the United States. Shachtman, like Rizzi, came to see the new Soviet social order as an example of "bureaucratic collectivism." The Stalinist bureaucracy was a new ruling class, inimical both to capitalism and to socialism. Its appeal, Shachtman felt, was to those elements of the old middle classes who had felt threatened under capitalism and were thus attracted to anticapitalist movements: intellectuals, professionals, government employees, labor bureaucrats. They had little to lose from the abolition of capitalism and much to gain from a system that would overturn capitalism without imposing the egalitarian principles of proletarian socialism.[16]

Burnham's *The Managerial Revolution* was probably the best-known formulation of the "new class" theory before the appearance of Milovan Djilas's *The New Class*. Burnham's book, writ-

ten in 1941, differed somewhat from previous discussions of the
"bureaucracy" in stressing technical and organizational control as
the source of political power, rather than vice versa. To Burnham it was the managers of modern industry who were supplant-
ing the capitalists as the new ruling class. The crucial position
of the managers stemmed from their monopoly of technical expertise, which was replacing private ownership as the source of
economic power, and the intensifying trend toward state take-
over of the means of production would ultimately bring them to
political power. Burnham's theory was similar to Rizzi's in viewing the rise of "managerial society" as a worldwide phenomenon,
an historical stage of postcapitalist development that Marx had
not foreseen. Burnham's "managerial class," however, bore a considerable similarity to Machajski's "intellectual workers."[17] Interestingly, in the figure of Burnham another strand of the long intellectual history of the "new class" theory joined the element
derived from Trotsky. Just two years after the appearance of *The
Managerial Revolution*, Burnham published a book called *The
Machiavellians*, a summary of the ideas of Michels, Sorel, Mosca,
and Pareto (theorists with whom the Italian Rizzi may also have
been familiar). Thus the sociological analysis of elite formation
which these figures had pioneered at the turn of the century to
some degree began to converge with the more strictly political
perceptions of anarchists and Marxists.

 • It was Milovan Djilas, a former leader of the Yugoslav Communist party, who did most to popularize the concept of the "new
class" with his book by that name, published in English in 1957.
Apparently unfamiliar with Machajski's ideas,[18] Djilas, like others
before him, took Trotsky's criticism of the Stalinist bureaucracy
as his starting point and carried it far beyond the limits Trotsky
himself had set for it.[19] Djilas maintained that the party bureaucracy in the Communist-ruled states of Eastern Europe was in fact
the core, or base, of a new owning and exploiting class consisting of those who derived economic privileges from their administrative positions. "In practice, the ownership privilege of the new
class manifests itself as an exclusive right, as a party monopoly,
for the political bureaucracy to distribute the national income,
to set wages, direct economic development, and dispose of nation-
alized and other property."[20] The book had a far-reaching impact,

and with its publication the term *new class* became a common-place description of the Soviet ruling elite.

As such, it has come to be used so broadly as to lose its explanatory value, often serving as little more than a polemical epithet or an ironical term for the privileged stratum of a professedly classless society.[21] To the extent that it continues to be used as a serious analytical concept, it demonstrates how wise Trotsky was in objecting to the application of the term *class* to the Soviet leadership. A ruling elite whose position is derived from political or administrative power, or even from technical expertise, may exhibit certain analogies to a property-owning class, but it is by no means the same thing. What Trotsky could not, or would not, acknowledge was the possibility that Soviet developments had outstripped the ability of traditional Marxist concepts to contain them. The categories of "property," "class," and "ownership" had melted down in the crucible of the Russian Revolution, and Stalin's Russia represented a new social, economic, and political alloy whose components required new forms of analysis. Attempts to comprehend Soviet political and social stratification in terms of the traditional economic, universalist categories of Marxism have therefore proved abstract and sterile, while efforts by Marxist analysts to move away from those traditional categories have led them into distinctly non-Marxist conceptual realms.[22]

This theoretical impasse is hardly surprising, for what was occurring under Stalin's auspices in the 1930s had little to do with class change or class conflict in the Marxist sense. It had a great deal to do, however, with the Russian intelligentsia, a specifically Russian phenomenon which had eluded Marxist attempts to capture it in the past and which the theory of the "new class" failed to deal with adequately now.

The resentments expressed in the criticism of the "bureaucracy" or the "new class" that marked the decade or so after 1917 were directed against two overlapping groups who seemed to be entrenching themselves as a new elite, the "bourgeois specialists" and the new party bosses. They composed what Machajski in 1918 had termed a "new bureaucracy" of *intelligenty* and semi-*intelligenty*, the latter consisting of former revolutionaries who had now become state officials. With the consolidation of Stalin's power and the introduction of the First Five-Year Plan came a growing assault on this new elite.

Even under Lenin, it had been made clear that the remnants of the old intelligentsia who worked for the new regime were merely being tolerated, grudgingly and temporarily, until such time as a new intelligentsia, politically more reliable and socially less suspect, could be formed. As a Soviet work puts it, a bit more euphemistically, "the Communist party and the Soviet state, while making use of the old intelligentsia, at the same time had to resolve the task of forming a new, authentically popular intelligentsia from the ranks of the workers and toiling peasants, for whom the construction of socialism was a heartfelt and desired cause."[23] There were two avenues open to the regime in creating "its own" intelligentsia. One was the expansion of educational opportunities for the children of workers and peasants, a process which, however, required at least an entire generation to complete. The other was the adoption of what came to be called *vydvizhenchestvo*, a crash program of "promoting" adult workers into courses of higher education or directly into responsible positions with on-the-job technical training. The First Five-Year Plan was accompanied by a massive expansion of this promotion policy. Precise figures are impossible to determine, but Western and Soviet estimates seem to agree that a million or so individuals were the beneficiaries of this policy.[24] The leading proponent of the promotion policy was Stalin, who declared in a speech of June 23, 1931, that the Soviet Union had entered a phase of development at which *the working class must create its own productive-technical intelligentsia, capable of standing up for its own interests in production as the interests of the working class.* "No ruling class," he added, "has managed without its own intelligentsia."[25]

The beneficiaries of the promotion policy were of a social and cultural background very different from that of the old intelligentsia. (Whether the term *intelligentsia* should be applied to the former raises once again the historical ambiguities of the word in Russian usage, but clearly it *was* applied to them.) They were in most cases authentically proletarian but, like much of the Russian working class, often had only recently emerged from the peasantry; they had no educational or cultural ties to the prerevolutionary past and its liberal values; they felt considerable loyalty to a system that was providing them with new opportunities for upward mobility; and they found Stalin a more congenial personality than most of the other top Bolshevik leaders. A prime example of this group was Nikita Khrushchev. Born in a peasant village, Khrushchev had gone to work as a metal fitter at a coal mine before the revolution. In 1929, at the age of thirty-five, he was sent to the Stalin Industrial Academy in Moscow to study metallurgy. In his background and his career he was typical of the "new men," even though he used the opportunity to move into the party apparatus rather than a managerial or technical post. His celebrated memoirs shed important light on the outlook of these men. On the one hand, they hint at a strong sense of self-identity by the provincial, poorly educated newcomers in opposition to the more sophisticated and solidly entrenched party leaders. In Khrushchev's description of the political line-up at the Industrial Academy in 1929, cultural cleavages seem to overshadow ideological divisions.

There was a group of us at the academy who stood for the General Line [i.e., Stalin] and who opposed the rightists: Rykov, Bukharin, and Uglanov, the Zinovievites, the Trotskyites, and the right-left bloc of Syrtsov and Lominadze. I don't even remember exactly what the differences were between Bukharin and Rykov on the one hand and Syrtsov and Lominadze on the other. Rightists, oppositionists, right-leftists, deviationists — these people were all moving in basically the same political direction, and our group was against them. We all came from the South — from the Donbass, from Dniepropetrovsk, and from Kharkov. Furthermore, we had all joined the Party after the Revolution. When someone's candidacy to a post in the academy organization was proposed at a meeting, he had to go to the podium and say where he was from and when he had joined the Party. This made it easy for the Old Guard in the Party cell to recognize and vote down anyone who was likely to oppose them.[26]

On the other hand, when he heard Stalin speak, he heard not the crude ideological reductionisms scorned by the more polished party members, but a firm and clear-headed leader, "a man who knows how to direct our minds and our energies toward the priority goals of industrializing our country and assuring the impregnability of our Homeland's borders against the capitalist world."[27]

The campaign to create a new intelligentsia occurred simultaneously with a wave of hostility against the old one. It was touched off by the Shakhty affair in the spring of 1928. In March of that year it was announced that a large group of coal-mining engineers from the town of Shakhty in the Donbass region were to be tried for sabotage in collusion with foreign powers. The case was given maximum publicity in the Soviet media, and it was made clear that the "bourgeois specialists" as a whole were under fire. Fifty Russians and three Germans were subsequently brought to trial in a public proceeding that featured confessions by some of the defendants and foreshadowed the "show trials" of the thirties.[28] At the same time, the Shakhty trial rekindled anti-intelligentsia sentiment from below, and a wave of "specialist-baiting" ensued. According to a Soviet source, worker suspicion of the old specialists mounted, accompanied by denunciations and purges. "There were also individual cases of unfounded accusations of sabotage, with ensuing consequences."[29]

The anti-intelligentsia themes sounded in the Shakhty affair continued to reverberate. The First Five-Year Plan was accompanied by the so-called cultural revolution, a radical wave of anti-elitism and anti-intellectualism amid the glorification of "proletarian" values in education, literature, and other areas of Soviet culture.[30] Meanwhile, the pressure on the technical intelligentsia specifically continued with the trial of the so-called Industrial party in late 1930. This trial involved eight prominent technologists who were charged with plotting the overthrow of the Soviet government in collaboration with foreign agents.[31] The campaign against the old technical intelligentsia is generally considered to have come to an end with Stalin's speech of June 23, 1931, which announced a new policy of reconciliation with the "bourgeois specialists" and condemned "specialist-baiting" *(spetseedstvo)*.[32] This was the same speech in which he reiterated the necessity for the working class to create its own technical intelligentsia. Thanks to the promotion policy, the formation of a "red" intelligentsia was well under way, and the regime, no longer entirely dependent on the "bourgeois" intelligentsia, could afford a more benign policy toward it.

The fateful intersection of the dual processes we have been tracing, the rapid promotion of a new, Soviet-trained intelligentsia and recurrent outbursts of hostility toward the old intelligentsia, occurred in the Great Purge of 1936–1938. The Great Purge decimated the old Russian intelligentsia, while at the same time consolidating the dominant position of the new Stalin elite. Many aspects of that bleak period remain shrouded in uncertainty, and at its height the Great Purge, or, as it was called after the secret police chief then in power, the Ezhovshchina, swept away individuals from top to bottom of the Soviet social structure. There is little doubt, however, that aside from the army, which underwent its own separate purge in 1937, the two groups upon which the Ezhovshchina fell most heavily were the educated elite, on the one hand, and party officials on the other.[33] A typical example of the stratum of Soviet society that was the main target of the purge is Eugenia Ginzburg. A journalist and teacher, with vast amounts of Russian poetry tucked away in her memory, she was a party member as well as the wife of an important provincial party official. She was both an *intelligent* in the traditional sense of the term and part of the entrenched postrevolutionary party elite, and her self-identification with these groups comes through as clearly in her memoirs as Khrushchev's sense of solidarity with the newcomers:

I had seen no men of this sort, our sort — the intellectuals, the country's former establishment — since transit camp. . . . The men here [in a Siberian prison-camp hospital] were like us. Here was Nathan Steinberger, a German Communist from Berlin. Next to him was Trushnov, a professor of language and literature from somewhere along the Volga, and over there by the window lay Arutyunyan, a former civil engineer from Leningrad. . . .
By some sixth sense they immediately divined that I was one of them and rewarded me with warm, friendly, interested glances. They were just as interesting to me. These were the people I used to know in my former life.[34]

The assault on the country's "establishment," as Ginzburg puts it, was obviously the product of political decisions taken from above. The amount of support it received from below, and the degree to which that support was spontaneous rather than contrived, are impossible to measure, but it appears that such support was not lacking. Just as the Shakhty affair and the "cultural revolution" stirred up anti-intelligentsia sentiment from below, the Great Purge bore a certain "populist" flavor, drawing on long-standing grass-roots grievances not only against the privileged specialists but against the entrenched party bosses, that "bureaucracy" which had for so long been an object of criticism. In J. Arch Getty's formulation, "*Spetseedstvo*, antibureaucratism, and class hatred reemerged in strength against the backdrop of a full-blown spy scare."[35] From the "cultural revolution" to the Ezhovshchina, the central authorities were able to draw on a reservoir of popular resentment against what was perceived to be a new privileged elite. At the very least, the apparent willingness of the Soviet public to accept the most vicious and outlandish charges of "wrecking," treason, and service to foreign powers that were leveled against the purge victims suggests a considerable social and cultural distance between that elite and much of the rest of society.

If the Eugenia Ginzburgs were the chief victims of the Great Purge, the Nikita Khrushchevs were its chief beneficiaries. The Great Purge provided the opportunity for the new political and technical elite to move into positions of authority vacated by the purge victims. Although some members of this new elite themselves fell victim to the Ezhovshchina, on the whole it survived not only the Great Purge but Stalin himself, remaining in power at least through the Brezhnev era.[36]

The precise relationship between this social change and the Great Purge must remain a matter of dispute. The two phenomena coincided, but whether by design or by accident, we cannot know. To regard it all as a deliberate plan on Stalin's part which he successfully carried out from 1928 to 1938 seems implausible; if Stalin had the kind of personal mastery over the country's political and social forces that such a plan required, he achieved it only at the end of this period, not at the beginning. It seems more reasonable to assume that the Great Purge, though it may have had its own political origins, gave Stalin the opportunity to promote more quickly a new intelligentsia which he had consistently fostered; with this new intelligentsia waiting in the wings, he could afford to dispense with the old, and the circumstances of the Great Purge permitted him to do so on a wholesale basis.[37]

Interestingly enough, Makhaevism figured in the demise of the old intelligentsia. The introduction of the First Five-Year Plan, the promotion policy, and the "cultural revolution" coincided with a flurry of interest in Makhaevism. In 1928, the first volume of an anthology of non-Bolshevik political views was published in Moscow which reprinted chapter 5 from part 2 of Machajski's *The Intellectual Worker*.[38] (It was a fairly innocuous section dealing mainly with the populists and legal Marxists.) In the same year, in Kremenchug, the still extant Evgenii Lozinskii published a little book in which he restated the essential elements of Makhaevism. Cautiously, he related them explicitly only to the Social-Democratic parties of the Second International and evaded the question of whether the Bolshevik regime represented the seizure of power by the intelligentsia.[39]

Also in 1928 and in 1930 the journal *Katorga i ssylka (Hard Labor and Exile)* published two memoir articles by revolutionaries of plebeian origins who had been attracted to Machajski's ideas, B. A. Breslav and M. Vetoshkin; their comments seemed to suggest that anti-intelligentsia sentiment of the sort Machajski had espoused had something to be said for it.[40] In 1929–1930, a critical but informative history of Makhaevism by L. Syrkin was published in the journal *Krasnaia letopis' (Red Annals)* and then issued in book form in 1931.[41] Finally, Baturin's 1926 *Pravda* obituary article on Makhaevism, "Pamiati 'makhaevshchiny'!" was reprinted in a collection of his writings in 1930.

Why was such attention being paid to Makhaevism at this time? In the highly charged political atmosphere of the First Five-Year Plan and the "cultural revolution," it seems unlikely that historical curiosity alone was at work. The contents of these publications, however, offer no clear explanation. Some were critical of Makhaevism, dismissing it, together with anarchism, as a retrograde "petty-bourgeois" ideology, while others found elements to praise in it. Was the resurrection of Makhaevism part of the intelligentsia-baiting of the time? Was it a *defense* against intelligentsia-baiting, an indirect attempt to condemn such sentiment by equating it with this discredited current of thought? Was it, perhaps, some of each, depending on the particular instance?

Much less ambiguous, and highly publicized, was the final reference to Makhaevism that appeared in this period. On November 15, 1938, as the Great Purge was drawing to a close, *Pravda* printed a lengthy Central Committee statement containing a passage on the intelligentsia. The statement declared the Soviet intelligentsia that had arisen during the years of Soviet power "an entirely new intelligentsia," unique in the world. "It is yesterday's workers and peasants, and sons of workers and peasants, promoted into commanding positions." Despite the intelligentsia's importance, however, "a disparaging attitude toward our intelligentsia has not yet been overcome. This is a highly pernicious transferral onto our Soviet intelligentsia of those views and attitudes toward the intelligentsia which were widespread in the prerevolutionary period, when the intelligentsia served the landowners and capitalists." The Central Committee then condemned such "Makhaevist" attitudes as "savage, hooliganistic, and dangerous for the Soviet state," and declared that they must cease.[42]

To drive the point home, three days later *Pravda* ran an article entitled "Answers to the Questions of Readers: What Is 'Makhaevism'?" The article took up three columns — an entire half-page of the newspaper. For the benefit of "readers" who had expressed puzzlement at the reference to Makhaevism in the Central Committee declaration, *Pravda* provided a fairly detailed account of its history and tenets, concluding, however, that Makhaevism's central principle could be reduced to the slogan "down with the intelligentsia." Quoting Stalin's speech of June 23, 1931, on the need for a more positive attitude toward the "bourgeois specialists," the paper declared that the party had always fought against the kind of specialist-baiting that Makhaevism encouraged. Furthermore, the article reiterated that the new Soviet intelligentsia, unlike the prerevolutionary intelligentsia, recruited its members chiefly from the workers and peasants. Socialist construction was creating a situation in which "the whole Soviet people will be thoroughly educated [*ves' sovetskii narod budet splosh' intelligentnym*]." Therefore the appearance of a "Makhaevist-hooligan attitude toward our Soviet intelligentsia" was scandalous and had to be condemned. This intelligentsia was "the salt of the Soviet earth," and those who scorned it could only be "aliens, degenerates, and enemies."[43] The message was clear: whatever justification may have existed for anti-intelligentsia sentiment in the past, it was no longer to be tolerated now that the new Soviet intelligentsia was firmly in place. With the subject of hostility to the intelligentsia now closed, official interest in Makhaevism came to an end. Subsequent Soviet references to it tended merely to repeat the terms of abuse *Pravda* had heaped upon it.[44]

It was fitting that Machajski's views were used for the last time in order to signal the definitive displacement of the old Russian intelligentsia by a new Soviet intelligentsia. The change in the country's elite that was being completed as the Great Purge drew to a close was actually more intelligible in Makhaevist than in Marxist terms. As Trotsky had recognized, it could not be explained in traditional Marxist "class" terms, but it was no less real for that. What was occurring was something startlingly akin to Machajski's "second revolution": upward mobility, through education, of men of authentic worker and peasant background.

In the fateful decade from 1928 to 1938, the awkwardness of the Russian intelligentsia's situation came back to haunt it. Despite the political radicalism of so many of its members, the intelligentsia's education had always set it apart as a privileged elite. Even after the revolution, the remnants of the old professional intelligentsia in the form of the "bourgeois specialists," along with the new party bosses — who, though in many cases they were at best semi-*intelligenty*, as Machajski termed them, did, after all, sit behind a desk — to a considerable degree continued to be seen from below as an extension of the old propertied and ruling classes. The elite which had entrenched itself after 1917 was largely of middle-class origin, tied to the old regime and to the West by virtue of its prerevolutionary education and culture, "bourgeois" in respect to its style of life. The attack on this establishment which began in 1928 may have been initiated by Stalin for his own purposes, but he was able to exploit popular sentiments that had their origin long before 1917. Worker-peasant Russia, having rid itself of the old rulers and property owners, now turned upon the equally alien and also privileged intelligentsia, passively accepting, if not actively participating in, its decimation, while supplying a new intelligentsia of plebeian origin to replace it.

This is not to suggest that the Makhaevist utopia had been achieved. The new men who came to power under Stalin used their position not to abolish privilege and establish equality for all, but to create new privileges for themselves. These former workers and peasants, unlike their champions in the old intelligentsia who were wont to project their own humanistic principles onto them, viewed the promises of the Russian Revolution in specific, down-to-earth terms. Their ambition was not to create a new world of abstract perfection but to better their own standing in the world as it existed. For all its failings and limitations, however, this new elite was more "democratic" in its origins and more accessible from below than the old. As such, and to the bewilderment of so many of the old *intelligenty*, it doubtless appeared to the laboring classes as a legitimate fulfillment of at least some of the promises the revolution had made.

It goes without saying that Stalin did not need Machajski to provide him with inspiration for any of his ideas or policies. If we take Makhaevism solely in its negative aspect, however, as an attack on the intelligentsia as a privileged and "exploiting" class, it is not entirely fanciful to accord Stalin one additional title among the many that were bestowed upon him: recognition as the greatest Makhaevist of them all, albeit an unwitting one. But if we take seriously the more visionary aspect of Makhaevism, that is, Makhaevism as one version of the intelligentsia's dream of universal freedom and equality to be achieved through the flames of popular revolution, then Machajski would scarcely have regarded Stalinism as the fulfillment of his hopes. He would have shared that disappointment with much of the rest of the old intelligentsia. For all his criticism of the intelligentsia, Machajski remained a member of it from beginning to end, sharing not only its aspirations and illusions but its deep ambivalence about itself and its rightful place in Russian life. Had he lived long enough, he would undoubtedly have shared also the fate that intelligentsia suffered at Stalin's hands.

Appendix
Notes
Bibliography
Index

Appendix

Machajski's May Day Appeal of 1902

The May Day appeal which I have translated below (and annotated) was circulated by Machajski's group in Irkutsk in 1902. He subsequently printed it as an appendix to the Geneva edition of part 1 of The Intellectual Worker. *It constitutes a representative sample of Machajski's writings. Although it was composed shortly after the two Siberian essays which marked the beginning of Makhaevism, it is a succinct summary of virtually all the major positions Makhaevism held on Social Democracy, the intelligentsia, working-class aims and tactics. In tone and vocabulary, too, it is typical of Machajski's writing style.*

APPEAL
(April 1902)

For several years now, the beginning of May of each year has brought the Russian government countless concerns. These are the days when the workers prepare themselves to rebel. Accordingly, the wealth created over the centuries and plundered by ruling society has to be defended from attack by the worker masses: the idleness, luxury, and depravity of the rich have to be safeguarded; the fat salaries of state officials, the incomes running into the thousands of all the ruling and learned men, also have to be safeguarded; the parasitism of educated bourgeois society, so stoutly nourished by the hands of the working class while hundreds of thousands of people starve to death in the towns and villages of Russia, has to be defended.

The whole of bourgeois society keeps a close eye on labor unrest, on the labor movement in general. Not only the police and the prose-

181

cutors but learned professors and writers, too, investigate which of the worker's thoughts and desires are to be extirpated as "criminal," that is, harmful to the existence of contemporary society, which is built on robbery. They painstakingly weigh what may be allowed to the workers without endangering the bondage of the working masses, which is so sweet for the exploiters.

Those strata of educated society whom the Russian autocratic order does not admit to full sway over the country, does not admit to any of the highest posts in the regime, keep a close eye on the labor movement and make use of it as a means to their own objectives. Those masses of unemployed intelligentsia who see how many profitable and cushy jobs, capable of feeding all the suffering *intelligenty* like lords, might be created in the enormous Russian state but are not made available solely because of the ignorant administration, the policemen and the priests — those are the ones who are making use of the labor movement. The intelligentsia observes the labor movement and asks with impatience when the working people will at last, with their struggle, build for it the kind of paradise educated society in Western Europe has long since come to enjoy.

As the First of May approaches, the day when workers all over the world think about and discuss their situation, they receive all kinds of advice from educated society.

The First of May, say the respectable socialist scholars, is a holiday which the workers in their comradely associations should spend in a solemn mood, thinking about that far-off day when there will be neither rich nor poor, neither capitalists nor workers. The bourgeoisie is happy with this socialist doctrine, which advises the workers to pray on their day of struggle, just as the gentry were happy when the priests preached that the serfs would be rewarded by God in the afterlife for their poverty, sufferings, and lashings at the hands of the landowners.

On May Day, says the Russian revolutionary intelligentsia, workers everywhere should organize political demonstrations against the autocratic government; they should demand that the state be governed by the will of the entire people freely electing their rulers the way it is done in the West, where the people themselves rule.

A fine fairy tale! Just half a century ago a French government elected "by the will of the entire people," with no autocratic tsar or hereditary monarch, a democratic, republican government, showed that it knew how to slaughter workers just as well as an autocracy. This government "freely elected by the people" killed tens of thousands of workers in the streets of Paris over four days. In that same France, another republican government repeated the carnage some twenty years later. And contemporary democratic governments elected by the entire people, like the French, the English, and the North American, know, of course, how to shoot down insurgent workers so as to make them remember that they are slaves.

Some thirty years ago the German workers with the utmost enthusiasm began to elect their own Social-Democratic deputies to the ruling German parliament. These deputies at the time promised that they would immediately and definitively emancipate the working class if only the workers elected them in large numbers. And now look: after the German workers have strained every nerve and collected their pennies to elect several dozen men as their deputies, these Social-Democratic, labor deputies are beginning to explain that it is impossible to emancipate the working class at the moment, that the greatest misfortunes would befall the land if the working class were suddenly victorious and took power into its own hands.

The French workers not long ago followed the example of the German ones in their politics. And they have already wound up with "representatives" such as the ones who produced the most faithful servant of the French bourgeoisie and the best friend of the Russian police government, Minister Millerand, who without hesitation approves an order to shoot down workers.

So, if the workers elect their own Social-Democratic representatives to governmental institutions, little by little these representatives develop not into emancipators of the working class but into its new masters. Why is this so?

Throughout the world, whether a country has an autocratic government or a "government elected by the people," the law expresses not the will of the people but the will of ruling society which plunders all earthly goods. This society, with the ownership of all material wealth, thereby owns all human knowledge as well, which it turns into a secret inaccessible to the working people. By the laws of the robbers, the working class is allowed only *popular* education, which is ignorance in comparison with the ruling learned world. By these laws of plunder the vast majority of mankind is doomed to be born slaves, to begin in childhood the penal labor of physical work; it is doomed to grow up from generation to generation as an inferior, uneducated race of people capable only of physical labor, of mechanically executing the orders of its masters. The masters, meanwhile, use their plunder to educate all of their own children — though many of them are utter nitwits — into a superior race whose business it is to rule.

Under such predatory laws, it hardly matters whether an autocratic tsar appoints the country's administrators or they are elected by the people.

In either case the government consists of *intelligenty* who bequeathe their administrative ability only to their own offspring, leaving to the majority of mankind the slave labor, the penal labor, of physical work. The elimination of this situation, in which millions even before they are born are fated to ignorance and slave labor, and the abolition of a government which expresses this law, a law of robbery and human bondage, can be accomplished only by a worldwide conspiracy of workers, a general uprising of the working class in a unanimous strike. This uprising will tear from the hands of ruling educated society the wealth created over the centuries and will put it into everyone's hands, proclaiming every human being an equal heir to all human wealth and knowledge.

The assurance that all the working class has to do to attain the possibility of participating in the running of the state is abolish the autocratic regime and win universal suffrage — that's an old fairy tale, repeated a thousand times by every conceivable bourgeois politician-fraud.

The workers, in discussing the question of how to observe the First of May, cannot put their trust in science, cannot put their trust in the revolutionary intelligentsia and its innumerable leaflets, which at present do nothing but loudly and brazenly repeat this old fairy tale.

But, it will be said, the Russian workers have Social-Democratic committees in all the large towns. Haven't these committees, whose membership includes conscious workers, shown the true path for the proletarian struggle to take?

The Social-Democratic committees train worker organizers and agitators. Each year they prepare the May First holiday, and in numerous leaflets they call upon the workers to set forth boldly to the struggle on this day. But when the workers respond to these appeals by suddenly rising en masse (as they did in Petersburg last year,[1] or in an entire city, as was the case three years ago in Riga[2]), putting forth their real labor demands in noisy strikes — then you don't see any Social-Democratic agitators or organizers at the place of struggle. Not a single committee has any thought of spreading a strike that flares up, of augmenting the strength of the aroused masses, of *backing up the workers' demands.*

In February of last year, when the police in Kazan Square beat up students and Petersburg intelligentsia,[3] all the Social-Democratic pamphlets and newspapers cried out with one voice that after such a disgraceful scandal the workers must immediately come out into the streets and without arguing expose themselves to bullets and bayonets. Of course! Have you ever heard of such a thing? On Kazan Square members of the well-bred public, the polite public, were beaten, not some rabble, strikers who might engage in unruly conduct, as in Riga.

On the streets of Riga it wasn't just a matter of a thrashing with whips and rifle butts, such as the students and intelligentsia are getting now, but of shooting and cutting down more than fifty workers. But since the people there were dying for the workers' cause and not for the cause dear to the heart of the intelligentsia, the Social-Democratic committees did not feel it necessary to raise the kind of ruckus throughout Russia that they are raising now in behalf of the students. It did not occur to a single Social-Democratic committee to appeal to the workers of other cities to revolt against the bestial massacre and butchering of the workers in Riga, to answer violence with an even greater general uprising, as they are now preaching.

The Social-Democratic committees patronizingly term stormy strikes like the one in Riga spontaneous outbursts of the unconscious, ignorant masses. They consider them unnecessary and useless, and during such mass disturbances they usually advise their own conscious workers to remain calm, to stay home.

And so, when they offend educated people, you, the worker, are supposed to get so indignant that you'll go right out and throw bombs; but when they shoot down workers in mass strikes — just sit quietly and appeal for calm . . . that's how the Social-Democratic committees, *the representatives of the working class,* reason.

Not too long ago, these "representatives" were beginning their work of so-called economic struggle, that is, they were organizing strikes to relieve the hardship of factory labor and increase wages (displaying unusual caution and moderation in this struggle, of course). Now, without being shy about it, they are explaining to the old Russian revolutionaries and to the whole intelligentsia that they conducted this struggle not for its own sake but in order to *interest* the workers in politics and to *draw* them into the struggle, so that the students might now have the workers for their ardent defenders and the whole of liberal society, in its quarrel with the tsar, might have the masses of the people behind it. (That, for example, is how the Russian Social-Democratic party's founder, Plekhanov, explains its task.)

Since last year, all the Social-Democratic committees have begun to declare that now is the time not for economic but for political struggle. None of the newly established committees, such as the ones in Siberia, even think of starting with economic struggle, but summon the workers directly to a political demonstration. They assume that without even having to throw the worker the penny they tossed him earlier, they can send him under the bayonets and bullets for the intelligentsia's cause.

Last year's congress of the Jewish Social-Democratic committees determined that in the economic respect the worker had already received almost everything that he could be given; therefore a political struggle should now be conducted to realize all the dreams of the Jewish intelligentsia, that is, to gain access for it to all the higher posts in the state, all those positions and fat salaries which it cannot get because it lacks equal rights.

The Petersburg committee, in regard to the Obukhov strike, informs us that there is a crisis throughout Russia, that the owners themselves are in distress, and that therefore those workers who remain out of work should abandon economic struggle and occupy themselves with politics. This means that at a time when workers are perishing from hunger and are seeking bread, they should demand only that the government not oppress *intelligenty* but set them all up in the honorable posts that are due them according to the laws of robbery.

When the workers began to help the students last year, the whole of Russian educated society rejoiced, for it determined that from now on the workers would help it absolutely free of charge. The whole revolutionary intelligentsia suddenly became Social-Democratic, once it understood that this doctrine is constructed in conformity with its aspirations. It is a doctrine that has tirelessly affirmed the impossibility of a proletarian revolution in Russia *only so that* the Russian intelligentsia could organize its own bourgeois revolution, with the workers serving merely as cannon fodder. Now the intelligentsia is sure that its cause is on the right track. The Social-Democratic committees have long since issued corresponding instructions. On May Day the workers should not undertake strikes for the relief of labor, but should organize demonstrations "of a sharply political character" and street processions with banners inscribed "down with the autocracy." When the Petersburg workers nevertheless organized in May a series of strikes and for weeks on end stubbornly fought with the police and troops, the Petersburg committee remained highly displeased. It is clear that the workers will organize the First of May for their *own* cause, in defiance of all the committees.

"Conscious" workers! You who participate in the Social-Democratic committees, cast off the fables with which pharisaical science has ensnared your minds, fables about the "immaturity" of industry and the immaturity of the proletariat for socialism, about the "narrow and unsocialist interests of the worker" and the "elevated ideas" of the intelligentsia; cast off these fables for just a moment and you will hear the mighty voice of the worker masses, loudly ringing out in May of each year. You will understand that science says only what educated society needs for holding sway over the proletariat, while what the worker needs the worker *masses* themselves know better than anyone. Hear out these masses to the end, for they have spoken more than once, they have spoken when bayonets and bullets were directed at them.

May Day, they say, is not a day for revolting against the autocracy because it has not admitted the whole of educated bourgeois society into the government. The May struggle is a revolt against the bondage which even before you were born doomed you to hunger-strikes, ignorance, penal labor, and uncomplaining service to the learned world; a revolt against the robbery by which only the offspring of the ruling classes are the heirs of human wealth and knowledge, and any idiot among them can be your master.

These worker masses unschooled by the Social Democrats, whom you regard as understanding nothing, are choosing a path of struggle so true that by comparison with it all the ideas of the learned people about "emancipating the proletariat" are a patent deception.

The worker masses on May Day do not run to demonstrations to protect the banner of the *intelligent*. They present demands for alleviating the conditions of labor, and they present them for *immediate* satisfaction. They do not "demonstrate in favor of" shortening the working day, something the Social-Democratic intelligentsia devised as a way of responding to the workers' demands with promises, a way of duping them, as they have been duped for decades, by promising every year to get an eight-hour working day through parliament.

The worker masses put forth demands not because their bosses' businesses are successful or unsuccessful, but because they have felt themselves to be human beings and are rebelling against their slave status. And therefore the masses untaught by the intelligentsia understand that their cause lies not in clever politics, not in legal principles, but in the *strength and numbers* of those rebelling; that the broader their strike, the stronger and higher their demands will be. Therefore the worker masses use an infallible method in their struggle which Social-Democratic programs never hit upon. Their first object is to *broaden* their strike. Stopping work in their own factory, they go en masse to the next one to bring it to a halt. In this way whole cities rise up.

The "revolutionary" intelligentsia understands that spreading such a struggle to the entire state signifies the start of a proletarian revolution. And since that would abolish not only the police and the capitalists but would take away property from the intelligentsia itself, all it can do is to call such disturbances "wild outbursts of the rabble" and hope that the tsar's bayonets will be able to quiet the rabble down.

But the masses expect something else from you "conscious" workers. Pointing to the dead bodies with which they cover the streets of one town or another, year in and year out, they have long been appealing to you to abandon the intelligentsia and its plans for a bourgeois revolution and to work *for labor's cause, for a universal conspiracy of workers, for the May general strike.*

Notes

PREFACE

1. Paul Avrich, *The Russian Anarchists* (Princeton, N.J.: Princeton University Press, 1967), pp. 102–06. See also his "What Is 'Makhaevism'?" *Soviet Studies*, July 1965, pp. 66–75.

2. Anthony D'Agostino, *Marxism and the Russian Anarchists* (San Francisco: Germinal Press, 1977), chap. 4.

3. See his brief critique of Machajski's ideas in "Prologue to a Theory of Revolutionary Intellectuals," *Telos*, no. 26 (Winter 1975–76): 31, n. 48, and his *The Future of Intellectuals and the Rise of the New Class* (New York: Seabury Press, 1979).

CHAPTER 1. *Poland and Siberia*

1. Machajski's date of birth sometimes appears incorrectly in the literature. The above date is the one he himself gave in a biographical *anketa* dated December 8, 1925, otherwise unidentified but apparently an official Soviet questionnaire. A copy of the *anketa* is in the Max Nomad Archive, International Institute of Social History, Amsterdam.

2. Stanisława Nieuważny, "Machajski Jan Wacław," *Polski Słownik Biograficzny* 18 (Wrocław and Warsaw: Polska Akademia Nauk, 1973), p. 619. Max Nomad, in *Dreamers, Dynamiters and Demagogues: Reminiscences* (New York: Waldon Press, 1964), p. 104, terms Machajski's father a "poor clerk," without further explanation. None of the other sources shed light on the father's occupation or social background.

3. Biographical information on Machajski is sparse and scattered, and his early life can be reconstructed only in broad outline. There are two primary sources for this period. One is a brief, unpaged manuscript in Russian by Machajski's widow Vera (her real name was Roza, née Levin). It was written in 1933, presumably on the basis of what she had

been told by Machajski himself, although in fact much of the information it contains can be found in sources published earlier. The manuscript is in the Max Nomad Archive under the English title "Machajski's Life to 1903." A Polish translation of this manuscript, which, however, omits the names of Machajski's sympathizers and adherents in Siberia that are listed in the original, was published as Wiera Machajska, "Życie i poglądy Wacława Machajskiego," *Wiadomości* (London), March 4, 1962, p. 2. The second source consists of the diaries, letters, and reminiscences of Machajski's longtime friend, the novelist Stefan Żeromski. This material was utilized in a lengthy article by the Żeromski scholar Stanisław Pigoń, "Zygzaki przyjaźni. Jan Wacław Machajski–Stefan Żeromski," in *Miłe życia drobiazgi* (Warsaw: Państwowy Instytut Wydawniczy, 1964), pp. 346–405. In particular, Pigoń's article quotes from some of Machajski's unpublished letters to Żeromski. A note in the article (p. 360, n. 15) states that Pigoń was planning to include Machajski's letters in an edition of Żeromski's correspondence that he was preparing; Pigoń died in 1968, and to the best of my knowledge these letters have never been published. An earlier version of Pigoń's article, "Żeromski–Machajski. Zygzaki przyjaźni," appeared in 1961, in four installments, in the Cracow weekly *Życie literackie*. It is considerably less informed and less accurate than the later version, which includes material subsequently supplied to Pigoń, or brought to his attention, by Max Nomad. In a few places, however, the reworked version omits passages from Machajski's letters that were included in the original version, which will therefore be cited where necessary, as specified. It should be noted also that the entry on Machajski in the *Polski Słownik Biograficzny*, cited in note 2 above, contains an extensive bibliography, particularly of Polish sources and references, and a good summary of Machajski's Polish activities.

4. Stefan Żeromski, *Dzienniki*, ed. Jerzy Kądziela (Warsaw: Czytelnik, 1963–1970), editor's notes, 7:288, 510; Pigoń, "Zygzaki przyjaźni," p. 351; Nieuważny, "Machajski Jan Wacław," p. 619.

5. Useful summaries of the history of Russian Poland from the 1860s to the 1880s are W. J. Rose, "Russian Poland in the Later Nineteenth Century," in *The Cambridge History of Poland (1697–1935)*, ed. W. F. Reddaway et al. (Cambridge: Cambridge University Press, 1941), 387–408; R. F. Leslie et al., *The History of Poland since 1863* (Cambridge: Cambridge University Press, 1980), pp. 35–61; the relevant sections of Norman Davies, *God's Playground: A History of Poland* (New York: Columbia University Press, 1982), vol. 2; and Stanislaus A. Blejwas, *Realism in Polish Politics: Warsaw Positivism and National Survival in Nineteenth-Century Poland* (New Haven: Yale Concilium on International and Area Studies, 1984), esp. chap. 3.

6. The following account of the early development of Polish so-

cialism is drawn largely from three studies: Ulrich Haustein, *Sozialismus und Nationale Frage in Polen* (Cologne and Vienna: Böhlau Verlag, 1969), chaps. 1–9; Lucjan Blit, *The Origins of Polish Socialism: The History and Ideas of the First Polish Socialist Party, 1878–1886* (Cambridge: Cambridge University Press, 1971); and Norman M. Naimark, *The History of the "Proletariat": The Emergence of Marxism in the Kingdom of Poland, 1870–1887* (Boulder, Colo.: East European Quarterly, 1979).

7. "The Proletariat never successfully came to terms with the conundrum of trying to build an internationalist movement among a nationally oppressed people" (Naimark, *History of the "Proletariat,"* p. 122). More bluntly, Norman Davies terms the Proletariat "obsessively antinationalist" (*God's Playground*, 2:65).

8. Naimark, *History of the "Proletariat,"* pp. 130–32; Blit, *Origins of Polish Socialism*, pp. 71–72; Blejwas, *Realism in Polish Politics*, p. 171.

9. Stefan Żeromski, "Wybieg instynktu" [1920], *Elegie i inne pisma literackie i społeczne* (Warsaw: Wydawnictwo J. Mortkowicza, 1928), p. 12.

10. Ibid., p. 13.

11. Żeromski, *Dzienniki*, 2:50, 56, 127 (1884–1885).

12. Żeromski, "Wybieg instynktu," p. 14.

13. Żeromski, *Dzienniki*, 2:290 (October 2, 1885). Żeromski depicted the life of these gymnasium students in his novel *Syzyfowe prace*. One of the central characters in this novel, Andrzej Radek — from whom the future Bolshevik Karl Radek (whose real name was Sobelsohn) apparently borrowed his *nom de guerre* — is often considered to have been modeled on Machajski. As Pigoń has shown, however, this judgment requires considerable qualification ("Zygzaki przyjaźni," pp. 346–47, 351, and, concerning possible reflections of Machajski in Żeromski's other works of fiction, *passim*).

14. Feliks Perl (Res), *Dzieje ruchu socjalistycznego w zaborze rosyjskim (do powstania PPS)* (Warsaw: Książka i Wiedza, 1958), pp. 270–307.

15. Żeromski, *Dzienniki*, 3:271; see also 3:15, 265–66, and Pigoń, "Zygzaki przyjaźni," p. 359, where 1887 is meant, not 1888.

16. Żeromski, *Dzienniki*, 3:26.

17. Editor's note, ibid., 7:568.

18. Perl, *Dzieje*, pp. 273–74, 276–79, 304–05; Stanisław Kozicki, *Historia Ligi Narodowej (Okres 1887–1907)* (London: "Myśl Polska," 1964), pp. 38–45; Naimark, *History of the "Proletariat,"* pp. 191–97.

19. Pigoń, "Zygzaki przyjaźni," pp. 353–60.

20. Perl, *Dzieje*, pp. 304–05; Kozicki, *Historia*, pp. 39–40; L. Frances Millard, "The Founding of Zet: A Chapter in the History of Polish Socialism," *The Polish Review* 17, no. 4 (Autumn 1972): 42–61.

21. Machajski himself specified 1888 as the first year of his participation in the revolutionary movement. *Anketa*, December 8, 1925.

22. Żeromski, "W sprawie Machajskiego" [1911], *Elegie i inne pisma*, p. 104; *Dzienniki*, 5:27 (March 7, 1888).

23. Żeromski, *Dzienniki*, 6:72 (January 8, 1889).

24. Perl, *Dzieje*, pp. 350–54; Naimark, *History of the "Proletariat,"* pp. 197–98.

25. Żeromski, *Dzienniki*, 6:130 (March 28, 1889), and editor's note, 7:388.

26. Perl, *Dzieje*, pp. 295–303.

27. Zygmunt Zaremba, *Słowo o Wacławie Machajskim* (Paris: Księgarnia Polska w Paryżu, 1967), pp. 25–26, 140–41.

28. Nieuważny, "Machajski Jan Wacław," p. 619; Machajska, "Machajski's Life to 1903." According to Żeromski, who saw him in Switzerland, Machajski was without financial resources and worked in Zurich as a house painter. Żeromski, "W sprawie Machajskiego," p. 106; Pigoń, "Zygzaki przyjaźni," p. 360.

29. J. W. M., "Z życia konspiracyjnego w Kongresówce," *Pobudka. Czasopismo narodowo-socjalistyczne* (January 1892): 3. The article was printed under the heading "komunikat" without comment by the editors. See also Perl, *Dzieje*, pp. 460–61, which contains excerpts from the article, and Pigoń, "Zygzaki przyjaźni," p. 361.

30. J. W. M., "Z życia konspiracyjnego," p. 4.

31. Ibid.

32. Machajska, "Machajski's Life to 1903."

33. Ibid.

34. Leslie, *History of Poland*, p. 57; Naimark, *History of the "Proletariat,"* p. 187.

35. Perl, *Dzieje*, p. 420.

36. Quoted ibid., p. 421.

37. Ibid.

38. Ibid.

39. On the development of the PPS and SDKPiL, and the differences between them, see J. P. Nettl, *Rosa Luxemburg* (London: Oxford University Press, 1966), 1:60–62, 69–77; Haustein, *Sozialismus und Nationale Frage in Polen*, chaps. 16–19.

40. Machajska, "Machajski's Life to 1903."

41. Żeromski, "W sprawie Machajskiego," p. 104.

42. Ibid. Machajski also experienced the bitterness of personal loss in his university years. In 1887, one of his brothers shot himself, leaving a wife and three children, and Żeromski recorded that Machajski was deeply affected by the event. Żeromski, *Dzienniki*, 4:236 (September 27, 1887). Zygmunt Zaremba (*Słowo*, p. 20) suggests that the incident may

have convinced Machajski that only by devoting himself to a freely chosen cause and leaving some achievement behind could he give meaning to his existence, and may have hardened his resolve to stick to the path he was choosing. This must be regarded as entirely speculative, however.

43. Blit, *Origins of Polish Socialism*, p. 5; Blejwas, *Realism in Polish Politics*, pp. 54, 59.

44. Blit, *Origins of Polish Socialism*, p. 92. "'Today,' admitted the party's newspaper, 'the intelligentsia sphere belongs almost completely to the camp of the privileged class and defends its interests'" (quoted in Naimark, *History of the "Proletariat,"* p. 122).

45. For an argument stressing the impact of Machajski's rejection of Polish nationalism on his later views, see Anthony D'Agostino, "Intelligentsia Socialism and the 'Workers' Revolution': The Views of J. W. Machajski," *International Review of Social History* 14 (1969): 55–63; also D'Agostino, *Marxism and the Russian Anarchists*, pp. 113–22.

46. Machajska, "Machajski's Life to 1903."

47. G. Lur'e, "Iakutskaia ssylka v devianostye i deviatisotye gody," in *100 let iakutskoi ssylki: sbornik iakutskogo zemliachestva*, ed. M. A. Braginskii (Moscow: Izdatel'stvo vsesoiuznogo obshchestva politkatorzhan i ssyl'no-poselentsev, 1934), pp. 184–85.

48. Adam B. Ulam, *The Bolsheviks* (New York: Macmillan, 1965), pp. 127–38.

49. S. N. Iuzhakov, ed., *Bol'shaia entsiklopediia* (St. Petersburg: Prosveshchenie, 1900–09), 5:60.

50. "Avtobiografiia Mikhaila Ivanovicha Romas', 1866–1927 gg.," *Katorga i ssylka*, no. 4 (33) (1927): 164–65.

51. Lur'e, "Iakutskaia ssylka," p. 181. The others whom Vera Machajska names as Machajski's adherents in Viliuisk are Shetlikh, Porębski, and Ratynskii ("Machajski's Life to 1903").

52. Romas', "Avtobiografiia," p. 166. Another exile, named Vinokur, related: "When I arrived in Viliuisk in 1898, Machajski's theory had not been fully completed. He worked a great deal, studied Marxism a great deal, and had a magnificent knowledge of political economy" (quoted in Lur'e, "Iakutskaia ssylka," p. 183).

53. Machajska, "Machajski's Life to 1903."

54. Lur'e, "Iakutskaia ssylka," pp. 182–83.

55. The precise contents of these hectographed pamphlets, which have long since been lost, are somewhat uncertain. The printed edition of *Umstvennyi rabochii*, published under the pseudonym A. Vol'skii (Geneva, 1904–1905), consisted of three parts. In this edition, Machajski stated that he had composed part 1, "The Evolution of Social Democracy," in 1898, although internal evidence suggests that it was completed in 1899; part 2 of the Geneva edition, "Scientific Socialism," is dated 1900.

Except for some new introductory material, they appear to be reproductions of the Siberian essays, though we cannot know what changes, if any, Machajski may have made. Part 3 of the Geneva edition was written subsequent to Machajski's Siberian exile; it was based on lectures that Machajski gave in Geneva, and its two sections are dated August 1904 and May 1905. Therefore, the hectographed pamphlets that circulated among the Siberian exiles appear to have consisted of parts 1 and 2 of the later printed edition (although in some cases the exiles may have seen only part of this material). Trotsky, however, refers below to *three* booklets by Machajski which reached him at his place of exile. This makes matters less clear, but it could simply have been a faulty recollection on Trotsky's part.

56. Lur'e, "Iakutskaia ssylka," p. 183.

57. S. N. Gozhanskii, quoted ibid.

58. "Listy Jana Strożeckiego do Kazimierza Pietkiewicza," *Dzieje Najnowsze (Kwartalnik Instytuta Pamięci Narodowej)* 1, part 1 (January-March 1947): 133-35.

59. B. Gorev, "Pered vtorym s"ezdom (vospominanii)," *Katorga i ssylka*, no. 1 (8) (1924): 45.

60. L. Trotskii, "Vospominaniia o moei pervoi sibirskoi ssylke," ibid., no. 5 (1923): 92; see also Leon Trotsky, *My Life: An Attempt at an Autobiography* (New York: Scribner, 1930), p. 129.

61. Trotskii, "Vospominaniia," p. 94.

62. Trotsky, *My Life*, p. 143.

63. Machajska, "Machajski's Life to 1903." Although there is no reason to doubt that Machajski was in fact mistaken for Steklov, it seems a bit odd, because Steklov, by his own account, was unusually tall. This added to the difficulties of being a fugitive, for the police (at least according to Steklov), with their professional interest in physical prowess, took particular notice of tall men. Machajski, however, is described below as being of average height. See Iu. M. Steklov, "Kak ia bezhal iz Iakutki," *Izbrannoe* (Moscow: "Izvestiia," 1973), p. 80.

64. A. Shetlikh, "Pamiati V. K. Makhaiskogo," *Izvestiia*, February 24, 1926, p. 4.

65. Vera Machajska names as Machajski's adherents in Irkutsk "Vera Davidovna Gurari, A. F. Zholtkevich, Bronislav Konstantinovich Mitkevich, Pavel Aleksandrovich Verkhoturov, Comrade Chuprina" ("Machajski's Life to 1903").

66. The manifesto was reprinted as an appendix to the Geneva edition of *Umstvennyi rabochii*, part 1. It is translated in its entirety in the appendix to this volume.

67. P. A. Garvi, *Vospominaniia sotsialdemokrata* (New York: Fond po izdaniiu literaturnogo nasledstva P. A. Garvi, 1946), p. 291n.

68. Machajska, "Machajski's Life to 1903."

69. Garvi, *Vospominaniia*, p. 289. Imprisoned with Machajski were Mitkevich, Verkhoturov, and Chuprina, a worker whom Garvi identifies as a baker.

70. Ibid., pp. 292–95.

71. Ibid., pp. 288–89, 290–91, 295.

72. Ibid., pp. 297–311. Machajski and his fellow prisoners may have been inspired by a celebrated instance of prisoner resistance which had occurred under somewhat similar circumstances in the town of Iakutsk on March 22, 1889. A group of political prisoners was about to be taken from Iakutsk to Verkhoiansk and Sredne-Kolymsk, two particularly remote exile colonies which had been specifically designated for Jewish revolutionaries. When a newly appointed governor resolved on the strict enforcement of regulations which would have made the journey both more arduous and more dangerous, the prisoners decided to resist. In the course of their protest shooting broke out and six prisoners were killed and a number wounded; three others were subsequently hanged. Most of the survivors were exiled for several years to Viliuisk—which, of course, was to be Machajski's destination a few years later. The story of this incident is told in M. A. Braginskii and K. M. Tereshkovich, eds., *Iakutskaia tragediia—22 marta (3 aprelia) 1889 goda—sbornik vospominanii i materialov* (Moscow: Obshchestvo politicheskikh katorzhan i ssyl'no-poselentsev, 1925).

73. Shetlikh, "Pamiati V. K. Makhaiskogo."

74. Garvi, *Vospominaniia*, pp. 311–18.

75. See, for example, the testimony of B. A. Breslav, M. Vetoshkin, and, on Irkutsk, M. M. Konstantinov, discussed below, pp. 129–31.

CHAPTER 2. *The "New Class"*

1. Nomad, *Dreamers, Dynamiters and Demagogues*, p. 105.

2. Pigoń, "Zygzaki przyjaźni," p. 364.

3. Ibid., p. 365. This was most likely a reference to part 3 of *Umstvennyi rabochii*.

4. Ibid., p. 366.

5. Ibid., pp. 366–67.

6. Ibid., p. 366.

7. Nomad, *Dreamers, Dynamiters and Demagogues*, p. 104.

8. Ibid., pp. 105, 196. For Janina Berson's subsequent adventures, see ibid., pp. 196–201.

9. All references here are to the Geneva edition (see the bibliography for reprinted editions). An English translation of brief excerpts

from *Umstvennyi rabochii* appeared in V. F. Calverton, ed., *The Making of Modern Society: An Outline of Sociology* (New York: Random House, 1937), pp. 427–36. Gary Kern is currently preparing a full-scale translation.

Machajski used the pseudonym A. Vol'skii for this and some of his other works. He should not be confused either with the Social Democrat Stanislav Vol'skii, whose real name was A. V. Sokolov, or with Nikolai Valentinov, whose real name was N. V. Vol'skii.

10. Neither work bears the author's name. In subsequent notes I cite the edition of *Burzhuaznaia revoliutsiia* published in St. Petersburg, 1906.

11. K. Marks i F. Engel's *Sviatoe semeistvo. Izbrannye mesta s primechaniiami perevodchika*, 2 (St. Petersburg: "Novyi golos," 1906). Machajski's name did not appear on the work, but it is attributed to him by Max Nomad, "Machajski, Waclaw," *Encyclopedia of the Social Sciences* (New York: Macmillan, 1930–1935), 9:655. The contents of the notes are unmistakably Makhaevist.

12. A photocopy of the Russian text is in the Slavonic Division of the New York Public Library under the English title "An Unfinished Essay in the Nature of a Critique of Socialism."

13. Rabochii zagovor, no. 1 [Geneva], September–October, 1907 (actually pub. early 1908); A. Vol'skii, ed., *Rabochaia revoliutsiia*, no. 1, Moscow, June–July, 1918. The latter is reprinted in the 1968 edition of *Umstvennyi rabochii*.

14. *Umstvennyi rabochii*, part 1, p. 20. For the quotations from the *Communist Manifesto*, see Karl Marx and Frederick Engels, *Selected Works in Two Volumes* (Moscow: Foreign Languages Publishing House, 1955), 1:65, 53.

15. Ibid., p. 19.

16. Ibid., pp. 17, 24.

17. Ibid., pp. 25–26.

18. Ibid., pp. 24–25, 30.

19. Ibid., pp. 41, 45.

20. George Lichtheim, *Marxism: An Historical and Critical Study* (London: Routledge and Kegan Paul, 1961), pp. 124–29.

21. *Umstvennyi rabochii*, part 1, pp. iii–iv.

22. Ibid., p. 70.

23. Ibid., pp. 18–19.

24. Ibid., p. 21.

25. I have retained the term "intellectual worker," the translation most often used for Machajski's *umstvennyi rabochii*. Although imperfect (the word "intellectual" is somewhat misleading), it seems to me less so than such alternatives as "mental worker" or "brain worker," which have an odd ring to them in present-day English. Machajski himself used the term

rather loosely, but in general he applied it to anyone who engaged in nonphysical work requiring some education — including, therefore, not only "intellectuals" in the strict sense but all professional and managerial personnel and much of the white-collar work force. As to the latter, however, he never specified the point at which the line should — or could — be drawn between the least skilled or lowest paid "intellectual workers" and skilled manual workers. Since this was the line separating exploiters and exploited in Machajski's doctrines it required clarification, and critics of Makhaevism frequently raised the issue.

26. Karl Kautsky, "Die Intelligenz und die Sozialdemokratie," part 1, *Die Neue Zeit*, no. 27 (1894–1895): 14.

27. Ibid., p. 16.

28. Ibid.

29. Ibid., part 2, no. 28 (1894–1895): 44.

30. Ibid., p. 45.

31. Ibid., part 3, no. 29 (1894–1895): 75–76.

32. *Umstvennyi rabochii*, part 1, p. 77.

33. Ibid., p. 81.

34. *Burzhuaznaia revoliutsiia i rabochee delo*, p. 86.

35. *Bankrotstvo sotsializma XIX stoletiia*, p. 28.

36. "An Unfinished Essay in the Nature of a Critique of Socialism," pp. 7–8.

37. Ibid., p. 14.

38. *Umstvennyi rabochii*, part 1, pp. 80–82.

39. The "new middle class" was to become a factor in the controversy over Revisionism. Eduard Bernstein, in contrast to Kautsky, regarded its growth as a sign of the greater diffusion of wealth and the amelioration of the class struggle. See Peter Gay, *The Dilemma of Democratic Socialism: Eduard Bernstein's Challenge to Marx* (New York: Collier Books, 1962), pp. 208–12. Machajski agreed with Bernstein that this phenomenon contradicted Marx's doctrine of the disappearance of the middle classes, but he felt that it in no way mitigated the class struggle. It merely indicated that the proletariat's exploiters were more numerous and more protean than Marxist doctrine was capable of revealing (*Umstvennyi rabochii*, part 1, p. 79). The problem of accommodating the new middle class within the tenets of Marxism has continued to bedevil Marxists, with one recent critic declaring that "it would not be exaggerating unduly to suggest that the problem of the new petty bourgeoisie or middle class exercises the minds of latter-day western Marxists to the same degree as did the problem of the peasantry among an earlier generation" (Frank Parkin, *Marxism and Class Theory: A Bourgeois Critique* [London: Tavistock, 1979], pp. 16–17; for a discussion of some of the solutions that have been advanced, see pp. 15–27). Machajski may claim

some credit for being one of the first to recognize the great significance of the "new middle class."

40. Vernon L. Lidtke, *The Outlawed Party: Social Democracy in Germany, 1878–1890* (Princeton: N.J.: Princeton University Press, 1966), pp. 305–19.

41. Perl, *Dzieje*, p. 326; Nettl, *Rosa Luxemburg*, 1:89.

42. Lur'e, "Iakutskaia ssylka," p. 182; *Umstvennyi rabochii*, part 1, pp. 11–12.

43. *Umstvennyi rabochii*, part 1, pp. 25–26. He would undoubtedly have had some exposure to Bakunin's writings as a student, for they circulated widely among the Polish radical youth in the 1870s and 1880s.

44. Michel Bakounine, "Articles écrits pour le journal *L'Égalité*," in *Oeuvres*, ed. Max Nettlau and James Guillaume (Paris: P. V. Stock, 1895–1913), 5:135. A translation of these articles appears in Mikhail Bakunin, *From out of the Dustbin: Bakunin's Basic Writings 1869–1871*, trans. and ed. Robert M. Cutler (Ann Arbor: Ardis, 1985), pp. 111–25.

45. Ibid., p. 129.

46. Ibid., p. 141.

47. Ibid., pp. 143–44.

48. Ibid., p. 135.

49. Arthur Lehning, ed., *Archives Bakounine* (Leiden: E. J. Brill, 1961–81), 7:121. Written in 1870–1871 as part of a work entitled *L'Empire knouto-germanique et la Révolution sociale*, this essay was first published in 1882 under the title *Dieu et l'état*. Subsequently translated into a number of languages, it became the best known of Bakunin's writings.

50. Ibid., pp. 102–03.

51. Ibid., pp. 123–25.

52. Ibid., p. 464.

53. Ibid., 2:204. This piece, which appears under the title "Écrit contre Marx" in the *Archives Bakounine*, was first published in 1910 in the six-volume *Oeuvres* edited by Nettlau and Guillaume, 4:397–510.

54. Michael Bakunin, "Statism and Anarchy," translated by Marshall S. Shatz, in Shatz, ed., *The Essential Works of Anarchism* (New York: Bantam Books, 1971), p. 160. For the complete Russian text of this work, see *Archives Bakounine*, vol. 3.

55. Ibid., p. 163.

56. Ibid.

57. Ibid., p. 166. Bakunin in part is paraphrasing the passage in part 2 of the *Communist Manifesto* which lists ten measures to be taken when the proletariat becomes the ruling class. The "state engineers," however, are Bakunin's own embellishment. See Marx and Engels, *Selected Works*, 1:53–54.

58. An extensive bibliography on the subject appears in N. A. Rubakin, *Sredi knig* (Moscow: "Nauka," 1911–1915), 1:393–400. In Rubakin's apt words, devoting a special section of his bibliographical work to "the question of the intelligentsia" was justified on the grounds of "the interest this question has provoked in Russian society for many years, a question which remains, as before, obscure and unresolved either in theory or in practice" (p. 393).

Useful surveys of the various usages of the term include Ivanov-Razumnik, *Ob intelligentsii* (St. Petersburg: M. Stasiulevich, 1910), pp. 6–18; Martin Malia, "What Is the Intelligentsia?" *Daedalus*, Summer 1960, pp. 441–58; Alan P. Pollard, "The Russian Intelligentsia: The Mind of Russia," *California Slavic Studies* (Berkeley and Los Angeles: University of California Press, 1964), 3:1–32; V. R. Leikina-Svirskaia, *Intelligentsiia v Rossii vo vtoroi polovine XIX veka* (Moscow: "Mysl'," 1971), pp. 3–12; Michael Confino, "On Intellectuals and Intellectual Traditions in Eighteenth- and Nineteenth-Century Russia," *Daedalus*, Spring 1972, pp. 117–49.

59. On the genesis of the intelligentsia, see Marc Raeff, *Origins of the Russian Intelligentsia: The Eighteenth-Century Nobility* (New York: Harcourt, Brace and World, 1966); Marshall S. Shatz, *Soviet Dissent in Historical Perspective* (Cambridge: Cambridge University Press, 1980), chap. 2.

60. Quoted in John L. H. Keep, *The Russian Revolution: A Study in Mass Mobilization* (New York: Norton, 1976), p. 40.

61. Alexander Herzen, *From the Other Shore and The Russian People and Socialism* (Cleveland: Meridian Books, 1963), p. 63.

62. Peter Lavrov, *Historical Letters*, trans. James P. Scanlan, in *Russian Philosophy*, ed. James M. Edie et al. (Chicago: Quadrangle Books, 1965), 2:138. To cite two additional examples by equally prominent *intelligenty*, Peter Kropotkin renounced a promising scholarly career on the grounds that its pleasures would have been financed by the labors of hungry people, while Nicholas Mikhailovskii called the intelligentsia the "people's debtors" because its consciousness and ideals had been "granted us only by the age-old sufferings of the people." P. Kropotkin, *Memoirs of a Revolutionist* (Boston: Houghton, Mifflin, 1899), p. 240; N. K. Mikhailovskii, *Sochineniia*, (St. Petersburg: "Russkoe Bogatstvo," 1896–1897), 1:868.

63. Ivanov-Razumnik, *Istoriia russkoi obshchestvennoi mysli* (St. Petersburg: M. M. Stasiulevich, 1911), 1:6–7.

64. Ibid., p. 12.

65. P. Struve, *Kriticheskie zametki k voprosu ob ekonomicheskom razvitii Rossii* (St. Petersburg: I. N. Skorokhodov, 1894), p. 70.

66. Ibid., p. 71.

67. See, for example, George Plekhanov's response to Ivanov-Razumnik's *Istoriia russkoi obshchestvennoi mysli*: "Ideologiia meshcha-nina nashego vremeni," in *Sochineniia*, ed. D. Riazanov (Moscow: Gosudarstvennoe izdatel'stvo, 1923-1927), 14:274 (article first pub. 1908); V. V. Vorovskii, "Predstavliaet li intelligentsiia obshchestvennyi klass?" in *Sochineniia* (Leningrad: Gosudarstvennoe sotsial'no-ekonomicheskoe izdatel'stvo, 1931), 2:16-17 (article first pub. 1904). In the *Communist Manifesto*, Marx referred to "bourgeois ideologists, who had raised themselves to the level of comprehending theoretically the historical movement as a whole," and thus go over to the proletariat. Marx and Engels, *Selected Works*, 1:43.

68. Although precise figures are very difficult to establish, the impressive dimensions of this growth are outlined in L. K. Erman, "Sostav intelligentsii v Rossii v kontse XIX i nachale XX v.," *Istoriia SSSR*, no. 1 (1963): 161-77, and Leikina-Svirskaia, *Intelligentsiia v Rossii*.

69. For example, M. Tugan-Baranovskii, "Chto takoe obshchestven-nyi klass?" *Mir Bozhii*, January 1904, p. 72; and Vorovskii, "Predsta-vliaet li intelligentsiia obshchestvennyi klass?" pp. 14-15. In his contribution to the celebrated *Vekhi* symposium of 1909 — which generated an entire chapter of its own to the continuing debate over the nature of the intelligentsia — Struve anticipated that "in the course of economic development the intelligentsia will be 'bourgeoisified' . . . it will organically and spontaneously be drawn into the existing social structure and distributed among the different classes of society." Peter Struve, "The Intelligentsia and Revolution," in *Vekhi (Signposts): A Collection of Articles on the Russian Intelligentsia*, trans. and ed. Marshall S. Shatz and Judith Zimmerman, *Canadian Slavic Studies* (Summer 1970): 197. This approach continues to be reflected in the official Soviet definition of the intelligentsia as a special interclass "stratum" composed of people engaged in intellectual labor — an "objective" definition which raises many of the same problems that it did in the late nineteenth and early twentieth centuries. See Leopold Labedz, "The Structure of the Soviet Intelligentsia," *Daedalus*, Summer 1960, pp. 503-19.

70. V. V. [Vasilii Vorontsov], "Kapitalizm i russkaia intelligentsiia," in *Ot semidesiatykh godov k desiatisotnym: Sbornik statei* (St. Petersburg: "Obshchestvennaia pol'za," 1907), p. 27.

71. Ibid., p. 31.

72. V. V. [Vasilii Vorontsov], *Nashi napravleniia* (St. Petersburg: M. Stasiulevich, 1893), p. 84.

73. Ibid., p. 107.

74. A. S. Izgoev, "Intelligentsiia, kak sotsial'naia gruppa," *Obrazo-vanie*, no. 1 (January 1904): 74-75.

75. Ibid., pp. 79-81. In chapter 52, entitled "The Classes," Marx took

up the question of what constitutes a class and raised the issue of how "physicians and officials," for example, fit into the capitalist class structure of wage laborers, capitalists, and landlords. At that point the manuscript comes to an end (Karl Marx, *Capital*, trans. Ernest Untermann [Chicago: C. H. Kerr, 1932-33], 3:1031-32).

76. Izgoev, "Intelligentsiia," p. 84. Izgoev used the term *umstvennye rabotniki* here, and *intellektual'nye rabotniki* elsewhere in the article.

77. Ibid., p. 86.

78. Ibid., p. 89.

79. Ibid., p. 94. Other Marxists encountered similar difficulties in trying to keep the intelligentsia within their class framework. Tugan-Baranovskii, for example, in his article "Chto takoe obshchestvennyi klass?", concluded that "the intelligentsia is a social group with an indefinite class character" (p. 72). Vorovskii expressed dissatisfaction with Tugan-Baranovskii's rather vague formulation, then proceeded to distinguish from the intelligentsia as a whole "the progressive [*peredovaia*] intelligentsia," which appeared in the 1860s as the bearer of the ideas of progress and democracy ("Predstavliaet li intelligentsiia obshchestvennyi klass?", pp. 14-15).

80. Nomad, *Dreamers, Dynamiters and Demagogues*, pp. 197-98.

81. Evgenii Lozinskii, *Chto zhe takoe, nakonets, intelligentsiia? (Kritiko-sotsiologicheskii opyt)* (St. Petersburg: "Novyi golos," 1907). In the 259 pages of this book, which consists entirely of an elaboration of Machajski's ideas, Lozinskii referred once, in a footnote on p. 221, to "A. Vol'skii's" *Umstvennyi rabochii*, and quoted from the anonymously published *Burzhuaznaia revoliutsiia i rabochee delo* without indicating who wrote it (pp. 229-31). Ivanov-Razumnik, reviewing the book, virtually accused him of plagiarizing from "A. Vol'skii" (*Kniga*, no. 10 [January 11, 1907]: 6-7). In a rejoinder to Ivanov-Razumnik, Lozinskii denied the charge and pointed out that he had tried to give his analysis of the intelligentsia a firm theoretical and sociological grounding, whereas "Vol'skii" rejected social science of any sort. Evgenii Lozinskii, "Kak pishet retsenzii g. Ivanov-Razumnik," *Protiv techeniia*, no. 1 (February 20, 1907): 10-14. Whether Lozinskii succeeded in providing a "scientific" foundation for Makhaevism's view of the intelligentsia is questionable, but his attempt to do so does distinguish him from Machajski, who, as we shall see in chapter 4, deeply distrusted social theory as a deception of the working class.

82. Ibid., pp. 159-60.

83. Ibid., pp. 162-64.

84. Ibid., pp. 127-37.

85. Ibid., p. 167.

86. Ibid., pp. 179-81.

87. Ibid., p. 167.
88. D. Zaitsev, "Marksizm i makhaevshchina," *Obrazovanie*, no. 3 (March 1908): 57–61.
89. Ibid., pp. 61–64.
90. Ibid., pp. 68–69.
91. Ibid., p. 69.
92. Ibid., pp. 69–70.
93. Ivanov-Razumnik, *Ob intelligentsii*, pp. 133–34. Ivanov-Razumnik was not referring specifically to Zaitsev, whose article appeared after the original edition of Ivanov-Razumnik's book. In his reply to Ivanov-Razumnik's criticism of the Marxist position, however, Zaitsev observed, not very persuasively, that it merely indicated the inability of the "ethical subjectivists" to cope with such complex social phenomena as the rise of ideologists ("Marksizm i makhaevshchina," p. 70).
94. Ivanov-Razumnik, *Ob intelligentsii*, pp. 135–44. Lozinskii claimed that the very fact of revealing the intelligentsia's true character absolved the Makhaevists of guilt by association and indicated their sincere adoption of the proletariat's cause: "only an *intelligent* who has betrayed his own class of intellectual workers to the proletariat and laid his cards down before the workers — he alone, by this very act, will prove his devotion to the interests of the proletariat, will prove that he has renounced lies and deceit, class hypocrisy and trickery. But many are called and few are chosen" (*Chto zhe takoe, nakonets, intelligentsiia?* p. 145).
95. Ivanov-Razumnik, *Ob intelligentsii*, pp. 146–47.

CHAPTER 3. *The Intelligentsia and Socialism*

1. *Umstvennyi rabochii*, part 2, pp. 1–2.
2. Lozinskii, *Chto zhe takoe, nakonets, intelligentsiia?* pp. 76–77.
3. *Burzhuaznaia revoliutsiia i rabochee delo*, p. 36.
4. Ibid., pp. 36–37.
5. Ibid., p. 37. For a similar theory of socialism as a reaction to the feudal remnants of the *ancien regime*, hence its failure in the United States, see Louis Hartz, *The Liberal Tradition in America* (New York: Harcourt, Brace, 1955), pp. 5–9.
6. "Even in England — where, in the last half-century, educated society has been thoroughly content with the economy of the capitalists and the intelligentsia has long had a reputation among its colleagues as a bourgeois intelligentsia — even in this England, in the first half of the century the intelligentsia *en masse* attack the capitalists and form a huge socialist party, the so-called Chartist party, which promises to introduce

a communist order upon the achievement of universal suffrage" (*Burzhuaznaia revoliutsiia i rabochee delo*, p. 37). See also *Bankrotstvo sotsializma*, pp. 17–18.

7. *Burzhuaznaia revoliutsiia i rabochee delo*, pp. 37–38.

8. Ibid., p. 38.

9. Ibid.

10. At the end of part 1 of *Umstvennyi rabochii* (pp. 70–71), Machajski remarked that Marx himself had cast light on this more basic conflict, but the Marxists had failed to draw the necessary conclusions. Machajski refers to *The Eighteenth Brumaire of Louis Bonaparte* in this connection, but he probably had in mind *The Class Struggles in France, 1848–1850*, which seems to have provided the inspiration for his own treatment of the June Days. At the beginning of this work, Marx listed the elements of the bourgeoisie that made up the February opposition to Louis Philippe and the rule of the "finance aristocracy," and then included "the *ideological* representatives and spokesmen of the above classes, their savants, lawyers, doctors, etc., in a word: their so-called men of *talent*" (Marx and Engels, *Selected Works*, 1:140). Earlier in this first essay (p. 21), Machajski had mentioned, though only in passing, that the June Days showed the proletariat that its enemy was not just the capitalists but the "*privileged employees* of the capitalist state: lawyers, journalists, scholars."

11. *Burzhuaznaia revoliutsiia i rabochee delo*, pp. 40–41.

12. *Umstvennyi rabochii*, part 3, section 1, p. 10.

13. *Burzhuaznaia revoliutsiia i rabochee delo*, p. 44.

14. *Bankrotstvo sotsializma*, p. 27. Cf. *The Class Struggles in France, 1848–1850*, in Marx and Engels, *Selected Works*, 1:162.

15. "An Unfinished Essay," pp. 35–37.

16. Ibid., pp. 38–40.

17. *Umstvennyi rabochii*, part 1, p. vi.

18. Ibid., p. 79.

19. Ibid., part 2, p. 59. See also *Burzhuaznaia revoliutsiia i rabochee delo*, p. 47.

20. *Umstvennyi rabochii*, part 1, p. 60.

21. *Umstvennyi rabochii*, part 3, section 1, pp. 11–12; *Burzhuaznaia revoliutsiia i rabochee delo*, p. 48.

22. *Burzhuaznaia revoliutsiia i rabochee delo*, pp. 46–47.

23. Ibid., p. 38.

24. *Umstvennyi rabochii*, part 2, pp. 61–62.

25. *Burzhuaznaia revoliutsiia i rabochee delo*, pp. 56–57.

26. *Umstvennyi rabochii*, part 3, section 1, pp. 21–23.

27. *Bankrotstvo sotsializma*, p. 8.

28. *Burzhuaznaia revoliutsiia i rabochee delo*, p. 49.

29. *Umstvennyi rabochii*, part 3, section 1, p. 49; section 2, p. 5. If Peter Stearns's analysis is correct, Machajski's opinion of French syndicalism was not unwarranted: as in the case of German Social Democracy, however, he refused to concede the possibility that the movement's reformist tendencies might have arisen in response to the demands of its own constituents. "French workers as a whole, despite their impressive strike activity, sought only limited and often traditional goals before World War I. They frequently disappointed the positive hopes of their leaders" (Peter N. Stearns, *Revolutionary Syndicalism and French Labor: A Cause Without Rebels* [New Brunswick, N.J.: Rutgers University Press, 1971], p. 43; see also pp. 100–01).

30. *Umstvennyi rabochii*, part 3, section 1, pp. 36–37.

31. Ibid., p. 49.

32. Ibid., pp. 48–49.

33. Ibid., p. 53.

34. "An Unfinished Essay," p. 18.

35. *Burzhuaznaia revoliutsiia i rabochee delo*, p. 5.

36. Ibid., p. 4.

37. Ibid., p. 12.

38. Ibid., pp. 12–13.

39. *Rabochii zagovor*, p. 10.

40. Ibid., pp. 11–12.

41. Ibid., pp. 14–19.

42. Ivanov-Razumnik, *Ob intelligentsii*, pp. 72–73.

43. *Bankrotstvo sotsializma*, p. 8.

44. Ibid.

45. George Fischer, *Russian Liberalism: From Gentry to Intelligentsia* (Cambridge, Mass.: Harvard University Press, 1958), chap. 2.

46. Martin Malia, *Alexander Herzen and the Birth of Russian Socialism, 1812–1855* (Cambridge, Mass.: Harvard University Press, 1961), p. 118.

47. Ibid., p. 108.

48. Allan Wildman, *The Making of a Workers' Revolution: Russian Social-Democracy, 1891–1903* (Chicago: University of Chicago Press, 1967), p. 252.

49. Malia, *Alexander Herzen*, p. 115.

50. V. I. Lenin, *Polnoe sobranie sochinenii* (Moscow: Gosudarstvennoe izdatel'stvo politicheskoi literatury, 1959–65), 6:30–31.

51. On Lenin in exile, see Ulam, *The Bolsheviks*, pp. 125–38.

52. Lenin, *Polnoe sobranie sochinenii*, 7:82.

53. Ibid., 43:378.

CHAPTER 4. *The "Socialization of Knowledge"*

1. The text of *The Holy Family* is as follows:

Not suspecting that the category "Progress" is completely empty and abstract, Absolute Criticism is so profound as to recognize "progress" as being absolute and to explain retrogression by supposing a "personal adversary" of progress, the mass. . . .

All communist and socialist writers proceeded from the observation that, on the one hand, even the most favorable brilliant deeds seemed to remain without brilliant results, to end in trivialities, and, on the other, all progress of the spirit had so far been progress against the mass of mankind, driving it to an ever more dehumanized predicament. They therefore declare "progress" (see Fourier) to be an inadequate abstract phrase.

K. Marx and F. Engels, *The Holy Family* (Moscow: Foreign Languages Publishing House, 1956), p. 113.

2. *Sviatoe semeistvo*, pp. 43–47.
3. Ibid., pp. 45, 53.
4. Ibid., pp. 54–55.
5. Ibid., p. 47.
6. *Burzhuaznaia revoliutsiia i rabochee delo*, pp. 102–03.
7. "An Unfinished Essay," p. 29.
8. Ibid., p. 30.
9. *Sviatoe semeistvo*, p. 47. "By the very recognition of civilized society — the state — as a scientific object of sociology, socialist science becomes the guardian of the existing order, the extinguisher of the slaves' revolt, an ordinary learned lie" (*Bankrotstvo sotsializma*, p. 10).
10. *Umstvennyi rabochii*, part 3, section 2, p. 17. Ivanov-Razumnik pointed out that while Machajski denied that social institutions and social development conformed to any laws, he nonetheless claimed that slaves and masters arose "inevitably" in each generation (*Ob intelligentsii*, pp. 78–79). On the Marxist side, Zaitsev observed that Machajski's rejection of sociological theory did not seem to prevent his borrowing heavily from Marx's doctrines of class struggle and historical materialism ("Marksizm i makhaevshchina," p. 37).
11. *Umstvennyi rabochii*, part 3, section 1, pp. 39–40.
12. Ibid., p. 40.
13. *Burzhuaznaia revoliutsiia i rabochee delo*, pp. 79–80.
14. Ibid., pp. 80–81.
15. Max Nomad, *Aspects of Revolt* (New York: Bookman Associates, 1959), p. 101n.

16. *Umstvennyi rabochii,* part 2, p. 1.

17. Marx, *Capital,* 2:509.

18. Ibid., p. 504.

19. Ibid., pp. 502–03.

20. *Umstvennyi rabochii,* part 2, pp. 5–7, 30–34.

21. Ibid., p. 38.

22. Lozinskii, *Chto zhe takoe, nakonets, intelligentsiia?* pp. 227–29.

23. Marx, *Capital,* 2:493.

24. *Burzhuaznaia revoliutsiia i rabochee delo,* pp. 88–89. Bakunin, like Machajski, rejected any evolutionary view of history that seemed to sanction past phases. In regard to Comte and the positivists, he wrote: "fatalists in their own way, they consider all governments, even the worst, to be not only necessary but *salutary* transitions in the historical development of humanity"; as a result, they were not "casseurs de vitres" (*Archives Bakounine,* 2:250). Similarly, in regard to the Marxists, Bakunin wrote that he, too, regarded the facts of history as inevitable, but still felt it necessary to protest against them (ibid., pp. 195–98).

25. *Umstvennyi rabochii,* part 3, section 2, p. 11.

26. *Burzhuaznaia revoliutsiia i rabochee delo,* pp. 89–90.

27. Vernon L. Lidtke, "German Social Democracy and German State Socialism, 1876–1884," *International Review of Social History* 9 (1964): 220–24, and *The Outlawed Party,* pp. 171–75. For a lucid summary of Rodbertus's views, see Alexander Gray, *The Socialist Tradition: Moses to Lenin* (New York: Harper & Row, 1968), pp. 343–51.

28. *Umstvennyi rabochii,* part 2, pp. 21–22.

29. Ibid., p. 57.

30. Ibid., p. 13.

31. Ibid., pp. 51–52; see also "An Unfinished Essay," pp. 26–29.

32. "An Unfinished Essay," p. 25.

33. Żeromski, "W sprawie Machajskiego," *Elegie i inne pisma,* p. 110.

34. Adam B. Ulam, *The Unfinished Revolution* (New York: Vintage Books, 1964), p. 44.

35. H. Stuart Hughes, *Consciousness and Society: The Reorientation of European Social Thought, 1890–1930* (New York: Vintage Books, 1977), p. 42.

36. Ibid., pp. 17, 35–36, 96–97.

37. James Burnham, *The Machiavellians: Defenders of Freedom* (New York: John Day, 1943); Hughes, *Consciousness and Society,* pp. 78–82 and chap. 7.

38. Gaetano Mosca, *The Ruling Class,* trans. Hannah D. Kahn, ed. Arthur Livingston (Westport, Conn.: Greenwood Press, 1980), p. 284. Mosca published the book in 1896 and 1923.

39. Vilfredo Pareto, *Les systèmes socialistes*, vol. 5 of *Oeuvres Complètes*, ed. Giovanni Busino (Geneva: Librairie Droz, 1965), 2:455.

40. Robert Michels, *Political Parties*, trans. Eden and Cedar Paul (New York: The Free Press, 1962), p. 278.

41. Georges Sorel, *Reflections on Violence*, trans. T. E. Hulme and J. Roth (New York: Collier Books, 1961), p. 177. See also Burnham, *The Machiavellians*, part 4, and Hughes, *Consciousness and Society*, pp. 90–96 and chap. 5.

42. Sorel, *Reflections on Violence*, p. 135.

43. Michels, *Political Parties*, pp. 313–14.

44. The following exposition of Machajski's program appeared in somewhat different form in my "The Makhaevists and the Russian Revolutionary Movement," *International Review of Social History* 15 (1970): 239–50.

45. *Burzhuaznaia revoliutsiia i rabochee delo*, pp. 13–15.

46. F. F. Ridley, *Revolutionary Syndicalism in France: The Direct Action of Its Time* (Cambridge: Cambridge University Press, 1970), p. 1.

47. *Burzhuaznaia revoliutsiia i rabochee delo*, p. 71.

48. "An Unfinished Essay," pp. 44–45.

49. *Rabochii zagovor*, no. 1, pp. 73–74. This journal, no further issues of which were published, deals mainly with Makhaevism's revolutionary program. Though bearing the publication date September-October 1907, it contains an editorial note dated January 1908, which states that an unsuccessful attempt to publish it in Russia itself delayed its appearance by three months. It consists of five unsigned articles. In a letter to Żeromski in 1913, Machajski said that he had written all but the third article. The latter was the work of a French sculptor known as Pontiez, who had settled in Russia and been a fellow exile of Machajski's in Viliuisk (Pigoń, "Zygzaki przyjaźni," pp. 372, 394). I have cited only the articles by Machajski himself.

50. *Umstvennyi rabochii*, part 1, p. 36.

51. Ibid., part 2, pp. 79–80.

52. *Burzhuaznaia revoliutsiia i rabochee delo*, p. 100.

53. Ibid., pp. 100–01.

54. *Rabochii zagovor*, p. 77.

55. *Burzhuaznaia revoliutsiia i rabochee delo*, pp. 72–73.

56. Ibid., pp. 73–74.

57. Ivanov-Razumnik, *Ob intelligentsii*, pp. 86–88.

58. *Umstvennyi rabochii*, part 3, section 1, p. 6. It should be noted also that Machajski expressed disapproval of individual terrorism as practiced by some anarchists and SRs, on the grounds that such acts were

ineffective in attacking the foundations of the existing order. Ibid., pp. 48–49.

59. Pigoń, "Żeromski–Machajski," *Życie literackie*, no. 36 (502) (September 3, 1961): 4.

60. For example, *Burzhuaznaia revoliutsiia i rabochee delo*, pp. 72–73.

61. E. Lozinskii, *Gde vykhod?* (St. Petersburg: "Novyi golos," 1909), p. 14. See also Evgenii Lozinskii, *Itogi i perspektivy rabochego dvizheniia* (St. Petersburg: "Novyi golos," 1909), pp. 350–53.

62. *Gde vykhod?* pp. 15–16.

63. Aleksandr Blok, "Narod i intelligentsiia," in *Sochineniia v dvukh tomakh* (Moscow: Goslitizdat, 1955), 2:90–91. For some additional examples of this theme and an informative introduction, see Martha Bohachevsky-Chomiak and Bernice Glatzer Rosenthal, eds., *A Revolution of the Spirit: Crisis of Value in Russia, 1890–1918* (Newtonville, Mass.: Oriental Research Partners, 1982); also, James Billington, *The Icon and the Axe: An Interpretive History of Russian Culture* (New York: Vintage Books, 1970), pp. 504–18, and Bernice Glatzer Rosenthal, "Eschatology and the Appeal of Revolution: Merezhkovsky, Bely, Blok," *California Slavic Studies*, 11, ed. Nicholas V. Riasanovsky et al. (Berkeley and Los Angeles: University of California Press, 1980), pp. 105–39.

64. Shatz, ed., *The Essential Works of Anarchism*, pp. 175–77.

65. *Umstvennyi rabochii*, part 3, section 1, p. 16. The term Machajski uses here is *bosiaki-proletarii*. A *bosiak*, literally a "barefoot," usually referred to an urban vagrant, and in places Machajski did use the word in this sense, as the equivalent of "hooligan." In this case, however, he was obviously talking about Russia's migratory workers, i.e., peasants who left their villages, usually on a seasonal basis, for industrial or construction work.

66. *Burzhuaznaia revoliutsiia i rabochee delo*, pp. 49–50.

67. Ibid., p. 77.

68. For views on the significance of the peasant-worker generally similar to Machajski's, see Ulam, *The Unfinished Revolution*, chaps. 3–4, esp. pp. 59–72; Theodore Von Laue, "Russian Peasants in the Factory, 1892–1904," *Journal of Economic History*, March 1961, pp. 61–80, and "Russian Labor Between Field and Factory, 1892–1903," *California Slavic Studies*, 3 (1964): 33–65; Leopold Haimson, "The Problem of Social Stability in Urban Russia, 1905–1917," *Slavic Review*, December 1964, pp. 619–42, and March 1965, pp. 1–22.

69. *Umstvennyi rabochii*, part 1, p. 88. See the appendix to this volume.

70. *Burzhuaznaia revoliutsiia i rabochee delo*, p. 67.

71. *Rabochii zagovor*, pp. 12–13.

72. *Burzhuaznaia revoliutsiia i rabochee delo*, p. 97.

73. Ibid., pp. 77–78. See also *Rabochii zagovor*, pp. 80–82.

74. *Umstvennyi rabochii*, part 2, p. 55.

75. *Burzhuaznaia revoliutsiia i rabochee delo*, p. 111.

76. Ibid., p. 113.

77. *Rabochii zagovor*, pp. 62–63.

78. Ibid., p. 63.

79. Vera Machajska maintained that her husband never denied the necessity of socialism: he considered it a necessary, but not a sufficient condition for the emancipation of the workers. "Machajski's Views," unpaged manuscript in Russian, Max Nomad Archive. A Polish translation appears in Machajska, "Życie i poglądy Wacława Machajskiego," p. 2. Presumably, then, socialization of the means of production would at some point follow the "socialization of knowledge," but Machajski himself never spelled this out.

80. This clearly delineated Makhaevism from Leo Tolstoy's attitude toward culture, with which, somewhat improbably, it was compared (Ivanov-Razumnik, *Ob intelligentsii*, p. 90). The sage of Iasnaia Poliana had in fact been made aware of the Makhaevists' views through Evgenii Lozinskii's writings, but aside from approving of their criticism of the intelligentsia he could have little in common with them. After reading several of Lozinskii's works, Tolstoy informed him that "I fully share your thoughts on the significance of the intelligentsia's activity, as well as on parliaments." He then went on, politely but insistently, to preach his philosophy of nonviolence. For Tolstoy's letter to Lozinskii of January 26, 1909, see L. N. Tolstoi, *Polnoe sobranie sochinenii* (Moscow: Gosudarstvennoe izdatel'stvo khudozhestvennoi literatury, 1928–58), 79:47–48. Lozinskii printed Tolstoy's letter, along with his own comments on it, in a pamphlet entitled *Lev Tolstoi ob intelligentsii i rabochem voprose* (St. Petersburg: "Severnaia pechatnia," 1911).

81. *Burzhuaznaia revoliutsiia i rabochee delo*, pp. 94–95.

82. *Umstvennyi rabochii*, part 2, pp. 77–78. See also ibid., part 1, p. 82.

83. Ibid., part 1, p. 30.

84. Ibid., p. viii. The same formulation appears in *Burzhuaznaia revoliutsiia i rabochee delo*, p. 19.

85. *Umstvennyi rabochii*, part 1, p. xxiv.

86. Ibid., part 2, p. 55.

87. *Rabochii zagovor*, pp. 80–82. One of his complaints against anarchism was that, by renouncing state power, it "frees the law from direct attack on it by the worker masses" instead of helping them attain "domination over state power, over the law" (*Bankrotstvo sotsializma*, p. 4).

88. B. I. Gorev, "Apoliticheskie i antiparlamentskie gruppy," in *Ob-*

shchestvennoe dvizhenie v Rossii v nachale XX-go veka, ed. L. Martov et al. (St. Petersburg: "Obshchestvennaia pol'za," 1909–14), 3:530. Lozinskii declared that the particular form the state took was actually irrelevant to the workers: "The kind of central state regime that satisfies the demands of the working masses will be a matter of complete indifference to them; whether it be the contemporary order, or a republican or a socialist one—it is all the same to them." E. L., "Sotsializm i egalitarizm," *Protiv techeniia,* no. 3 (May 8, 1907): 11. He even went so far as to suggest that it might be preferable to retain the tsarist government. Absolutism had certain advantages over parliamentary governments, he stated, for in trying to preserve itself an absolutist regime sometimes offered the proletariat protection against the bourgeoisie (*Itogi parlamentarizma. Chto on dal i mozhet li on chto-libo dat' rabochim massam?* [St. Petersburg: "Novyi golos," 1907], pp. 56–57).

89. M. R-skii in *Burevestnik* (March–April 1908): 31–32.

90. Donald C. McKay, *The National Workshops: A Study in the French Revolution of 1848* (Cambridge, Mass.: Harvard University Press, 1933), pp. 136–50.

91. Robert Eugene Johnson, *Peasant and Proletarian: The Working Class of Moscow in the Late Nineteenth Century* (New Brunswick, N.J.: Rutgers University Press, 1979).

92. *Burzhuaznaia revoliutsiia i rabochee delo,* p. 115.

93. Nomad, *Aspects of Revolt,* pp. 103–04, and *Dreamers, Dynamiters and Demagogues,* pp. 202–05. Nomad bases his conclusion in part on a conversation he had in 1934 with Vera Machajska in which, speaking for herself and her late husband, she claimed quite frankly that they had been thinking all along in terms of a seizure of power.

CHAPTER 5. *The "Workers' Conspiracy" and the Russian Revolutionary Movement*

1. Franco Venturi, *Roots of Revolution,* trans. Francis Haskell (London: Weidenfeld and Nicolson, 1960), pp. 512–15, 538–40; Reginald E. Zelnik, "Populists and Workers: The First Encounter Between Populist Students and Industrial Workers in St. Petersburg, 1871–74," *Soviet Studies,* October 1972, pp. 265–69; Pamela Sears McKinsey, "The Kazan Square Demonstration and the Conflict Between Russian Workers and *Intelligenty,*" *Slavic Review,* Spring 1985, pp. 89–90, 101–03.

2. For accounts of Tochiskii's life and the activities of his Petersburg organization, see R. A. Kazakevich, *Sotsial-demokraticheskie organizatsii Peterburga kontsa 80-kh–nachala 90-kh godov (Kruzhki P. V. Tochisskogo i M. I. Brusneva)* (Leningrad: Izdatel'stvo Leningradskogo

Universiteta, 1960), pp. 31–76; N. K. Lisovskii, *P. V. Tochisskii* (Moscow: Gosudarstvennoe izdatel'stvo politicheskoi literatury, 1963); Norman M. Naimark, *Terrorists and Social Democrats: The Russian Revolutionary Movement Under Alexander III* (Cambridge, Mass.: Harvard University Press, 1983), pp. 84–89. Tochiskii himself spelled his name with one *s*, as I have done here, but this surname is usually spelled with two, which accounts for the inconsistency in the literature about him.

3. Andrei Breitfus, "Tochiskii i ego kruzhok," *Krasnaia letopis'*, no. 7 (1923): 326.

4. M. Lebedeva (Tochisskaia), "K biografii P. V. Tochisskogo (Vospominaniia sestry)," in *Istoriko-revoliutsionnyi sbornik*, ed. V. I. Nevskii (Moscow-Leningrad: Gosudarstvennoe izdatel'stvo, 1926), 3:298.

5. Breitfus, "Tochiskii," p. 326.

6. Lebedeva, "K biografii," p. 298; Breitfus, "Tochiskii," p. 328.

7. N. L. Sergievskii, "O kruzhke Tochiskogo. Doklad departamenta politsii ministru vnutrennikh del," *Krasnaia letopis'*, no. 7 (1923): 354–55, 367–68. Tochiskii remained active in the labor movement but does not seem to have maintained his anti-intelligentsia sentiments, or at least not to the same degree. Soviet works such as Lisovskii's claim that he eventually joined the Bolsheviks and was killed during the civil war, but this account is open to question. Tochiskii's sister, for example, refers to his suicide in 1918 (Lebedeva, "K biografii," p. 299; Naimark, *Terrorists*, pp. 264–65, n. 82).

In his recent study of underground groups in the 1880s and early 1890s, Norman Naimark presents a mixed picture of worker-intelligentsia relations. The relationship between intelligentsia propagandists and workers within these organizations, he concludes, "was usually a good one, though exceptions were numerous and general statements difficult to substantiate. There was trust and there were instances of enmity" (*Terrorists*, p. 240). Even aside from the Tochiskii Circle, there were cases of disagreement and friction arising from social and cultural differences, intelligentsia efforts to politicize the movement at the expense of economic issues, and the desire of workers for greater control over their organizations (ibid., pp. 49, 194–96). Interestingly, even at this early date the tsarist authorities had become aware of these frictions and attempted to exploit them. In something of a preview of the Zubatov experiment, Major-General V. S. Strel'nikov, a military prosecutor posted to Kiev in the wake of Alexander II's assassination in 1881, attempted to drive a wedge between the workers and the propagandists (whom he considered to be "Jewish intellectuals"). He released or failed to prosecute arrested workers and seems to have made some headway in winning their confidence. He was assassinated by terrorists in March 1882 (ibid., pp. 51–52).

8. Ezra Mendelsohn, *Class Struggle in the Pale: The Formative Years of the Jewish Workers' Movement in Tsarist Russia* (Cambridge: Cambridge University Press, 1970), pp. 56-57.

9. Ibid., p. 57. See also his "Worker Opposition in the Russian Jewish Socialist Movement from the 1890s to 1903," *International Review of Social History* 10 (1965): 271-72.

10. Mendelsohn, *Class Struggle*, pp. 57-62.

11. Ibid., pp. 126-39; also, "Worker Opposition," pp. 276-77.

12. For the history of the Russian Social-Democratic movement to the 1905 revolution I have drawn on Leopold H. Haimson, *The Russian Marxists and the Origins of Bolshevism* (Cambridge, Mass.: Harvard University Press, 1955); Dietrich Geyer, *Lenin in der Russischen Sozialdemokratie* (Cologne: Böhlau Verlag, 1962); Richard Pipes, *Social Democracy and the St. Petersburg Labor Movement, 1885-1897* (Cambridge, Mass.: Harvard University Press, 1963); J. L. H. Keep, *The Rise of Social Democracy in Russia* (Oxford: Clarendon Press, 1963); and Wildman, *Making of a Workers' Revolution*. Significantly, all of these works focus on the relationship between intelligentsia and workers.

13. Peterburzhets [K. M. Takhtarev], *Ocherk peterburgskogo rabochego dvizheniia 90-kh gg.* (London: Tip. Zhizni, 1902), pp. 61-72, provides a first-hand account of these events. In his treatment of the St. Petersburg labor movement in this period, Richard Pipes emphasizes the cleavage between workers and intelligentsia and the labor movement's vigorous independence of the Social-Democratic *intelligenty*. "Labor," he concludes, "was mainly concerned with intellectual and economic self-improvement, the Social-Democratic intelligentsia mainly with politics . . . the workers never yielded to the socialists' efforts to politicize their movement; nor did they concede leadership to the intelligentsia" (*Social Democracy*, p. 117). Allan Wildman, in *Making of a Workers' Revolution*, takes exception to this view (pp. 28-29, n. 2, 59-60, 73-77). He credits the Social Democrats in the nineties with an important role in fostering a mass labor movement; he argues, however, that they proved incapable of dealing tactfully with it once they had helped call it into being and soon "lost the ties that once firmly bound [the Social-Democratic intelligentsia] to the working class" (p. 117). Much of the rest of his book traces the increasingly bitter process of alienation and distrust that marked intelligentsia-worker relations within the Russian Social-Democratic party up to 1903. Reginald Zelnik expresses support for Wildman's position and finds that hostility toward the intelligentsia was to be found not just among workers who rejected politics but also among politically minded and militantly revolutionary workers. "Russian Bebels: An Introduction to the Memoirs of Semen Kanatchikov and Matvei Fisher," part 2, *Russian Review*, October 1976, pp. 425-37. He also describes (ibid., pp.

425–26, n. 37) the dilemma Soviet historiography faces in trying to deal with anti-intelligentsia sentiment among the workers, since it was often directed at Marxists. While the issue of the intelligentsia's contribution to the formation of the Russian labor movement is not directly germane here, these different positions lend support to the central point of this chapter: that anti-intelligentsia sentiment was a recurrent and pervasive phenomenon, emanating from many different levels of the working class.

14. The first two issues were published in St. Petersburg, and the editorial operation was then shifted to Berlin. The newspaper became an official organ of the Petersburg Union of Struggle and of the Social-Democratic party. Toward the end of its existence both its tone and its format changed considerably. By issue no. 12, in 1901, the emphasis had shifted to political matters, and most of the paper was taken up with long, theoretical articles. Wildman, *Making of a Workers' Revolution*, chap. 5, provides a detailed history of *Rabochaia mysl'*.

15. Translated in Pipes, *Social Democracy*, p. 129.

16. Ibid., p. 130.

17. "Zametki," *Rabochaia mysl'*, no. 4 (October 1898): 4.

18. Ibid.

19. "Nash iubilei," ibid., no. 5 (January 1899): 1. A special supplement, issued in September 1899, provided a theoretical elaboration of this viewpoint and reflected the influence of Eduard Bernstein.

20. He termed the students "the future administrators, directors, engineers, judges, procurators" of the proletariat (*Umstvennyi rabochii*, part 3, section 1, p. 23).

21. Ibid., pp. 21–23, 59–60; *Burzhuaznaia revoliutsiia i rabochee delo*, pp. 64–65.

22. V. Levitskii [Tsederbaum], *Za chetvert' veka* (Moscow-Leningrad: Gosudarstvennoe izdatel'stvo, 1926–27), 1: part 2, p. 58.

23. Ibid., pp. 133–62; Wildman, *Making of a Workers' Revolution*, pp. 103–07, 243–44.

24. Garvi, *Vospominaniia*, p. 109.

25. Ibid., pp. 107–12; Jeremiah Schneiderman, *Sergei Zubatov and Revolutionary Marxism: The Struggle for the Working Class in Tsarist Russia* (Ithaca: Cornell University Press, 1976), pp. 295, 329–30; Wildman, *Making of a Workers' Revolution*, pp. 110–12.

26. N. Angarskii, ed., *Doklady sots.-demokraticheskikh komitetov vtoromu s"ezdu RSDRP* (Moscow-Leningrad: 1930), esp. p. 93, on St. Petersburg, and pp. 244–45, on Tula.

27. Wildman, *Making of a Workers' Revolution*, pp. 107–10, 116, n.48; see also Keep, *Rise of Social Democracy*, pp. 95–103. In Wildman's words, "there is hardly a single center of Social Democratic activity which did not encounter similar tendencies" (p. 116, n.48).

28. Petr Garvi, describing the rise of a "workers' opposition" in Odessa, chose to blame it in part on the spread of anti-intelligentsia sentiment from the Bund (*Vospominaniia*, p. 109).

29. V. Akimov-Makhnovets, "Stroiteli budushchego," part 2, *Obrazovanie*, no. 5 (May 1907): 70.

30. Schneiderman, *Sergei Zubatov*, p. 63, n.39. This is the most thorough study of the Zubatov episode to have appeared in English.

31. "Trepov o rabochem dvizhenii. Doklad moskovskogo ober-politseistera (po okhrannomu otdeleniiu) Trepova, moskovskomu general-gubernatoru, velikomu kniaziu Sergeiu," dated April 8, 1898, *Rabochaia mysl'*, no. 6 (April 1899), *Prilozhenie*, p. 1. The newspaper printed Trepov's report with only a mild editorial comment referring to him ironically as "our new colleague." Interestingly, Trepov's report was also published in the other newspaper of Economist persuasion, *Rabochee delo*.

32. Ibid.

33. On Zubatov's early career, see K. Tereshkovich, "Moskovskaia molodezh' 80-kh godov i Sergei Zubatov," *Minuvshie gody*, no. 5-6 (May–June 1908): 207-15.

34. D. Zaslavskii, "Zubatov i Mania Vil'bushevich," *Byloe*, no. 3 (31) (1918): 117.

35. N. A. Bukhbinder, "Nezavisimaia evreiskaia rabochaia partiia. Po neizdannym arkhivnym dokumentam," *Krasnaia letopis'*, no. 2-3 (1922): 208-09.

36. B. M. Frumkin, "Zubatovshchina i evreiskoe rabochee dvizhenie," *Perezhitoe*, 3 (St. Petersburg, 1911), pp. 202-09; Zaslavskii, "Zubatov i Mania Vil'bushevich," pp. 99-128; A. M. Chemerisskii, in "Novoe o zubatovshchine," *Krasnyi arkhiv* 1 (1922): 315-16. Zubatov himself referred to the large number of "green youths" in the Jewish labor movement ("Novoe o zubatovshchine," p. 292). It should be noted, however, that veteran workers and revolutionaries also succumbed to his persuasion (Schneiderman, *Sergei Zubatov*, p. 81).

37. Bukhbinder, "Nezavisimaia . . . partiia," pp. 242-43.

38. Frumkin, "Zubatovshchina," pp. 211-13. See also Mendelsohn, "Worker Opposition," pp. 279-80, and *Class Struggle*, pp. 139-52.

39. Bukhbinder, "Nezavisimaia . . . partiia," pp. 210-16; "Novoe o zubatovshchine," p. 293.

40. "Novoe o zubatovshchine," p. 293.

41. Frumkin, "Zubatovshchina," pp. 228-29; A. Morskoi, *Zubatov-shchina. Stranichka iz istorii rabochego voprosa v Rossii* (Moscow: I. D. Sytin, 1913), pp. 123-24.

42. The connection between Zubatovism and Zionism, to which Vil'bushevich, Genrikh Shaevich in Odessa, and other Zubatovites adhered, is only one of the many bizarre aspects of this episode. See Schnei-

derman, *Sergei Zubatov*, pp. 232–34, 252–54; Mendelsohn, *Class Struggle*, p. 150, n.2. Another is the spectacle of the tsarist police acquiescing in, or in some cases engaging in, illegal activities in behalf of the Zubatov organizations (Schneiderman, *Sergei Zubatov*, pp. 149, 244–45).

43. Schneiderman, *Sergei Zubatov*, pp. 103–04.

44. M. Grigor'evskii, *Politseiskii sotsializm v Rossii (Zubatovshchina)* (St. Petersburg: "Obrazovanie," 1906), pp. 13–14; Schneiderman, *Sergei Zubatov*, pp. 194–95.

45. On developments in Moscow, see Schneiderman, *Sergei Zubatov*, chaps. 4–6.

46. Bukhbinder, "Nezavisimaia . . . partiia," p. 230.

47. N. A. Bukhbinder, "O zubatovshchine," *Krasnaia letopis'*, no. 4 (1922): 307.

48. Ibid., pp. 310–11.

49. Bukhbinder, "Nezavisimaia . . . partiia," p. 270.

50. Ibid., p. 281.

51. Schneiderman, *Sergei Zubatov*, pp. 304, 310–11.

52. On the Odessa general strike, see ibid., chaps. 12–13.

53. Shaevich, for example, wrote after his arrest: "My exile will force all the revolutionaries to understand that I was never a servant of the government, only a friend of the workers." "K istorii zubatovshchiny," *Byloe*, no. 1 (23) (July 1917): 93. There seems little reason to doubt his idealism, or that of other participants in the movement.

54. Letter of Zubatov to L. A. Rataev, April 2, 1902, "Novoe o Zubatovshchine," p. 314.

55. I have come across no interchange of personnel between the two, nor any evidence that Machajski's ideas influenced the Zubatovites.

56. *Umstvennyi rabochii*, part 3, section 1, pp. 10, 21.

57. Quoted in V. Astrov, "Sotsial-demokratiia pered revoliutsiei 1905 goda," in *1905: Istoriia revoliutsionnogo dvizheniia v otdel'nykh ocherkakh*, ed. M. N. Pokrovskii (Moscow-Leningrad: Gosudarstvennoe izdatel'stvo, 1925–27), 2:115. Astrov comments that here the workers' basically healthy desire for party unity assumed somewhat unwholesome forms "which smack of Makhaevism" (pp. 115–16).

58. Akimov-Makhnovets, "Stroiteli budushchego," part 1, *Obrazovanie*, no. 4 (April 1907): 107; S. I. Somov, "Iz istorii sotsial-demokraticheskogo dvizheniia v Peterburge v 1905 godu," part 2, *Byloe* (May 1907): 169–71.

59. Somov, "Iz istorii," part 2, p. 172.

60. Ibid., pp. 173–74. Cf. the complaint of a dissatisfied group of workers in Cherkassy, which adopted the familiar name "Workers' Will": "Even now we see that all the higher posts are occupied by intellectuals. One has to hunt for workers with a lamp. . . . When a worker, even

if an 'advanced' one, suggests some means of improving the agitation, he is told to mind his business and do as he is told, so that the voice of every worker in this so-called 'workers' party' is reduced to nil." From a leaflet dated May 18, 1905, quoted in Keep, *Rise of Social Democracy*, p. 169.

61. Cited in Laura Engelstein, *Moscow, 1905: Working-Class Organization and Political Conflict* (Stanford: Stanford University Press, 1982), p. 122n. In reference to 1905, Engelstein comments: "Repression . . . drove large sections of educated society, not merely the self-styled revolutionary intelligentsia, toward a symbolic alliance with the working class. A flesh-and-blood alliance was not always possible, since the ordinary worker was more often than not hostile to all intellectuals and professionals" (p. 122). A different view, however, is presented in Victoria E. Bonnell's *Roots of Rebellion: Workers' Politics and Organizations in St. Petersburg and Moscow, 1900–1914* (Berkeley and Los Angeles: University of California Press, 1983), pp. 130–33, 164, which argues that in some cases workers actively sought the assistance of intelligentsia organizers, who were instrumental in forming trade unions in 1905.

62. On efforts to democratize the party, see Solomon M. Schwarz, *The Russian Revolution of 1905*, trans. Gertrude Vakar (Chicago: University of Chicago Press, 1967), chap. 5, esp. pp. 209–30; Abraham Ascher, *Pavel Axelrod and the Development of Menshevism* (Cambridge, Mass.: Harvard University Press, 1972), chap. 7.

63. Parts of the following section, in more summary form, appeared in my article "The Makhaevists and the Russian Revolutionary Movement."

64. B. A. Breslav, "Chtenie Gor'kogo v tiur'me," *Katorga i ssylka*, no. 4 (41) (1928): 123. The line is spoken by Foma in act 1: "Ono, pozhalui, barstvo-to—kak ospa . . . i vyzdoroveet chelovek, a znaki-to ostaiutsia" (M. Gor'kii, *Polnoe sobranie sochinenii* [Moscow: "Nauka," 1968–76], 7:124).

65. Breslav, "Chtenie Gor'kogo v tiur'me," p. 123.

66. Ibid.

67. Ibid., p. 124. This reminiscence was originally given as a speech at a Gorky evening at the Obshchestvo politkatorzhan i ssyl'no-poselentsev, which published *Katorga i ssylka*. Curiously, it ends with no criticism, by author or editors, of Makhaevism or of anti-intelligentsia attitudes.

68. M. Vetoshkin, "Stranichki revoliutsionnogo proshlogo," *Katorga i ssylka*, no. 2 (63) (1930): 8.

69. Ibid., pp. 10–11.

70. Ibid., no. 3 (64) (1930): 75.

71. Ibid.

72. Ibid., p. 76. Social and cultural envy of this sort seems to have been common among "conscious" workers who took the intelligentsia as their model but lacked the formal education to measure up to it. The memoirs of the Bolshevik worker Semen Kanatchikov contain strong expressions of this sentiment (*A Radical Worker in Tsarist Russia: The Autobiography of Semën Ivanovich Kanatchikov*, trans. and ed. Reginald E. Zelnik [Stanford, Calif.: Stanford University Press, 1986], pp. 91–92, 102–08, 382–84). See also Zelnik, "Russian Bebels," part 2, *Russian Review* (October 1976): 432–34. Kanatchikov's memoirs are a virtual compendium of the various sources of worker hostility, or at least deep ambivalence, in regard to the intelligentsia. Besides the kind of cultural and educational love-hate feelings mentioned above, he or the other workers whose views he reports voice resentment over the intelligentsia's material privileges and social ties to the propertied classes (even in prison and exile this created frictions), suspicion that the intelligentsia would at some point abandon the workers' cause, and even accusations that *intelligenty* were economic parasites on the workers. Although Kanatchikov never mentions Makhaevism, it is clear from his account that the intelligentsia's relationship to the privileged classes, and hence the workers' relationship to the intelligentsia, were serious and recurrent issues among "conscious" workers like Kanatchikov and his friends (*A Radical Worker*, pp. 142–43, 204–05, 248–49, 283, 369).

73. M. M. Konstantinov, "Dvadtsat' let nazad," *Katorga i ssylka*, no. 8–9 (45–46) (1928): 113.

74. Ibid., p. 114.

75. On Lur'e's Social-Democratic career, see Wildman, *Making of a Workers' Revolution*, pp. 192–98, 203–06. On his activities in the PPS, see Haustein, *Sozialismus und Nationale Frage in Polen*, pp. 237–38.

76. B. L. Eidel'man, "Imeniny Rossiiskoi Kommunisticheskoi Partii," in *K dvadtsatipiatiletiiu pervogo s"ezda partii (1898–1923)* (Moscow-Petrograd: Gosudarstvennoe izdatel'stvo, 1923), p. 37. In this respect, his views had a good deal in common with Avram Gordon's "opposition" in the Bund. Mendelsohn, *Class Struggle*, pp. 58–59. Lur'e, however, was a political-minded and highly militant revolutionary.

77. S. Gel'man and N. Kudrin, "Pamiati Romanovtsa M. V. Lur'e," *Katorga i ssylka*, no. 56 (1929): 155.

78. Ibid.; S. Gel'man, "Pervaia podpol'naia tipografiia gruppy 'Rabochee Znamia,'" *Katorga i ssylka*, no. 6 (27) (1926): 55.

79. D. Gershanovich, "O Moisee Vladimiroviche Lur'e," in *K dvadtsatipiatiletiiu pervogo s"ezda partii*, pp. 173–74.

80. Eidel'man, "Imeniny," p. 37. No name or place is given.

81. E. Mikhailova, "Iz kommentariev k 'Chto delat'?'. Gruppa

samoosvobozhdeniia rabochego klassa," *Krasnaia letopis'*, no. 1 (12) (1925): 239, n.2.

82. Naimark, *Terrorists and Social Democrats*, pp. 123, 224–25.

83. Mikhailova, "Iz kommentariev," pp. 243–44.

84. Ibid., pp. 241, 246–48; N. P. Paialin, *Zavod imeni Lenina, 1857–1918* (Moscow-Leningrad: Gosudarstvennoe sotsial'no-ekonomicheskoe izdatel'stvo, 1933), pp. 78–80. Lenin lumped the Group for the Self-Emancipation of the Working Class together with *Rabochaia mysl'* in his denunciation of Economism in *Chto delat'?* See his *Polnoe sobranie sochinenii*, 6:43–44.

85. Vera Machajska, "Machajski's Life to 1903."

86. Levitskii, *Za chetvert' veka*, 1: part 2, p. 172.

87. Garvi, *Vospominaniia*, p. 291; I. I. Genkin, *Po tiur'mam i etapam* (Petersburg: Gosudarstvennoe izdatel'stvo, 1922), pp. 288–90.

88. Genkin, *Po tiur'mam*, pp. 287–88. Genkin, a Social Democrat, provides some valuable information on the Makhaevists, but his memoirs contain numerous inaccuracies and unverified assertions and have to be used with caution.

89. Vera Machajska, letter to Max Nomad (in Russian), July 25, 1932, Max Nomad Archive (an English translation, under the title "Short History of the Machajski Group Written by His Wife," typescript, is also in the Max Nomad Archive); "Ocherk anarkhicheskogo dvizheniia v Odesse," *Buntar'* (December 1, 1906): 30–32; Mikhail Znamenskii, "Tiuremnye vpechatleniia," in *Al'manakh: Sbornik po istorii anarkhicheskogo dvizheniia v Rossii* (Paris, 1909), 1:149–55. According to Genkin, some Socialist-Revolutionaries were also members of this group. "Sredi preemnikov Bakunina (Zametki po istorii rossiiskogo anarkhizma)," *Krasnaia letopis'*, no. 1 (22) (1927): 190.

90. Belostochanin, "Iz istorii anarkhicheskogo dvizheniia v Belostoke," *Al'manakh*, 1:7.

91. Vera Machajska to Max Nomad, July 25, 1932.

92. Genkin, "Sredi preemnikov Bakunina," p. 177; Avrich, *Russian Anarchists*, pp. 48–49, 67–68.

93. "Tovarishchu i drugu," *Buntar'* (December 1, 1906): 32–34; D. I. Novomirskii, "Anarkhicheskoe dvizhenie v Odesse," in A. A. Borovoi, ed., *Mikhailu Bakuninu, 1876–1926* (Moscow: "Golos truda," 1926), p. 248.

94. Avrich, *Russian Anarchists*, chap. 4; D'Agostino, *Marxism and the Russian Anarchists, passim*.

95. [D. I.] Novomirskii, *Iz programmy sindikal'nogo anarkhizma* (n. p., 1907), pp. 87–101. See also his *Chto takoe anarkhizm* (1907; New York, 1919), pp. 57–63, and his newspaper *Novyi mir*, no. 1, October 15, 1905. In addition, see Avrich, *Russian Anarchism*, pp. 110–12.

96. Maksim Dubinskii, "Intelligentsiia pered sudom g. E. Lozinskogo," *Burevestnik*, no. 8 (November 1907): 16.

97. Besides a general similarity of outlook, some anarchists showed an interest in the same social stratum as the Makhaevists. The anarchist *beznachal'tsy*, for instance, declared their intention of working among "the unemployed, vagabonds, migrants," and other outcasts from society. Zagranichnaia gruppa "Beznachalie," "Zaiavlenie," *Listok Gruppy Beznachalie*, no. 1 (April 1905): 1-2. See also Avrich, *Russian Anarchists*, pp. 49-54.

98. Gorev, "Apoliticheskie i antiparlamentskie gruppy," p. 512; Manfred Hildermeier, *Die Sozialrevolutionäre Partei Russlands: Agrarsozialismus und Modernisierung im Zarenreich (1900-1914)* (Cologne and Vienna: Böhlau Verlag, 1978), chap. 4; A. F. Zhukov, *Ideino-politicheskii krakh eserovskogo maksimalizma* (Leningrad: Izdatel'stvo Leningradskogo Universiteta, 1979), pp. 12-14. On Ustinov as Lozinskii, see I. F. Masanov, *Slovar' psevdonimov russkikh pisatelei, uchenykh i obshchestvennykh deiatelei* (Moscow, 1956-60), 3:186. Besides Ustinov, Lozinskii also used the pseudonyms Podolianin and Karmeliuk.

99. See, for example, L., "Burzhuaznaia ili sotsialisticheskaia revoliutsiia?" in no. 1 (May 1, 1905): 2-4; S. Samoilov, "Chto my: 'minimal'nye' ili 'maksimal'nye' sotsialisty?" ibid., p. 7; Karmeliuk, "O liberalizme voobshche, i o russkikh liberalakh v chastnosti i v osobennosti," no. 2 (June 10, 1905): 8-10. On the "minimum" and "maximum" programs of the Socialist-Revolutionary party, see Oliver H. Radkey, *The Agrarian Foes of Bolshevism: Promise and Default of the Russian Socialist Revolutionaries, February to October, 1917* (New York: Columbia University Press, 1958), chap. 2; Hildermeier, *Die Sozialrevolutionäre Partei*, pp. 99-105.

100. E. Ustinov, "Petr Lavrov o vozmozhnosti sotsialisticheskoi revoliutsii v Rossii," *Vol'nyi diskussionnyi listok*, no. 3 (July 5, 1905): 1-4.

101. Ibid., no. 2, p. 12. Quoted from *Revoliutsionnaia Rossiia*, no. 67.

102. *Kommuna*, no. 1 (December 1905): 8.

103. "Kak organizovat' revoliutsionnuiu kommunu?" ibid., pp. 5-7.

104. He now criticized the Maximalists in typically Makhaevist terms, taking them to task for harboring a sympathetic attitude toward the intelligentsia and the landowning peasantry. See "Sushchnost' maksimalizma," *Protiv techeniia*, no. 2 (March 22, 1907): 10-13; "Maksimalizm i intelligentsiia," ibid., no. 3 (May 8, 1907): 12.

105. One example of such interaction, as well as a further indication of the spread of Machajski's ideas, is a little newspaper entitled *Proletarskoe delo (The Proletarian Cause)*, two issues of which appeared in Geneva in March and April 1905. It was published by a "Group of Worker Communists," whose further identity remained a mystery: the paper

gave no indication of party affiliation, and none of its articles were signed. It was militantly revolutionary in its stance, and much of it reads like a paraphrase of Machajski. In particular, it was stamped with the hallmark of Makhaevism, the accusation that socialism represented the class interests of the intelligentsia. *Proletarskoe delo* expressly recommended to its readers "an interesting book by A. Vol'skii," namely, part 1 of *Umstvennyi rabochii*, and at the same time it hailed the publication of *Vol'nyi diskussionnyi listok* (no. 2 [April 1905]: 8).

106. E. Ustinov, *Sovremennyi anarkhizm. Ego konechnye idealy, programma, taktika i nravstvenno-klassovaia sushchnost'* (Geneva: Izdanie gruppy sotsialistov-revoliutsionerov, 1905), p. 2. This was an expanded version of an article originally published in the second issue of *Vol'nyi diskussionnyi listok.*

107. Vera Machajska to Max Nomad, July 25, 1932, Max Nomad Archive. Aside from Vera Gurari, the identity of the other members of the Petersburg Workers' Conspiracy cannot be determined. Genkin identifies as the principal members Gurari and "a seventeen- or eighteen-year-old worker, Rafalovich," who was "the son of a well-off entrepreneur-artisan" (*Po tiur'mam*, p. 288; also pp. 303–04). In a later version of his memoirs, however, he refers to "a young worker, Rafail Margolin," who may be the same individual ("Sredi preemnikov Bakunina," p. 190). Genkin claims that the Petersburg Makhaevists merged with the anarchist *beznachal'tsy* in 1906 ("Sredi preemnikov Bakunina," p. 190), but this is incorrect; although some individuals may possibly have done so, the Workers' Conspiracy remained active at least until the end of 1907.

108. Vladimir S. Voitinskii, *Peterburgskii sovet bezrabotnykh, 1906–1907* (New York: Russian Institute, Columbia University, 1969), p. 84. According to Voitinskii (p. 83), the anarchists and Maximalists were also active among the unemployed of St. Petersburg, and, like the Makhaevists, sought to provoke "anarchic outbursts" among them.

109. "Iz zhizni partii," *Tovarishch*, no. 245 (April 18, 1907): 4.

110. "Iz zhizni partii," ibid., no. 300 (June 23, 1907): 3.

111. "Iz zhizni partii," ibid., no. 355 (August 26, 1907): 4.

112. "Iz zhizni partii," ibid., no. 368 (September 11, 1907): 2.

113. "Iz zhizni partii," ibid., no. 384 (September 29, 1907): 4.

114. "Iz zhizni partii," ibid., no. 399 (October 17, 1907): 4.

115. V. Voitinskii, *Gody pobed i porazhenii* (Berlin, 1923–24), 2:194–95.

116. Ibid., p. 195. Voitinskii also repeats a rumor that Makhaevists were responsible for the murder of two municipal engineers in the port in May 1907, the perpetrators of which were never caught (p. 196).

117. Pigoń, "Żeromski–Machajski," *Życie literackie*, no. 36 (502) (September 3, 1961): 4.

118. Ibid.; also Pigoń, "Zygzaki przyjaźni," pp. 385–86.

119. Voitinskii, *Gody pobed*, 2:194.

120. Max Nomad, "Looking Backward," typescript, Max Nomad Archive, p. 14.

121. Pigoń, "Zygzaki przyjaźni," p. 368.

122. Ibid., p. 387.

123. Ibid., pp. 387–88.

124. Nomad, *Aspects of Revolt*, pp. 220–22. See also Gorev, "Apoliticheskie i antiparlamentskie gruppy," p. 525.

125. Genkin refers to Makhaevist groups in Vilna and Belostok ("Sredi preemnikov Bakunina," p. 190), and Garvi states that Chuprina (who had been a member of Machajski's group in Irkutsk) formed one in Kiev (*Vospominaniia*, p. 291), but I have found no information on these groups or confirmation that they actually existed.

126. Pigoń, "Zygzaki przyjaźni," p. 368; Nomad, "Looking Backward," p. 14.

127. Gorev, "Apoliticheskie i antiparlamentskie gruppy," p. 523.

128. I. Grosman, "Makhaevtsy sverkhu i makhaevtsy snizu," *Kievskie vesti*, May 28, 1909, p. 2.

CHAPTER 6. *Cracow–Paris–Moscow*

1. Pigoń, "Zygzaki przyjaźni," p. 373, and "Żeromski-Machajski," *Życie literackie*, no. 36 (502) (September 3, 1961): 4.

2. Max Nomad, "Wacław Machajski — Prophet Without Glory: Reflections and Reminiscences of an Ex-Follower," typescript, Max Nomad Archive, pp. 9–10; Nomad, *Dreamers, Dynamiters and Demagogues*, pp. 8–10.

3. Nettl, *Rosa Luxemburg*, 1:342–43, 2:560–65; Kazimiera Janina Cottam, *Boleslaw Limanowski (1835–1935): A Study in Socialism and Nationalism* (Boulder, Colo.: East European Quarterly, 1978), pp. 156–57, 160–62. The Polish Social Democratic party of Galicia and Teschen Silesia (Polska Partia Socjal-Demokratyczna, or PPSD), which was federated with the Austrian Social Democratic party, was the Galician counterpart of the PPS. Cottam, *Limanowski*, pp. 115–16, 290, n.42; Haustein, *Sozialismus und Nationale Frage in Polen*, pp. 258–61.

4. Pigoń, "Zygzaki przyjaźni," pp. 375–79; Nomad, *Dreamers, Dynamiters and Demagogues*, pp. 110–33.

5. Quoted in Pigoń, "Zygzaki przyjaźni," p. 376.

6. Nomad, *Dreamers, Dynamiters and Demagogues*, pp. 111–14.

7. Pigoń, "Zygzaki przyjaźni," pp. 380–81.

8. Ibid., pp. 361–62, 382–83.

9. Ibid., p. 385.

10. Ibid., p. 386.

11. The Max Nomad Archive contains a set of clippings from Austrian Polish newspapers concerning Machajski's arrest, filed under the heading "Polish (Galician) papers about Machajski's arrest in Zakopane," all dating from January 1911.

12. Pigoń, "Zygzaki przyjaźni," pp. 356, 383.

13. "Polish (Galician) papers about Machajski's arrest in Zakopane"; Pigoń, "Zygzaki przyjaźni," p. 389.

14. Żeromski, "W sprawie Machajskiego," pp. 110-11.

15. Pigoń, "Zygzaki przyjaźni," p. 389.

16. Zaremba, Słowo o Wacławie Machajskim, pp. 87-95; Pigoń, "Zygzaki przyjaźni," pp. 390-92.

17. Machajski to Max Nomad, September 28, 1916, Max Nomad Archive.

18. Machajski to Max Nomad, June 29, 1917, Max Nomad Archive.

19. Zaremba, Słowo o Wacławie Machajskim, p. 95.

20. This account of the Makhaevists in Petrograd is drawn from ibid., pp. 103-07, which is based on information provided to Zaremba by Max Nomad. According to Nomad, Mitkevich subsequently joined the Bolsheviks and became a commissar in Siberia, where he was killed in the civil war (ibid., p. 146, n.65).

21. Lenin's elaboration of this new policy appeared in his article "Ocherednye zadachi sovetskoi vlasti," published April 28, 1918. See his Sochineniia, 36:165-208.

22. A. Vol'skii, ed., Rabochaia revoliutsiia, no. 1 (June-July, 1918): 2, 18-20. A reprint of this publication is included in the 1968 edition of Umstvennyi rabochii.

23. Ibid., p. 24.

24. Ibid., p. 17.

25. Ibid., p. 16.

26. Ibid., pp. 20-21.

27. Ibid., pp. 7-9.

28. Ibid., p. 9.

29. Ibid., p. 6.

30. Ibid., p. 26.

31. Ibid., p. 6.

32. Ibid.

33. Ibid., p. 10.

34. Ibid., p. 28.

35. A. Sokolov, in The Anarchists in the Russian Revolution, ed. Paul Avrich (Ithaca: Cornell University Press, 1973), p. 121.

36. M. Sergven, ibid., p. 123.

37. Robert V. Daniels, ed., *A Documentary History of Communism* (New York: Vintage Books, 1962), 1:154. On the Left Communists, see also his *The Conscience of the Revolution: Communist Opposition in Soviet Russia* (Cambridge, Mass.: Harvard University Press, 1965), pp. 70–87; Stephen F. Cohen, *Bukharin and the Bolshevik Revolution: A Political Biography, 1888–1938* (New York: Knopf, 1973), pp. 60–78.

38. Cohen, *Bukharin*, p. 75.

39. Shetlikh, "Pamiati V. K. Makhaiskogo,"

40. Daniels, *Conscience of the Revolution*, pp. 125–53; Leonard Schapiro, *The Origin of the Communist Autocracy: Political Opposition in the Soviet State* (Cambridge, Mass.: Harvard University Press, 1977), pp. 314–37.

41. Lenin, *Polnoe sobranie sochinenii*, 43:378.

42. *Desiatyi s"ezd RKP/b. Mart 1921 goda. Stenograficheskii otchet* (Moscow: Gospolitizdat, 1963), pp. 654–55. Iaroslavskii later wrote a scurrilous book on Russian anarchism which contained a distorted description of Makhaevism. E. Yaroslavsky, *History of Anarchism in Russia* (New York: International Publishers, 1937), pp. 38–39.

43. *Desiatyi s"ezd*, p. 657. The Soviet annotator of the proceedings of the congress defines Makhaevism as "an anarchist current" which became "a synonym for a hooligan attitude toward the intelligentsia" and accuses the Democratic Centralists of displaying traces of it themselves (p. 869, n. 78).

44. For a detailed account of Miasnikov's life and political career, see Paul Avrich, "Bolshevik Opposition to Lenin: G. I. Miasnikov and the Workers' Group," *Russian Review*, January 1984, pp. 1–29, and, on Miasnikov's affinities with Machajski, pp. 18, 26–27.

45. V. Sorin, *Rabochaia gruppa: "Miasnikovshchina"* (Moscow, 1924), p. 94. This book quotes extensively from the manifesto of the Workers' Group and other documents compiled by the police.

46. Ibid., pp. 63–64.

47. Ibid., pp. 64, 109.

48. Daniels, ed., *Documentary History of Communism*, 1:53.

49. Nik. Karev, "O gruppe 'Rabochaia Pravda,'" *Bol'shevik*, no. 7–8 (1924): 32–33.

50. "Vozzvanie gruppy 'Rabochaia pravda,'" *Sotsialisticheskii vestnik*, January 31, 1923, p. 13.

51. Karev, "O gruppe 'Rabochaia Pravda,'" p. 33.

52. Avrich, "Bolshevik Opposition," pp. 22–24; Daniels, *Conscience of the Revolution*, pp. 159–61.

53. Ulam, *The Bolsheviks*, p. 210.

54. Quoted by David Joravsky, "The Construction of the Stalinist Psyche," in Sheila Fitzpatrick, ed., *Cultural Revolution in Russia, 1928–*

1931 (Bloomington: Indiana University Press, 1978), p. 105. The Soviet editors of Lenin's works print only the initial letter of the last Russian word: "g . . ." (*Polnoe sobranie sochinenii*, 51:48). We can assume that Lenin himelf was less reticent.

55. Lenin, *Polnoe sobranie sochinenii*, 54:265.

56. Michel Heller, "Premier avertissement: un coup de fouet. L'histoire de l'expulsion des personalités culturelles hors de l'Union Soviétique en 1922," *Cahiers du monde russe et soviétique*, April–June 1979, p. 131. The exact number of those forced to emigrate cannot be determined. The number 160 appears in the literature but seems to include some who were sent into internal exile (ibid., p. 163).

57. In Heller's words, this action against the intelligentsia, one of Lenin's last political initiatives before he was incapacitated, "was a capital point of the testament the founder of the Russian state left to his heirs" (ibid., p. 132).

58. "Wacław Machajski—Prophet Without Glory," p. 14. Nomad adds, rather vaguely, that Machajski's ideas influenced some dissident Bolshevik groups but that he had no direct contact with them.

59. Machajski to Nomad, December 6, 1922, Max Nomad Archive.

60. Machajski to Nomad (in Polish), January 29, 1924, Max Nomad Archive.

61. Shetlikh, "Pamiati V. K. Makhaiskogo."

62. N. Baturin, "Pamiati 'makhaevshchiny'!" *Pravda*, March 2, 1926, p. 2.

63. Pigoń, "Zygzaki przyjaźni," p. 403.

CHAPTER 7.   *Makhaevism After Machajski*

1. Some parts of this chapter appeared in different form in my historiographical article "Stalin, the Great Purge, and Russian History: A New Look at the 'New Class,'" The Carl Beck Papers in Russian and East European Studies, no. 305 (Pittsburgh: University of Pittsburgh, 1984).

2. N. Bukharin, *Proletarskaia revoliutsiia i kul'tura* (Petrograd: Priboi, 1923), pp. 23–38; "Burzhuaznaia revoliutsiia i revoliutsiia proletarskaia," in N. Bukharin, *Ataka: Sbornik teoreticheskikh statei* (Moscow: Gosudarstvennoe izdatel'stvo, 1924), pp. 234–36.

3. Bukharin, *Proletarskaia revoliutsiia*, p. 43.

4. Ibid., p. 44.

5. Bukharin, "Burzhuaznaia revoliutsiia," p. 239; also *Proletarskaia revoliutsiia*, p. 44.

6. Bukharin, *Proletarskaia revoliutsiia*, p. 47. For a discussion of Bukharin's thinking, see Cohen, *Bukharin*, pp. 141–44.

7. G. I. Miasnikov, *Ocherednoi obman* (Paris, 1931), p. 28.

8. Avrich, "Bolshevik Opposition to Lenin," p. 25.

9. Leon Trotsky, "The Class Nature of the Soviet State" [October 1, 1933], in *Writings of Leon Trotsky, 1933-34* (New York: Pathfinder Press, 1972), pp. 101-22.

10. Leon Trotsky, *The Revolution Betrayed: What Is the Soviet Union and Where Is It Going?* trans. Max Eastman (1937; New York: Pathfinder Press, 1972), pp. 248-49.

11. Ibid., pp. 249-50.

12. Ibid., pp. 86-94.

13. Robert H. McNeal, "Trotskyist Interpretations of Stalinism," in *Stalinism: Essays in Historical Interpretation*, ed. Robert C. Tucker (New York: Norton, 1977), p. 51. On Trotsky's theory, in addition to McNeal's article, see Baruch Knei-Paz, *The Social and Political Thought of Leon Trotsky* (Oxford: Clarendon Press, 1978), chap. 10.

14. Bruno R.[izzi], *La Bureaucratisation du Monde* [Paris, 1939], p. 23.

15. Ibid., pp. 25-29. An English translation of part 1 of Rizzi's book, which deals with the Soviet Union, has recently been published: Bruno Rizzi, *The Bureaucratization of the World*, trans. Adam Westoby (New York: The Free Press, 1985).

As late as September 1939, Trotsky, in response to Rizzi, was still rejecting the idea that the bureaucracy constituted a "ruling class" and continued to describe the situation in the Soviet Union as "the deformity of a transitional period." Leon Trotsky, "The USSR in War" [September 25, 1939], *In Defense of Marxism (Against the Petty-Bourgeois Opposition)* (New York: Pioneer Publishers, 1942), pp. 3-21.

16. Max Shachtman, *The Bureaucratic Revolution: The Rise of the Stalinist State* (New York: Donald Press, 1962). A collection of articles written 1940-1957.

17. James Burnham, *The Managerial Revolution* (New York: John Day, 1941).

18. Max Nomad, who was ever alert to the unacknowledged influence of his one-time mentor, conceded that Djilas seems never to have heard of Machajski until he came to the United States in 1968 ("Wacław Machajski—Prophet Without a Cause," p. 17). He did not let James Burnham off so easily, however: see *Aspects of Revolt*, p. 15.

19. Milovan Djilas, *The New Class: An Analysis of the Communist System* (New York: Praeger, 1957), pp. 50-51.

20. Ibid., pp. 44-45. A recent variation on Djilas's theme is the attempt to define the "new class" in the Soviet Union specifically as the so-called *nomenklatura*, the holders of key official positions whose appointment requires party approval. See Michael Voslensky, *Nomen-*

klatura: The Soviet Ruling Class, trans. Eric Mosbacher, with a preface by Milovan Djilas (Garden City, N. Y.: Doubleday, 1984). An earlier *samizdat* document that takes the same position is S. Zorin and N. Alekseev, *Vremia ne zhdet* (Frankfurt/Main: Posev, 1970).

21. Aside from its continued use by various offshoots of Trotskyism, other echoes of the term can still be heard. For example, a work by two Hungarian dissidents entitled *The Intellectuals on the Road to Class Power*, drawing on ideas from Bakunin to Djilas (but not, apparently, Machajski), depicted the Eastern European intelligentsia as a "new class" whose interest lay in the replacement of private property by a planned economy dependent on specialized knowledge (George Konrád and Ivan Szelényi, *The Intellectuals on the Road to Class Power*, trans. Andrew Arato and Richard E. Allen [New York: Harcourt Brace Jovanovich, 1979]). At almost the same time the American sociologist Alvin Gouldner, in *The Future of Intellectuals and the Rise of the New Class*, analyzed what he saw as the worldwide phenomenon of struggle within the bourgeois elite between property owners, on the one hand, and a "new class" of intellectuals and technical specialists whose "capital" consists of education and knowledge. Gouldner was familiar with Machajski's ideas and included a critique of them in his "Prologue to a Theory of Revolutionary Intellectuals," p. 31, n.48.

The term has also enjoyed a certain vogue among the so-called neoconservatives in American thought, in reference to those possessors of higher education who, in the name of the "public interest," press for a widening of government regulatory power — and with it an increase in their own administrative power at the expense of the business class. For a variety of statements of this position, see B. Bruce-Briggs, ed., *The New Class?* (New Brunswick, N.J.: Transaction Books, 1979). See also Peter Steinfels, *The Neoconservatives* (New York: Simon and Schuster, 1979), esp. chap. 8. At least some of the individuals associated with this current of thought, Daniel Bell, for example, are familiar with Machajski's ideas. Bell has written of Machajski in his *The End of Ideology: On the Exhaustion of Political Ideas in the Fifties* (New York: Free Press, 1962), pp. 355–57, and *The New Class?* is dedicated to the memory of Max Nomad. To complete the circle, many of the neoconservatives were Trotskyists in their younger days.

22. For a lucid and stimulating discussion of the problem of finding "new categories, new labels to attach to a phenomenon which Marx did not analyze," and a critique of the various formulations of the "new class" theory, see A. Nove, "Is There a Ruling Class in the USSR?" *Soviet Studies*, October 1975, pp. 615–38. See also Stephen F. Cohen, "Bolshevism and Stalinism," in Tucker, ed., *Stalinism*, pp. 26–27. On neo-Marxist attempts

to move away from property as the central determinant of class relations, see Parkin, *Marxism and Class Theory*, pp. 23-25, 59.

23. G. P. Andreiuk, "Vydvizhenchestvo i ego rol' v formirovanii intelligentsii (1921-1932 gg.)," in *Iz istorii sovetskoi intelligentsii*, ed. M. P. Kim (Moscow: "Mysl'," 1966), p. 6.

24. Sheila Fitzpatrick, in her study of the *vydvizhenchestvo*, estimates that perhaps a million and a half workers moved out of manual positions and into white-collar and administrative posts or higher education from 1928 to 1933. "Stalin and the Making of a New Elite, 1928-1939," *Slavic Review*, September 1979, p. 387. Andreiuk gives a figure of 8-900,000 *vydvizhentsy* by 1933 ("Vydvizhenchesto," p. 38).

25. I. V. Stalin, "Novaia obstanovka — novye zadachi khoziaistvennogo stroitel'stva," *Sochineniia* (Moscow: Gosudarstvennoe izdatel'stvo politicheskoi literatury, 1946-52), 13:66-67. On Stalin's role in pressing this policy, see also Kendall E. Bailes, *Technology and Society Under Lenin and Stalin: Origins of the Soviet Technical Intelligentsia, 1917-1941* (Princeton: N.J.: Princeton University Press, 1978), chap. 7.

26. [Nikita Khrushchev], *Khrushchev Remembers*, trans. and ed. Strobe Talbott (Boston: Little, Brown, 1970), p. 39.

27. Ibid., p. 37. Another beneficiary of the promotion policy was the future dissident Petro Grigorenko. Like Khrushchev, he had been born and brought up in a peasant village. He attended a *rabfak*, a special school that prepared young workers for higher education, and was sent to the Kharkov Technical Institute to study construction engineering. He subsequently rose to the rank of general in the army (Petro G. Grigorenko, *Memoirs*, trans. Thomas P. Whitney [New York: Norton, 1982]). For biographical sketches of other *vydvizhentsy*, including Leonid Brezhnev, see Fitzpatrick, "Stalin and the Making of a New Elite," pp. 385-86, 397-98.

28. Bailes, *Technology and Society*, chap. 3.

29. M. P. Kim, ed., *Sovetskaia intelligentsiia (Istoriia formirovaniia i rosta 1917-1965 gg.)* (Moscow: "Mysl'," 1968), pp. 127-28. See also Bailes, *Technology and Society*, p. 73.

30. For various aspects of this phenomenon, see the articles in Fitzpatrick, ed., *Cultural Revolution in Russia*.

31. Bailes, *Technology and Society*, chap. 4. According to Bailes, this case "was the high point of the terror against the old technical intelligentsia" (p. 96).

32. Stalin, "Novaia obstanovka," pp. 69-73. For an analysis of this aspect of his speech, see Bailes, *Technology and Society*, pp. 153-56. There was one further show trial of technical specialists: the Metro-Vickers trial of 1933, which featured a group of Soviet engineers and foreign

specialists accused of sabotage. This episode was not followed by a terror campaign against the technical intelligentsia on the scale of 1928-31,
however. See Bailes, *Technology and Society*, pp. 280-81; Robert Conquest, *The Great Terror: Stalin's Purges of the Thirties* (New York: Collier Books, 1973), pp. 736-39.

33. Conquest, *The Great Terror*, chap. 9.

34. Eugenia Ginzburg, *Within the Whirlwind*, trans. Ian Boland (New
York: Harcourt Brace Jovanovich, 1981), p. 112.

35. J. Arch Getty, *Origins of the Great Purges: The Soviet Communist Party Reconsidered, 1933-1938* (Cambridge: Cambridge University Press, 1985), p. 178. On the continuities between the "cultural revolution" and the purges, see Fitzpatrick, "Stalin and the Making of a New
Elite," pp. 393-402; Jerry F. Hough, "The Cultural Revolution and Western Understanding of the Soviet System," in Fitzpatrick, ed., *Cultural
Revolution in Russia*, pp. 245-47; Getty, *Origins of the Great Purges*,
pp. 102-05, 117-18, 126, 184.

36. Fitzpatrick, "Stalin and the Making of a New Elite," pp. 393-
402. Soviet publications have sometimes called attention to the large-
scale promotion of new men as a result of the Great Purge. In 1966,
Voprosy istorii made the following statement: "In 1937-38 Soviet industry
suffered a heavy blow as a result of mass repressions. The loss thus inflicted was difficult to make good. A large number of young engineers
who had graduated from technical college as late as 1933 or 1934 became
directors of enterprises, and many gifted organizers of production arose
from their ranks as the new commanders gradually gained experience"
(quoted in Boris Levytsky, ed., *The Stalinist Terror in the Thirties:
Documentation from the Soviet Press* [Stanford: Hoover Institution,
1974]), p. 421.

37. This is Sheila Fitzpatrick's conclusion in "Stalin and the Making
of a New Elite," p. 401. Similarly, Bailes writes: "One is tempted to conclude . . . that without the massive formation of a new technical intelligentsia, the Stalinist purges of the later 1930s could not have taken
place in the way they did" (*Technology and Society*, p. 285).

38. F. Anderson et al., comp., *Nashi protivniki. Sbornik materialov
i dokumentov* (Moscow: Kommunisticheskii universitet imeni Ia. M.
Sverdlova, 1928-29), 1:141-60.

39. Evgenii Lozinskii, *Revoliutsionnaia rol' prava i gosudarstva v
epokhu proletarskoi diktatury* (Kremenchug: Krempechat', 1928), pp.
12-21.

40. See above, chap. 5, pp. 129-30. It is worth noting also that the
Bolshevik worker Semen Kanatchikov's memoirs, which do not refer to
Machajski but are replete with anti-intelligentsia sentiments, began to
appear in 1929.

41. L. N. Syrkin, "Makhaevshchina," *Krasnaia letopis'*, no. 6 (33) (1929): 184–212, and no. 1 (34) (1930): 117–45; L. Syrkin, "*Makhaev-shchina*" (Moscow-Leningrad: Gosudarstvennoe sotsial'no-ekonomicheskoe izdatel'stvo, 1931).

42. "O postanovke partiinoi propagandy v sviazi s vypuskom 'Kratkogo kursa istorii VKP(b)'," *Pravda*, November 15, 1938, p. 2.

43. "Chto takoe 'makhaevshchina'?" *Pravda*, November 18, 1938, p. 2.

44. See, for instance, the article "Makhaevshchina" in *Bol'shaia sovetskaia entsiklopediia* (Moscow: "Bol'shaia sovetskaia entsiklopediia," 1950–59), 26:544, where the Central Committee statement of 1938 is quoted. Subsequently, however, a better balanced appraisal of the subject appeared in the article "Makhaevshchina" in the *Sovetskaia istoricheskaia entsiklopediia* (Moscow: "Sovetskaia entsiklopediia," 1961–76), 9:193–94.

APPENDIX

1. In May 1901, striking workers of the Obukhov arms factory in St. Petersburg erected barricades and resisted the mounted police sent against them, with considerable bloodshed.

2. In 1899, the May Day demonstration in Riga turned into a citywide armed clash between striking Latvian workers and tsarist police and troops.

3. In February 1901, a Socialist-Revolutionary former student assassinated Minister of Education Nikolai Bogolepov. A wave of public demonstrations of students and intelligentsia, with some worker support, ensued. On March 4 a demonstration took place in Kazan Square in St. Petersburg, and the demonstrators, mostly from the intelligentsia, were manhandled by Cossack troops.

Bibliography

Unpublished Sources

Machajska, Vera. "Short History of the Machajski Group Written by His Wife." Typescript. Max Nomad Archive, International Institute of Social History, Amsterdam. An English translation of a letter from Machajska to Max Nomad (in Russian), July 25, 1932.

Machajski, Jan Wacław. "An Unfinished Essay in the Nature of a Critique of Socialism." Manuscript in Russian, 1910–1911. Slavonic Division, New York Public Library. A Russian translation from Polish by Machajski's wife.

Nomad, Max. "Looking Backward." Typescript. Max Nomad Archive, International Institute of Social History, Amsterdam.

———. "Wacław Machajski—Prophet Without Glory: Reflections and Reminiscences of an Ex-Follower." Typescript. Max Nomad Archive, International Institute of Social History, Amsterdam.

Note: The Max Nomad Archive at the International Institute of Social History (Internationaal Instituut voor Sociale Geschiedenis) in Amsterdam contains the papers of the late Max Nomad. When his archive was still in his personal possession in New York City, Nomad kindly allowed me to use a series of letters written to him by Machajski and his wife, in Polish, Russian, and French, between 1912 and 1935. These have been cited in the text. An examination of the archive in Amsterdam in the summer of 1978, however, failed to turn up the letters, and the staff of the International Institute was unaware of their whereabouts. They appear to have been lost in the archive's transition from New York City to Amsterdam.

Newspapers

Buntar' (Paris), no. 1, December 1, 1906.
Burevestnik (Paris), nos. 1–19, 1906–1910.

Kommuna (Paris), no. 1, December 1905.
Listok Gruppy Beznachalie (Paris), nos. 1–4, 1905.
Novyi mir (Paris), no. 1, October 15, 1905.
Proletarskoe delo (Geneva), nos. 1–2, 1905.
Rabochaia mysl' (London), nos. 4–11, 1898–1901.
Tovarishch (St. Petersburg), 1907.
Vol'nyi diskussionnyi listok (Paris), nos. 1–3, 1905.

PUBLISHED WORKS BY JAN WACŁAW MACHAJSKI
(pseudonym: A. Vol'skii)

J. W. M. "Z życia konspiracyjnego w Kongresówce." *Pobudka. Czaso-pismo narodowo-socjalistyczne.* Paris. January 1892, pp. 3–4.
A. Vol'skii. *Umstvennyi rabochii.* Part 1, *Evoliutsiia sotsialdemokratii: Novoe izdanie s predisloviem i prilozheniem.* Geneva, 1905. Part 2, *Nauchnyi sotsializm.* Geneva, 1905. Part 3, section 1, *Sotsializm i rabochee dvizhenie v Rossii.* Geneva, 1904. Part 3, section 2, *So-tsialisticheskaia nauka, kak novaia religiia.* Geneva, 1904. Parts 1 and 2 were reprinted in St. Petersburg: V. Iakovenko, 1906. The entire Geneva edition has been reprinted, with prefaces by Albert Parry and R. N. Redlikh: New York: Mezhdunarodnoe Literatur-noe Sodruzhestvo/Inter-Language Literary Associates, 1968. Brief excerpts appear in English translation in V. F. Calverton, ed., *The Making of Society: An Outline of Sociology*, pp. 427–36. New York: Random House, 1937.
Bankrotstvo sotsializma XIX stoletiia. Geneva, 1905.
Burzhuaznaia revoliutsiia i rabochee delo. Geneva, 1905. Reprint. St. Petersburg: "Rabochaia Bor'ba," 1906.
[Jan Wacław Machajski, trans.]. K. Marks i F. Engel's, *Sviatoe semeistvo. Izbrannye mesta. S primechaniiami perevodchika.* Vol. 2. St. Peters-burg: "Novyi golos," 1906.
[Jan Wacław Machajski, ed.]. *Rabochii zagovor.* No. 1, Geneva, Sep-tember–October 1907. Published early 1908.
A. Vol'skii, ed. *Rabochaia revoliutsiia.* No. 1, Moscow, June–July 1918. Reprinted in the 1968 edition of *Umstvennyi rabochii.*

WORKS BY EVGENII LOZINSKII
(pseudonyms: Karmeliuk, Podolianin, E. Ustinov)

E. Ustinov. "Chto takoe sotsialisticheskaia nravstvennost'? (Po povodu sovremennykh eticheskikh shatanii)." *Vestnik russkoi revoliutsii,* no. 4, March 1905, pp. 137–86. Reprinted as separate work, St. Petersburg: "Severnaia Rus'," 1906.

———. *Kakova dolzhna byt' programma russkoi revoliutsii?* Geneva: Izdanie gruppy sotsialistov-revoliutsionerov, 1905.

———. *Parlamentarizm i predstavitel'naia sistema s tochki zreniia revoliutsionnogo sotsializma.* Geneva: Izdanie soiuza revoliutsion-nykh sotsialistov, 1905.

———. *Sovremennyi anarkhizm. Ego konechnye idealy, programma, taktika i nravstvenno-klassovaia sushchnost'.* Geneva: Izdanie gruppy sotsialistov-revoliutsionerov, 1905. Reprint. Moscow: "Molodaia Rossiia," 1906, under the name Podolianin.

Podolianin. "Klassovaia proletarskaia bor'ba v strane vsetor-zhestvuiushchego kapitalizma." *Vestnik russkoi revoliutsii,* no. 4, March 1905, pp. 262–98. Reprinted as separate work, Moscow: "Molodaia Rossiia," 1905.

Evgenii Lozinskii. "Iz istorii munitsipal'nogo khoziaistva." *Mir Bozhii,* September 1905, pp. 112–30.

———. *Chego zhdat' russkim rabochim ot vseobshchego izbiritel'nogo prava.* St. Petersburg: "Novyi golos," 1907.

———. *Chto zhe takoe, nakonets, intelligentsiia? (Kritiko-sotsiologiche-skii opyt).* St. Petersburg: "Novyi golos," 1907.

———. *Itogi parlamentarizma. Chto on dal i mozhet li on chto-libo dat' rabochim massam?* St. Petersburg: "Novyi golos," 1907.

———, ed. *Protiv techeniia. Dvukhnedel'nyi obshchestvenno-satiricheskii i literaturno-kriticheskii zhurnal.* Nos. 1–3, St. Petersburg, 1907.

———. *Gde vykhod?* St. Petersburg: "Novyi golos," 1909.

———. *Itogi i perspektivy rabochego dvizheniia.* St. Petersburg: "Novyi golos," 1909.

———. *Lev Tolstoi ob intelligentsii i rabochem voprose.* St. Petersburg: "Severnaia pechatnia," 1911.

Karmeliuk. *Novaia nagornaia propoved'.* Elizavetgrad: Partiia sotsiali-stov-revoliutsionerov, 1917. Published as J. Karmeluk, *Die prole-tarische Bergpredigt. Ein Intermezzo aus der Umwertung aller Werte.* Zurich: Kommissions-Verlag der Grütli-Buchhandlung, 1904, and in a number of subsequent Russian editions.

Evgenii Lozinskii. *Revoliutsionnaia rol' prava i gosudarstva v epokhu proletarskoi diktatury.* Kremenchug: Krempechat', 1928.

OTHER PUBLICATIONS

A., P. [Petr Arshinov]. "Pamiati V. K. Makhaiskogo." *Delo truda,* no. 11, 1926, pp. 5–8.

Akimov-Makhnovets, V. "Stroiteli budushchego." *Obrazovanie*, part 1: no. 4, April 1907, pp. 91–118; part 2: no. 5, May 1907, pp. 66–98; part 3: no. 6, June 1907, pp. 54–88.

Al'manakh: Sbornik po istorii anarkhicheskogo dvizheniia v Rossii. Vol. 1. Paris, 1909.

Anderson, F., et al., comp. *Nashi protivniki. Sbornik materialov i dokumentov.* 2 vols. Moscow: Kommunisticheskii universitet imeni Ia. M. Sverdlova, 1928–29.

Andreiuk, G. P. "Vydvizhenchestvo i ego rol' v formirovanii intelligentsii (1921–1932 gg.)." In *Iz istorii sovetskoi intelligentsii*, ed. M. P. Kim, pp. 5–38. Moscow: "Mysl'," 1966.

Angarskii, N., ed. *Doklady sots.-demokraticheskikh komitetov vtoromu s"ezdu RSDRP.* Moscow-Leningrad, 1930.

Ascher, Abraham. *Pavel Axelrod and the Development of Menshevism.* Cambridge, Mass.: Harvard University Press, 1972.

Astrov, V. "Sotsial-demokratiia pered revoliutsiei 1905 goda." In *1905: Istoriia revoliutsionnogo dvizheniia v otdel'nykh ocherkakh*, ed. M. N. Pokrovskii, 2:79–124. 3 vols. Moscow-Leningrad: Gosudarstvennoe izdatel'stvo, 1925–27.

Avrich, Paul. "What Is 'Makhaevism'?" *Soviet Studies*, July 1965, pp. 66–75.

————. *The Russian Anarchists*. Princeton, N.J.: Princeton University Press, 1967.

————, ed. *The Anarchists in the Russian Revolution.* Ithaca: Cornell University Press, 1973.

————. "Bolshevik Opposition to Lenin: G. I. Miasnikov and the Workers' Group." *Russian Review*, January 1984, pp. 1–29.

Bailes, Kendall E. *Technology and Society Under Lenin and Stalin: Origins of the Soviet Technical Intelligentsia, 1917–1941.* Princeton, N.J.: Princeton University Press, 1978.

Bakunin, Mikhail [Michel Bakounine]. *Oeuvres.* Ed. Max Nettlau and James Guillaume. 6 vols. Paris: P. V. Stock, 1895–1913.

————. *Archives Bakounine.* Ed. Arthur Lehning. 7 vols. Leiden: E. J. Brill, 1961–81.

————. *From out of the Dustbin: Bakunin's Basic Writings, 1869–1871.* Trans. and ed. Robert M. Cutler. Ann Arbor: Ardis, 1985.

Baturin, N. "Pamiati 'makhaevshchiny'!" *Pravda*, March 2, 1926, p. 2. Reprinted in his *Sochineniia*, pp. 352–55. Moscow-Leningrad: Gosudarstvennoe izdatel'stvo, 1930.

Bell, Daniel. *The End of Ideology: On the Exhaustion of Political Ideas in the Fifties.* Rev. ed. New York: Free Press, 1962.

Berlin, P. A. *Apostoly anarkhii. Bakunin. Kropotkin. Makhaev.* Petrograd: "Nov. Rossiia," 1917.

Billington, James. *The Icon and the Axe: An Interpretive History of Russian Culture.* New York: Vintage Books, 1970.

Blejwas, Stanislaus A. *Realism in Polish Politics: Warsaw Positivism and National Survival in Nineteenth-Century Poland.* New Haven: Yale Concilium on International and Area Studies, 1984.

Blit, Lucjan. *The Origins of Polish Socialism: The History and Ideas of the First Polish Socialist Party, 1878–1886.* Cambridge: Cambridge University Press, 1971.

Blok, Aleksandr. *Sochineniia v dvukh tomakh.* 2 vols. Moscow: Goslitizdat, 1955.

Bohachevsky-Chomiak, Martha, and Bernice Glatzer Rosenthal, eds. *A Revolution of the Spirit: Crisis of Value in Russia, 1890–1918.* Newtonville, Mass.: Oriental Research Partners, 1982.

Bonnell, Victoria E. *Roots of Rebellion: Workers' Politics and Organizations in St. Petersburg and Moscow, 1900–1914.* Berkeley and Los Angeles: University of California Press, 1983.

Borovoi, A. A., ed. *Mikhailu Bakuninu, 1876–1926. Ocherki istorii anarkhicheskogo dvizheniia v Rossii.* Moscow: "Golos truda," 1926.

Braginskii, M. A., and K. M. Tereshkovich, eds. *Iakutskaia tragediia — 22 marta (3 aprelia) 1889 goda — sbornik vospominanii i materialov.* Moscow: Obshchestvo politicheskikh katorzhan i ssyl'no-poselentsev, 1925.

Breitfus, Andrei. "Tochiskii i ego kruzhok." *Krasnaia letopis',* no. 7, 1923, pp. 324–39.

Breslav, B. A. "Chtenie Gor'kogo v tiur'me." *Katorga i ssylka,* no. 4 (41), 1928, pp. 120–24.

Bruce-Briggs, B., ed. *The New Class?* New Brunswick, N.J.: Transaction Books, 1979.

Bukharin, N. "Burzhuaznaia revoliutsiia i revoliutsiia proletarskaia." 1922. In *Ataka: Sbornik teoreticheskikh statei,* pp. 216–41. 2d ed. Moscow: Gosudarstvennoe izdatel'stvo, 1924.

———. *Proletarskaia revoliutsiia i kul'tura.* Petrograd: Priboi, 1923.

Bukhbinder, N. A. "Nezavisimaia evreiskaia rabochaia partiia. Po neizdannym arkhivnym dokumentam." *Krasnaia letopis',* no. 2–3, 1922, pp. 208–84.

———. "O zubatovshchine." *Krasnaia letopis',* no. 4, 1922, pp. 289–335.

Burnham, James. *The Managerial Revolution.* New York: John Day, 1941.

———. *The Machiavellians: Defenders of Freedom.* New York: John Day, 1943.

"Chto takoe 'makhaevshchina'?" *Pravda,* November 18, 1938, p. 2.

Cohen, Stephen F. *Bukharin and the Bolshevik Revolution: A Political Biography, 1888–1938.* New York: Knopf, 1973.

———. "Bolshevism and Stalinism." In *Stalinism: Essays in Historical*

Interpretation, ed. Robert C. Tucker, pp. 3–29. New York: Norton, 1977.

Confino, Michael. "On Intellectuals and Intellectual Traditions in Eighteenth- and Nineteenth-Century Russia." *Daedalus*, Spring 1972, pp. 117–49.

Conquest, Robert. *The Great Terror: Stalin's Purges of the Thirties.* Rev. ed. New York: Collier Books, 1973.

Cottam, Kazimiera Janina. *Boleslaw Limanowski (1835–1935): A Study in Socialism and Nationalism.* Boulder, Colo.: East European Quarterly, 1978.

D'Agostino, Anthony. "Intelligentsia Socialism and the 'Workers' Revolution': The Views of J. W. Machajski." *International Review of Social History* 14 (1969): 54–89.

———. *Marxism and the Russian Anarchists.* San Francisco: Germinal Press, 1977.

Daniels, Robert V., ed. *A Documentary History of Communism.* 2 vols. New York: Vintage Books, 1962.

———. *The Conscience of the Revolution: Communist Opposition in Soviet Russia.* Cambridge, Mass.: Harvard University Press, 1965.

Davies, Norman. *God's Playground: A History of Poland.* 2 vols. New York: Columbia University Press, 1982.

Desiatyi s"ezd RKP/b. Mart 1921 goda. Stenograficheskii otchet. Moscow: Gospolitizdat, 1963.

Djilas, Milovan. *The New Class: An Analysis of the Communist System.* New York: Praeger, 1957.

Eidel'man, B. L. "Imeniny Rossiiskoi Kommunisticheskoi Partii." In *K dvadtsatipiatiletiiu pervogo s"ezda partii (1898–1923)*, pp. 32–52. Moscow-Petrograd: Gosudarstvennoe izdatel'stvo, 1923.

Engelstein, Laura. *Moscow, 1905: Working-Class Organization and Political Conflict.* Stanford: Stanford University Press, 1982.

Erman, L. K. "Sostav intelligentsii v Rossii v kontse XIX i nachale XX v." *Istoriia SSSR*, no. 1, 1963, pp. 161–77.

Fischer, George. *Russian Liberalism: From Gentry to Intelligentsia.* Cambridge, Mass.: Harvard University Press, 1958.

Fitzpatrick, Sheila, ed. *Cultural Revolution in Russia, 1928–1931.* Bloomington: Indiana University Press, 1978.

———. "Stalin and the Making of a New Elite, 1928–1939." *Slavic Review*, September 1979, pp. 377–402.

Fountain, Alvin Marcus, II. *Roman Dmowski: Party, Tactics, Ideology, 1895–1907.* Boulder, Colo.: East European Monographs, 1980.

Frumkin, B. M. "Zubatovshchina i evreiskoe rabochee dvizhenie." In *Perezhitoe. Sbornik, posviashchennyi obshchestvennoi i kul'turnoi istorii evreev v Rossii*, 3:199–230. 4 vols. St. Petersburg, 1908–13.

Garvi, P. A. *Vospominaniia sotsialdemokrata*. New York: Fond po izdaniiu literaturnogo nasledstva P. A. Garvi, 1946.

Gay, Peter. *The Dilemma of Democratic Socialism: Eduard Bernstein's Challenge to Marx*. 1952. Reprint. New York: Collier Books, 1962.

Gel'man, S. "Pervaia podpol'naia tipografiia gruppy 'Rabochee Znamia.'" *Katorga i ssylka*, no. 6 (27), 1926, pp. 44–56.

———, and N. Kudrin. "Pamiati Romanovtsa M. V. Lur'e." *Katorga i ssylka*, no. 56, 1929, pp. 152–64.

Genkin, I. I. *Po tiur'mam i etapam*. Petersburg: Gosudarstvennoe izdatel'stvo, 1922. Rev. ed. under the title *Sredi politkatorzhan*. Moscow, 1930.

———. "Sredi preemnikov Bakunina (Zametki po istorii rossiiskogo anarkhizma)." *Krasnaia letopis'*, no. 1 (22), 1927, pp. 170–205.

Gershanovich, D. "O Moisee Vladimiroviche Lur'e." In *K dvadtsatipiatiletiiu pervogo s"ezda partii (1898–1923)*, pp. 165–74. Moscow-Petrograd: Gosudarstvennoe izdatel'stvo, 1923.

Getty, J. Arch. *Origins of the Great Purges: The Soviet Communist Party Reconsidered, 1933–1938*. Cambridge: Cambridge University Press, 1985.

Geyer, Dietrich. *Lenin in der Russischen Sozialdemokratie*. Cologne: Böhlau Verlag, 1962.

Ginzburg, Eugenia. *Within the Whirlwind*. Trans. Ian Boland. New York: Harcourt Brace Jovanovich, 1981.

Gorev, B. I. "Apoliticheskie i antiparlamentskie gruppy." In *Obshchestvennoe dvizhenie v Rossii v nachale XX-go veka*, ed. L. Martov et al., 3:473–534. 4 vols. St. Petersburg: "Obshchestvennaia pol'za," 1909–14. Published separately as *Anarkhisty, maksimalisty i makhaevtsy*. Petrograd: "Kniga," [1917].

———. "Pered vtorym s"ezdom (vospominanii)." *Katorga i ssylka*, no. 1 (8), 1924, pp. 42–65.

Gouldner, Alvin W. "Prologue to a Theory of Revolutionary Intellectuals." *Telos*, no. 26, Winter 1975–76, pp. 3–36.

———. *The Future of Intellectuals and the Rise of the New Class*. New York: Seabury Press, 1979.

Gray, Alexander. *The Socialist Tradition: Moses to Lenin*. New York: Harper & Row, 1968.

Grigorenko, Petro G. *Memoirs*. Trans. Thomas P. Whitney. New York: Norton, 1982.

Grigor'evskii, M. *Politseiskii sotsializm v Rossii (Zubatovshchina)*. St. Petersburg: "Obrazovanie," 1906.

Grosman, I. "Makhaevtsy sverkhu i makhaevtsy snizu." *Kievskie vesti*, May 28, 1909, p. 2.

Haimson, Leopold H. *The Russian Marxists and the Origins of Bolshevism.* Cambridge, Mass.: Harvard University Press, 1955.
_____. "The Problem of Social Stability in Urban Russia, 1905–1917." *Slavic Review,* part 1: December 1964, pp. 619–42; part 2: March 1965, pp. 1–22.
Hartz, Louis. *The Liberal Tradition in America.* New York: Harcourt, Brace, 1955.
Haustein, Ulrich. *Sozialismus und Nationale Frage in Polen.* Cologne and Vienna: Böhlau Verlag, 1969.
Heller, Michel. "Premier avertissement: un coup de fouet. L'histoire de l'expulsion des personnalités culturelles hors de l'Union Soviétique en 1922." *Cahiers du monde russe et soviétique,* April–June 1979, pp. 131–72.
Herzen, Alexander. *From the Other Shore and The Russian People and Socialism.* Cleveland: Meridian Books, 1963.
Hildermeier, Manfred. *Die Sozialrevolutionäre Partei Russlands: Agrarsozialismus und Modernisierung im Zarenreich (1900–1914).* Cologne and Vienna: Böhlau Verlag, 1978.
Hughes, H. Stuart. *Consciousness and Society: The Reorientation of European Social Thought, 1890–1930.* Rev. ed. New York: Vintage Books, 1977.
Ivanov-Razumnik. Review of Evgenii Lozinskii, *Chto zhe takoe, nakonets, intelligentsiia? Kniga,* no. 10, January 11, 1907, pp. 6–7.
_____. *Ob intelligentsii.* 1908. 2d ed. St. Petersburg: M. Stasiulevich, 1910.
_____. *Istoriia russkoi obshchestvennoi mysli.* 3d ed. 2 vols. St. Petersburg: M. M. Stasiulevich, 1911.
Izgoev, A. S. "Intelligentsiia, kak sotsial'naia gruppa." *Obrazovanie,* no. 1, January 1904, pp. 72–94.
Johnson, Robert Eugene. *Peasant and Proletarian: The Working Class of Moscow in the Late Nineteenth Century.* New Brunswick, N.J.: Rutgers University Press, 1979.
[Kanatchikov, Semen Ivanovich]. *A Radical Worker in Tsarist Russia: The Autobiography of Semën Ivanovich Kanatchikov.* Trans. and ed. Reginald E. Zelnik. Stanford, Calif.: Stanford University Press, 1986.
Karev, Nik. "O gruppe 'Rabochaia Pravda.'" *Bol'shevik,* no. 7–8, 1924, pp. 27–39.
Kautsky, Karl. "Die Intelligenz und die Sozialdemokratie." *Die Neue Zeit,* 1894–1895, part 1: no. 27, pp. 10–16; part 2: no. 28, pp. 43–49; part 3: no. 29, pp. 74–80.
Kazakevich, R. A. *Sotsial-demokraticheskie organizatsii Peterburga kontsa 80-kh–nachala 90-kh godov (Kruzhki P. V. Tochisskogo i M. I.*

Brusneva). Leningrad: Izdatel'stvo Leningradskogo Universiteta, 1960.

Keep, J. L. H. *The Rise of Social Democracy in Russia.* Oxford: Clarendon Press, 1963.

————. *The Russian Revolution: A Study in Mass Mobilization.* New York: Norton, 1976.

[Khrushchev, Nikita]. *Khrushchev Remembers.* Trans. and ed. Strobe Talbott. Boston: Little, Brown, 1970.

Kim, M. P., ed. *Sovetskaia intelligentsiia (Istoriia formirovaniia i rosta 1917–1965 gg.).* Moscow: "Mysl'," 1968.

"K istorii zubatovshchiny." *Byloe,* no. 1 (23), July 1917, pp. 86–99.

Knei-Paz, Baruch. *The Social and Political Thought of Leon Trotsky.* Oxford: Clarendon Press, 1978.

Konrád, George, and Ivan Szelényi. *The Intellectuals on the Road to Class Power.* Trans. Andrew Arato and Richard E. Allen. New York: Harcourt Brace Jovanovich, 1979.

Konstantinov, M. M. "Dvadtsat' let nazad." *Katorga i ssylka,* no. 8–9 (45–46), 1928, pp. 110–28.

Kozicki, Stanisław. *Historia Ligi Narodowej (Okres 1887–1907).* London: "Myśl Polska," 1964.

Kropotkin, P. *Memoirs of a Revolutionist.* Boston: Houghton, Mifflin, 1899.

Labedz, Leopold. "The Structure of the Soviet Intelligentsia." *Daedalus,* Summer 1960, pp. 503–19. Reprinted in Richard Pipes, ed., *The Russian Intelligentsia.* New York: Columbia University Press, 1961.

Lavrov, Peter. *Historical Letters.* Trans. James P. Scanlan. In *Russian Philosophy,* ed. James M. Edie et al., 2:123–69. 3 vols. Chicago: Quadrangle Books, 1965.

Lebedeva (Tochisskaia), M. "K biografii P. V. Tochisskogo (Vospominaniia sestry)." In *Istoriko-revoliutsionnyi sbornik,* ed. B. I. Nevskii, 3:296–99. Moscow-Leningrad: Gosudarstvennoe izdatel'stvo, 1926.

Leikina-Svirskaia, V. R. *Intelligentsiia v Rossii vo vtoroi polovine XIX veka.* Moscow: "Mysl'," 1971.

Lenin, V. I. *Polnoe sobranie sochinenii.* 5th ed. 55 vols. Moscow: Gosudarstvennoe izdatel'stvo politicheskoi literatury, 1959–65.

Leslie, R. F., et al. *The History of Poland since 1863.* Cambridge: Cambridge University Press, 1980.

Levitskii, V. [Tsederbaum]. *Za chetvert' veka.* Vol. 1, pts. 1–2. Moscow-Leningrad: Gosudarstvennoe izdatel'stvo, 1926–27.

Levytsky, Boris, ed. *The Stalinist Terror in the Thirties: Documentation from the Soviet Press.* Stanford: Hoover Institution, 1974.

Lichtheim, George. *Marxism: An Historical and Critical Study.* London: Routledge and Kegan Paul, 1961.

Lidtke, Vernon L. "German Social Democracy and German State Socialism, 1876–1884." *International Review of Social History* 9 (1964): 202–25.

——. *The Outlawed Party: Social Democracy in Germany, 1878–1890.* Princeton, N.J.: Princeton University Press, 1966.

Lisovskii, N. K. *P. V. Tochisskii.* Moscow: Gosudarstvennoe izdatel'stvo politicheskoi literatury, 1963.

Lur'e, G. "Iakutskaia ssylka v devianostye i deviatisotye gody." In *100 let iakutskoi ssylki: sbornik iakutskogo zemliachestva,* ed. M. A. Braginskii, pp. 174–207. Moscow: Izdatel'stvo vsesoiuznogo obshchestva politkatorzhan i ssyl'no-poselentsev, 1934.

Machajska, Wiera. "Życie i poglądy Wacława Machajskiego." *Wiadomości* (London), March 4, 1962, p. 2. A Polish translation of two Russian manuscripts in the Max Nomad Archive.

McKay, Donald C. *The National Workshops: A Study in the French Revolution of 1848.* Cambridge, Mass.: Harvard University Press, 1933.

McKinsey, Pamela Sears. "The Kazan Square Demonstration and the Conflict Between Russian Workers and *Intelligenty.*" *Slavic Review,* Spring 1985, pp. 83–103.

McNeal, Robert H. "Trotskyist Interpretations of Stalinism." In *Stalinism: Essays in Historical Interpretation,* ed. Robert C. Tucker, pp. 30–52. New York: Norton, 1977.

"Makhaevshchina." *Bol'shaia sovetskaia entsiklopediia.* 2d ed. 53 vols. Moscow: "Bol'shaia sovetskaia entsiklopediia," 1950–59.

"Makhaevshchina." *Sovetskaia istoricheskaia entsiklopediia.* 16 vols. Moscow: "Sovetskaia entsiklopediia," 1961–76.

Malia, Martin. "What Is the Intelligentsia?" *Daedalus,* Summer 1960, pp. 441–58. Reprinted in Richard Pipes, ed., *The Russian Intelligentsia.* New York: Columbia University Press, 1961.

——. *Alexander Herzen and the Birth of Russian Socialism, 1812–1855.* Cambridge, Mass.: Harvard University Press, 1961.

Marx, Karl. *Capital.* Trans. Ernest Untermann. 3 vols. Chicago: C. H. Kerr, 1932–33.

——, and F. Engels. *Selected Works in Two Volumes.* Moscow: Foreign Languages Publishing House, 1955.

——. *The Holy Family.* Moscow: Foreign Languages Publishing House, 1956.

Masanov, I. F. *Slovar' psevdonimov russkikh pisatelei, uchenykh i obshchestvennykh deiatelei.* 4 vols. Moscow, 1956–60.

Mendelsohn, Ezra. "Worker Opposition in the Russian Jewish Socialist Movement, from the 1890s to 1903." *International Review of Social History* 10 (1965): 268–82.

———. *Class Struggle in the Pale: The Formative Years of the Jewish Workers' Movement in Tsarist Russia.* Cambridge: Cambridge University Press, 1970.

Miasnikov, G. I. *Ocherednoi obman.* Paris, 1931.

Michels, Robert. *Political Parties: A Sociological Study of the Oligarchical Tendencies of Modern Democracy.* 1911. Trans. Eden and Cedar Paul. New York: The Free Press, 1962.

Mikhailova, E. "Iz kommentariev k 'Chto delat'?'. Gruppa samoosvobozhdeniia rabochego klassa." *Krasnaia letopis'*, no. 1 (12) (1925): 239–48.

Mikhailovskii, N. K. *Sochineniia.* 6 vols. St. Petersburg: "Russkoe Bogatstvo," 1896–1897.

Millard, L. Frances. "The Founding of Zet: A Chapter in the History of Polish Socialism." *The Polish Review* 17, no. 4 (Autumn 1972): 42–61.

Morskoi, A. [Vladimir von Shtein]. *Zubatovshchina. Stranichka iz istorii rabochego voprosa v Rossii.* Moscow: I. D. Sytin, 1913.

Mosca, Gaetano. *The Ruling Class.* Trans. Hannah D. Kahn. Ed. Arthur Livingston. Westport, Conn.: Greenwood Press, 1980.

Naimark, Norman M. *The History of the "Proletariat": The Emergence of Marxism in the Kingdom of Poland, 1870–1887.* Boulder, Colo.: East European Quarterly, 1979.

———. *Terrorists and Social Democrats: The Russian Revolutionary Movement Under Alexander III.* Cambridge, Mass.: Harvard University Press, 1983.

Nettl, J. P. *Rosa Luxemburg.* 2 vols. London: Oxford University Press, 1966.

Nieuważny, Stanisława. "Machajski Jan Wacław." *Polski Słownik Biograficzny.* Vol. 18. Wrocław and Warsaw: Polska Akademia Nauk, 1973.

Nomad, Max. "Machajski, Waclaw." *Encyclopedia of the Social Sciences.* 15 vols. New York: Macmillan, 1930–35.

———. *Aspects of Revolt.* New York: Bookman Associates, 1959.

———. *Dreamers, Dynamiters and Demagogues: Reminiscences.* New York: Waldon Press, 1964.

Nove, A. "Is There a Ruling Class in the USSR?" *Soviet Studies*, October 1975, pp. 615–38.

"Novoe o zubatovshchine." *Krasnyi arkhiv* 1 (1922): 289–328.

Novomirskii, D. I. *Iz programmy sindikal'nogo anarkhizma.* N. p., 1907.

———. *Chto takoe anarkhizm.* 1907. Reprint. New York, 1919.

"O postanovke partiinoi propagandy v sviazi s vypuskom 'Kratkogo kursa istorii VKP(b).'" *Pravda*, November 15, 1938, p. 2.

Paialin, N. P. *Zavod imeni Lenina, 1857–1918*. Moscow-Leningrad: Gosudarstvennoe sotsial'no-ekonomicheskoe izdatel'stvo, 1933.

Pareto, Vilfredo. *Les systèmes socialistes*. 1902–03. Vol. 5 of *Oeuvres Complètes*, ed. Giovanni Busino. Geneva: Librairie Droz, 1965.

Parkin, Frank. *Marxism and Class Theory: A Bourgeois Critique*. London: Tavistock, 1979.

Perl, Feliks [Res]. *Dzieje ruchu socjalistycznego w zaborze rosyjskim (do powstania PPS)*. 1910. Reprint. Warsaw: Książka i Wiedza, 1958.

Pigoń, Stanisław. "Żeromski–Machajski. Zygzaki przyjaźni." *Życie literackie* (Cracow), no. 17 (483), April 23, 1961, pp. 3, 9; no. 20 (486), May 14, 1961, pp. 4, 7; no. 36 (502), September 3, 1961, p. 4; no. 39 (505), September 24, 1961, pp. 4–5.

—————. "Zygzaki przyjaźni. Jan Wacław Machajski–Stefan Żeromski." In *Miłe życia drobiazgi*, pp. 346–404. Warsaw: Państwowy Instytut Wydawniczy, 1964. A revised version of the preceding work.

Pipes, Richard. *Social Democracy and the St. Petersburg Labor Movement, 1885–1897*. Cambridge, Mass.: Harvard University Press, 1963.

Plekhanov, G. V. "Ideologiia meshchanina nashego vremeni." 1908. In *Sochineniia*, ed. D. Riazanov, 14:259–344. 24 vols. Moscow: Gosudarstvennoe izdatel'stvo, 1923–27.

Pollard, Alan P. "The Russian Intelligentsia: The Mind of Russia." *California Slavic Studies*, 3, ed. Nicholas V. Riasanovsky and Gleb Struve, pp. 1–32. Berkeley and Los Angeles: University of California Press, 1964.

Radkey, Oliver H. *The Agrarian Foes of Bolshevism: Promise and Default of the Russian Socialist Revolutionaries, February to October, 1917*. New York: Columbia University Press, 1958.

Raeff, Marc. *Origins of the Russian Intelligentsia: The Eighteenth-Century Nobility*. New York: Harcourt, Brace and World, 1966.

Ridley, F. F. *Revolutionary Syndicalism in France: The Direct Action of Its Time*. Cambridge: Cambridge University Press, 1970.

R.[izzi], Bruno. *La Bureaucratisation du Monde*. [Paris, 1939].

[Romas', Mikhail Ivanovich]. "Avtobiografiia Mikhaila Ivanovicha Romas', 1866–1927 gg." *Katorga i ssylka*, no. 4 (33), 1927, pp. 162–67.

Rose, W. J. "Russian Poland in the Later Nineteenth Century." In *The Cambridge History of Poland (1697–1935)*, ed. W. F. Reddaway et al., 2:387–408. Cambridge: Cambridge University Press, 1941.

Rosenthal, Bernice Glatzer. "Eschatology and the Appeal of Revolution: Merezhkovsky, Bely, Blok." *California Slavic Studies*, 11, ed. Nicholas V. Riasanovsky et al., pp. 105–39. Berkeley and Los Angeles: University of California Press, 1980.

Rubakin, N. A. *Sredi knig.* 2d ed. 3 vols. Moscow: "Nauka," 1911–15.

Schapiro, Leonard. *The Origin of the Communist Autocracy: Political Opposition in the Soviet State.* 2d ed. Cambridge, Mass.: Harvard University Press, 1977.

Schneiderman, Jeremiah. *Sergei Zubatov and Revolutionary Marxism: The Struggle for the Working Class in Tsarist Russia.* Ithaca: Cornell University Press, 1976.

Schwarz, Solomon M. *The Russian Revolution of 1905.* Trans. Gertrude Vakar. Chicago: University of Chicago Press, 1967.

Sergievskii, N. L. "O kruzhke Tochiskogo. Doklad departamenta politsii ministru vnutrennikh del." *Krasnaia letopis',* no. 7, 1923, pp. 340–88.

Shachtman, Max. *The Bureaucratic Revolution: The Rise of the Stalinist State.* New York: Donald Press, 1962.

Shatz, Marshall S. "Jan Waclaw Machajski: The 'Conspiracy' of the Intellectuals." *Survey,* January 1967, pp. 45–57.

———. "The Makhaevists and the Russian Revolutionary Movement." *International Review of Social History* 15 (1970): 235–65.

———. *Soviet Dissent in Historical Perspective.* Cambridge: Cambridge University Press, 1980.

———. "Stalin, the Great Purge, and Russian History: A New Look at the 'New Class.'" The Carl Beck Papers in Russian and East European Studies, no. 305. Pittsburgh: University of Pittsburgh, 1984.

———, ed. *The Essential Works of Anarchism.* New York: Bantam Books, 1971.

Shetlikh, A. "Pamiati V. K. Makhaiskogo." *Izvestiia,* February 24, 1926, p. 4.

Somov, S. I. [M. I. Peskin]. "Iz istorii sotsial-demokraticheskogo dvizheniia v Peterburge v 1905 godu. (Lichnye vospominaniia.)" *Byloe,* part 1: April 1907, pp. 22–55; part 2: May 1907, pp. 152–78.

Sorel, Georges. *Reflections on Violence.* 1906. Trans. T. E. Hulme and J. Roth. New York: Collier Books, 1961.

Sorin, V. *Rabochaia gruppa: "Miasnikovshchina."* Moscow, 1924.

Stalin, I. V. "Novaia obstanovka—novye zadachi khoziaistvennogo stroitel'stva." [Speech of June 23, 1931.] In *Sochineniia,* 13:51–80. 13 vols. Moscow: Gosudarstvennoe izdatel'stvo politicheskoi literatury, 1946–1952.

Stearns, Peter N. *Revolutionary Syndicalism and French Labor: A Cause Without Rebels.* New Brunswick, N.J.: Rutgers University Press, 1971.

Steinfels, Peter. *The Neoconservatives*. New York: Simon and Schuster, 1979.

Steklov, Iu. M. "Kak ia bezhal iz Iakutki." 1918. In *Izbrannoe*, pp. 51–90. Moscow: "Izvestiia," 1973.

[Strożecki, Jan]. "Listy Jana Strożeckiego do Kazimierza Pietkiewicza." *Dzieje Najnowsze (Kwartalnik Instytuta Pamięci Narodowej)*, 1, part 1 (January–March 1947): 90–138.

Struve, P. *Kriticheskie zametki k voprosu ob ekonomicheskom razvitii Rossii*. St. Petersburg: I. N. Skorokhodov, 1894.

Syrkin, L. N. "*Makhaevshchina*." Moscow-Leningrad: Gosudarstvennoe sotsial'no-ekonomicheskoe izdatel'stvo, 1931. First published in *Krasnaia letopis'*, no. 6 (33), 1929, pp. 184–212; no. 1 (34), 1930, pp. 117–45.

Takhtarev, K. M. [Peterburzhets]. *Ocherk peterburgskogo rabochego dvizheniia 90-kh gg.: po lichnym vospominaniiam*. London: Tip. Zhizni, 1902.

Tereshkovich, K. "Moskovskaia molodezh' 80-kh godov i Sergei Zubatov. (Iz vospominanii.)" *Minuvshie gody*, no. 5–6, May–June 1908, pp. 207–15.

Tolstoi, L. N. Letter to E. I. Lozinskii. In *Polnoe sobranie sochinenii*, 79:47–48. 90 vols. Moscow: Gosudarstvennoe izdatel'stvo khudozhestvennoi literatury, 1928–58.

Trotskii, L. [Leon Trotsky]. "Vospominaniia o moei pervoi sibirskoi ssylke." *Katorga i ssylka*, no. 5, 1923, pp. 91–95.

———. *My Life: An Attempt at an Autobiography*. New York: Scribner, 1930.

———. "The Class Nature of the Soviet State." [October 1, 1933.] In *Writings of Leon Trotsky, 1933–34*, pp. 101–22. New York: Pathfinder Press, 1972.

———. *The Revolution Betrayed: What Is the Soviet Union and Where Is It Going?* Trans. Max Eastman. 1937. Reprint. New York: Pathfinder Press, 1972.

———. "The USSR in War." [September 25, 1939.] In *In Defense of Marxism (Against the Petty-Bourgeois Opposition)*, pp. 3–21. New York: Pioneer Publishers, 1942.

Tugan-Baranovskii, M. "Chto takoe obshchestvennyi klass?" *Mir Bozhii*, January 1904, pp. 64–72.

Ulam, Adam B. *The Unfinished Revolution*. New York: Vintage Books, 1964.

———. *The Bolsheviks*. New York: Macmillan, 1965.

V., V. [Vasilii Vorontsov]. *Nashi napravleniia*. St. Petersburg: M. Stasiulevich, 1893.

————. "Kapitalizm i russkaia intelligentsiia." 1884. In *Ot semidesiatykh godov k desiatisotnym: Sbornik statei*, pp. 27–57. St. Petersburg: "Obshchestvennaia pol'za," 1907.

Vekhi (Signposts): A Collection of Articles on the Russian Intelligentsia. Trans. and ed. Marshall S. Shatz and Judith Zimmerman. 7 parts. *Canadian Slavic Studies*, Summer 1968–Fall 1971.

Venturi, Franco. *Roots of Revolution.* Trans. Francis Haskell. London: Weidenfeld and Nicolson, 1960.

Vetoshkin, M. "Stranichki revoliutsionnogo proshlogo." *Katorga i ssylka*, no. 2 (63), 1930, pp. 7–21; no. 3 (64), 1930, pp. 63–79.

Voitinskii, Vladimir S. *Gody pobed i porazhenii.* 2 vols. Berlin, 1923–24.

————. *Peterburgskii sovet bezrabotnykh, 1906–1907.* New York: Russian Institute, Columbia University, 1969.

Von Laue, Theodore H. "Russian Peasants in the Factory, 1892–1904." *Journal of Economic History*, March 1961, pp. 61–80.

————. "Russian Labor Between Field and Factory, 1892–1903." *California Slavic Studies*, 3, ed. Nicholas V. Riasanovsky and Gleb Struve, pp. 33–65. Berkeley and Los Angeles: University of California Press, 1964.

Vorovskii, V. V. "Predstavliaet li intelligentsiia obshchestvennyi klass?" 1904. In *Sochineniia*, 2:3–20. 3 vols. Leningrad: Gosudarstvennoe sotsial'no-ekonomicheskoe izdatel'stvo, 1931.

Voslensky, Michael. *Nomenklatura: The Soviet Ruling Class.* Trans. Eric Mosbacher. Preface by Milovan Djilas. Garden City, N.Y.: Doubleday, 1984.

"Vozzvanie gruppy 'Rabochaia pravda.'" *Sotsialisticheskii vestnik*, January 31, 1923, pp. 12–14.

Wildman, Allan K. *The Making of a Workers' Revolution: Russian Social-Democracy, 1891–1903.* Chicago: University of Chicago Press, 1967.

Yaroslavsky [Iaroslavskii], E. *History of Anarchism in Russia.* New York: International Publishers, 1937.

Zaitsev, D. "Marksizm i makhaevshchina." *Obrazovanie*, no. 3, March 1908, pp. 35–71.

Zaremba, Zygmunt. *Słowo o Wacławie Machajskim.* Paris: Księgarnia Polska w Paryżu, 1967.

Zaslavskii, D. "Zubatov i Mania Vil'bushevich." *Byloe*, no. 3 (31), March 1918, pp. 99–128.

Zelnik, Reginald E. "Populists and Workers: The First Encounter Between Populist Students and Industrial Workers in St. Petersburg, 1871–74." *Soviet Studies*, October 1972, pp. 251–69.

————. "Russian Bebels: An Introduction to the Memoirs of Semen Kanatchikov and Matvei Fisher." *Russian Review*, part 1: July 1976, pp. 249–89; part 2: October 1976, pp. 417–47.

Żeromski, Stefan. *Elegie i inne pisma literackie i społeczne.* Warsaw: Wydawnictwo J. Mortkowicza, 1928.

———. *Dzienniki.* Ed. Jerzy Kądziela. 7 vols. Warsaw: Czytelnik, 1963–70.

Zhukov, A. F. *Ideino-politicheskii krakh eserovskogo maksimalizma.* Leningrad: Izdatel'stvo Leningradskogo Universiteta, 1979.

Zorin, S., and N. Alekseev. *Vremia ne zhdet.* Frankfurt/Main: Posev, 1970.

Index

Aizenshtadt, Liubov', 20
Anarchism, 37–42, 64–66, 81, 103, 108, 137, 162, 174, 207–08n58; and anti-intelligentsia sentiment, 134–35; on Bolsheviks, 154; and Makhaevism, 37, 42, 64–66, 81, 134–35, 160, 209n87; and "revolt against positivism," 91–92, 167. See also Bakunin, Michael; Kropotkin, Peter; Makhaevists, and anarchists; Syndicalism
Andreev, Leonid: Tsar Hunger, 97
Apukhtin, Aleksandr, 7

Bakunin, Michael, 5, 23, 69, 89, 134, 153, 154, 226n21; on intellectuals, 37–42, 72, 78, 91–92; on Marxists, 30, 37–42, 154, 161–62, 198n57, 206n24; on "new class," 39–42, 162; in Poland, influence of, 5, 198n43; Statism and Anarchy, 40–42, 98–100
Baturin, N., 160, 174
Berlin, Isaiah: The Hedgehog and the Fox, 54
Bernstein, Eduard, 21, 121, 197n39, 213n19. See also Revisionism
Berson, Janina, 28, 50
Blok, Alexander, 97
Bogdanov, Aleksandr, 157
Breitfus, Andrei, 112
Breslav, B. A., 129, 174, 216n67
Brezhnev, Leonid, 173, 227n27
Bukharin, Nikolai, 154, 170; on "new class," 162–63

Bund (General Jewish Workers' Union in Russia and Poland), 29, 66, 185; anti-intelligentsia sentiment in, 114–15, 119, 214n28, 217n76; and Zubatovism, 115, 121–23, 126, 214n36
Burnham, James, 166–67, 225n18

Chaikovskii Circle, 111–12
Chernyshevskii, Nikolai, 5, 20
Chuprina, 133, 194n65, 195n69, 221n125
Cohen, Stephen, 154

Daszyński, Ignacy, 146
Democratic Centralists, 155–56, 223n43
Djilas, Milovan, 225n20, 226n21; and Machajski, 167, 225n18; The New Class, 166, 167–68
Dłuski, Kazimierz, 147
Dmowski, Roman, 9, 148–49
Dulęba, Henryk, 20
Dzerzhinskii, Feliks, 158

Economism, 20, 115, 117, 126, 132, 160, 214n31, 218n84. See also Rabochaia mysl'
Engels, Friedrich, 6, 21, 46, 78, 80, 86. See also Marx, Karl
Erdelovskii, N. M., 133

Gapon, Georgii, 123
Garvi, Petr, 23–25, 214n28, 221n125
German Social-Democratic party, 17–18, 29–32, 72, 183; Die Jungen, 36–37

Pitt Series in Russian and
East European Studies
Jonathan Harris, Editor